¶ THE TREE OF MEANING

LANGUAGE, MIND

AND ECOLOGY

ROBERT BRINGHURST

¶ THE TREE OF MEANING

LANGUAGE, MIND

AND ECOLOGY

ROBERT BRINGHURST

COUNTERPOINT · Berkeley

Library of Congress Cataloguing-in-Publication Data

Bringhurst, Robert.

   The Tree of meaning : language, mind, and ecology / Robert
Bringhurst ; foreword by Jim Harrison.

      p. cm.

      Includes index.

   ISBN-13: 978-1-59376-179-0
   ISBN-10: 1-59376-179-1

         1. American literature – Indian authors – History and criticism.
         2. Indians of North America – Intellectual life.
         3. Indians in literature.
         4. Nature in literature.
         5. Indians of North America – Philosophy.
         I. Title.

   PS153.I52B75 2008

      810.9'897 – dc22   2007032981

COUNTERPOINT
2117 Fourth Street
Suite D
Berkeley, CA 94710
www.counterpointpress.com

   9 8 7 6 5 4 3 2 1

In Memoriam

GEORGE HEBER BRINGHURST
1915–1992

MARION JEANETTE BRINGHURST
1917–2006

CONTENTS

Occasionally, but rarely, in my lifetime I've come across a criti-cal intelligence whom I can fairly describe by the word *genius*. George Steiner, Roberto Calasso, and Walter Benjamin come easily to mind among a few others, and now I must add Robert Bringhurst, who has set my old mind off in an altogether pleas-ant whirl. Aristophanes said, "Whirl is king," but then this is an aspect of life I've tried to control by living rather remotely. I haven't, however, been able to resist Bringhurst's vast and persistent energies in the past few weeks, so that even my trout fishing and cooking have been invaded by his thought and the utter lucidity of his language, activities normally immune to deep thinking of any sort. The banal and illusory perceptions of day-to-day reality are very far from the world of the seem-ingly limitless intelligence of Robert Bringhurst.

I recall that in the late eighties on a trip to Toronto, no one seemed enthused about the work of Bringhurst, which I had come across while I was researching an aborted screenplay to be set partly among the Haida Indians in the Queen Charlotte Islands (all of my screenplays were aborted or simply born dead). I had corresponded with Gary Snyder at the time, who was also familiar with Bringhurst. When I visited Toronto a few days ago, all of my Canadian writer friends seemed quite familiar with the work. It takes a while.

The Tree of Meaning is a book that before your eyes magically enlarges itself from 336 pages to many volumes. The prose is never reductive but tends to push at the confines of whatever room you are reading in so that the four corners seem much farther away than normal. I suspect that this is because Bringhurst has been willing to immerse himself in Native cultures to the point of drowning, especially the Haida, who to us are the soul of *otherness*. When you read the great Haida poet Ghandl in Bringhurst's translation, for instance, you try to hold back at first out of fear for your mental safety but then you give up and let yourself plunge into the work. While studying *The Tree of Meaning* I felt the same trepidation I had when reading Rimbaud and Dostoevsky in my late teens fifty years ago. Here I am a tiny isolate island in Michigan; dare I welcome these intruders ashore to keep me company the rest of my life? *The Tree of Meaning* will stay with you until you reach your deathbed, beyond which no one apparently has a clue, though there is a specific desire to be reincarnated as a raven in the Queen Charlotte Islands – either male or female would do.

I had a modest insight into Bringhurst in Toronto last week. This is a vast and intensely sophisticated city, seemingly more so than New York where the citizenry is suffocated under the immense carapace of greed. The melting pot of dozens of immigrant cultures appears more melted in Toronto, though all the ingredients can still be detected. Curiously, from the air much of Toronto in June appears to be forested, though, of course, this is a vast City of Man. Toronto, luckily, is bifurcated by a number of ravines, and while walking the spacious riverine thicket along a small river called the Don, I began to identify the imagination of Bringhurst along with all the birds I was seeing, the prodigious variety of flora, even the passing dogs and the many shades of skin color in people who moved along the path. I thought that perhaps Bringhurst is the logical fruition of many of the ideas to be read about in Gary Snyder's *The Practice of the Wild* where he speaks of the Spanish notion of *gramática parda*, the tawny grammar of earth herself. Walking along the ravine, I detected that Bringhurst tends to write in the spoken (inaudibly) pattern of the wild, the patterns of uncultivated nature. He is in no haste to turn a tree into a geometric pile of two-by-fours, to reduce the incalculable tree into lumber for easy usage. Bringhurst himself is a wild ravine through the leftovers of the French Enlightenment we suffer from, the logical positivism that continues to make war our main accoutrement, a wild ravine through what he insists is the continuing colonialization of North America. Bringhurst has immersed his imagination in the people and their literature who have not made a life out of separating themselves from their surroundings, who have not turned wild nature into a linear metaphoric golf course. As the ancient Chinese folk wisdom says, "He breathes through his feet."

Meanwhile, *The Tree of Meaning* identifies the uneven war between those who think they belong in the world and those who think the world belongs to them. Once during a walk in the mountains along the Mexican border, a friend of mine, Neil Claremon, a scholar of Apache thinking, said, "Don't you think reality is an aggregate, an accretion of the perceptions of all creatures?" This is certainly a Bringhurstian idea. When we read the stories and poems of Native cultures, it is proper to wonder how and why we managed to evict these gods from our collective literature.

In an interview with Bringhurst by Noah Richler, I was reminded of D. H. Lawrence's dictum, "The only aristocracy is that of consciousness." There is a natural playfulness of language from someone who totally lives his forest and ocean material in British Columbia. "Well, I'm not much of a ritualist by inclination. I go to church to look at the art when I'm in Europe, and occasionally listen to the music ... but not for the sake of the ceremonies. When I come out here [in the forest] I am constantly conversing with the plants and whatever animals I happen to meet. And, you know, often in the course of a walk something strikes me between the eyes and I have to stop for a while and try to grasp it.... About the only regular ritual activity that I do is to take the salmon skins and bones down to the water and return them to the ocean, with a little sub-vocal prayer that the salmon might survive and continue to feed me."

The peculiar, very difficult genius of Bringhurst is in the news he brings back from his forays into this unknown country. When you begin reading you're not sure this country exists because it has a shape no cartographer can parse. Dreams and poetry emerge from this landscape. In The Tree of Meaning he deals fluently with mythology, poetry, comparative literature, humanity, the breadth of culture, and what he calls "ecological linguistics." Bringhurst's early training in the sciences is evident, as is his foremost vocation as a poet, though he certainly can't be piecemealed. The essay "Poetry and Thinking" should be obligatory reading in all of our three hundred MFA factories in the States. The event of the publication of The Tree of Meaning is especially striking in the United States where, more than occasionally. publishing reminds one of a monstrous Wal-Mart of words.

To read Bringhurst is to discover an unknown spring or deep creek way back in the forest. His language owns a delightful liquidity so far from the academic stutter-step. At one point in the laborious process of writing this foreword, laborious because I was dealing with the taxonomy of a new species of mammal in my own existence, I questioned whether I was half-daft with wonderment because I had taken a big forced step out of my own consciousness, something we do when we come upon a rare, fine book. I was reassured of my own, somewhat tenuous sanity when I read a quote from the renowned

Margaret Atwood writing about Bringhurst's trilogy of translations from the Haida, which was chosen as the literary book of the year by the London *Times*: "Bringhurst's achievement is gigantic, as well as heroic. It's one of those works that rearranges the inside of your head—a profound meditation on the nature of oral poetry and myth, and on the habits of thought and feeling that inform them." This made me feel like I was in good company indeed. I will temporarily recover by spending all day tomorrow rowing and floating and fishing on a huge river, an activity similar to reading this fine book. We must welcome this man across our massive border fence.

THE TREE OF MEANING

LANGUAGE, MIND

AND ECOLOGY

PROLOGUE

There are a lot of rocks in western Montana, and several creeks called Rock Creek. One of them, draining the north slope of the Anacondas and the eastern flank of the Sapphire Mountains, became my father's favorite trout-fishing stream around 1949. That watershed is where my brain was born. It wasn't the first world I'd ever explored, and it's a place I never stayed for more than a week or two at a time, but that is the first landscape I began to learn to read.

Reading, for me, is the proof of being at home: a quintessential part of the equation that enables us to reach across the fence between the world and ourselves without destroying what we find. The most basic parts of that equation, surely, are eating and being eaten. Can't have one without the other. May not seem so in the restaurant or the bookstore, but walking in the forest or sitting by the stream, we know it works both ways: being fed and feeding, reading and being read.

When I was a child, the family I belonged to moved at least once every year and did a lot of fidgeting from one place to another between moves. By 1952, home was western Alberta, and the fish came out of creeks that fed the Athabasca, not the Clark Fork. Pages of rocks and vegetation turned; new volumes opened; and the reading went right on.

Vexed by the demands of an ill-mannered only child, my mother taught me first to write and then to read the Latin alphabet, and started me reading the English language, about the same time I was introduced to Rock Creek. Whether this kept me out of more trouble than it got me into, I do not really know. But it allowed me, early on, to see the entire world of written language, along with the whole of the Rocky Mountains, as part of my own version of the private world every child knows: the one where no one else gives orders and the child gets to practice being free.

Languages are things I feel perpetually slipping through my fingers and melting in my ears like snowflakes on the tongue. But that is how it is with languages and trout streams. They go their way, like air flowing in and back out of our lungs, sounds bouncing off our eardrums, light careening past our eyes. They go their way like meaning: the meaning they are part of; the meaning that is part of what they are. Writing isn't, for me, a way of arresting the flow but of jumping in and swimming with the current, going for a ride.

The way my father fished was this. He rose in the tent before dawn. By candlelight, he found some bread and dried beef and stuffed them in the pocket of his fishing vest, then started in the half dark, walking silently upstream. He had no use for lakes or rivers: too open, too exposed. He wanted trees and fallen logs and brush, to discourage lesser fishermen, to hide his shadow from the trout, and of course to serve as an obstacle course for his cast.

He'd return to camp at dark, with a string of trout meticulously cleaned and the beef sandwich still in his pocket. He had not had time to eat; he had been fishing. After tending to his gear, he'd eat the bread and beef and sit reflectively by the fire, cracking the delicate shells of *chá'oł bineeshch'íí'* – pinyon seeds from the Navajo country, a food which even in Alberta, a thousand miles north of where it grows, he did not like to be without. The trout were for my mother and for me. Nothing short of genuine starvation could move my father to eat fish. His calling was to catch them.

He read creekwater and rocks and vegetation; he read the behavior of horses, sheep, and cows; and like the rest of us, he read the signals sent by other human beings. He delighted in deciphering the logic of complicated machines. Books to him were as useless as lakes, perhaps for the same reasons. The fish there might be big, but the sterility of sitting in a boat or standing on the shore in open view in order to catch them was more than he could bear. He was perplexed, and none too secretly insulted, by my disinterest in any kind of fishing. I loved the creeks, and I remember to this day the shapes they cut, the sounds they made, the shallows paved with colored pebbles, the thickets of dwarf willows, how the riffles broke the light; but from the moment camp was pitched, I was content to spend my time with rocks and trees, quadrupeds and birds, instead of fish.

My love of books perplexed him too, and sometimes that perplexity turned into deep suspicion. Still I insist – and it is not from filial piety or devotion to gender equality – that my father as much as my mother taught me to read.

As a small child, in Utah and California, I heard a lot of Navajo and Spanish. Then of course my family moved, and moved again. I lost both tongues before I had them. A few years later, I had the same experience with Cree. For a couple of years in my early teens I took lessons in Latin, reading *De Bello gallico* (it seemed the only book my teacher knew) with very little pleasure or success. At seventeen, intrigued by the script, I began to study Arabic. A few months later I was living in Beirut. I turned twenty-one living in Israel, twenty-two living in Panama. I remember a brief trip back to North America near the end of the 1960s, when I heard the Beatles played on American radio and wondered who these Englishmen might be, singing remarkably good translations of songs I'd only ever heard in Spanish in a Panamanian bar.

At twenty-four, in Indiana, nudged by Ezra Pound, I started trying to teach myself classical Greek. At thirty, in Vancouver, I learned at last to read a little (very little) classical Chinese. Eight or nine years later, after a decade on the British Columbia coast, when I had written a few books, it dawned on me that really I knew nothing of the literary heritage of the land in which I lived, nor the mountains I'd grown up in, nor any other part of North America. I began to study Haida, which led me back to Navajo and Cree. And my sense of the relations between humans, language, literature, writing, and nonhumans underwent a much belated change.

I have no special aptitude for language, only a nagging suspicion there might be something it's trying to say. And I've never learned any language well, including English. But as it happens, I have no special aptitude for human relations either. I'm therefore happy to think of language as the natural (and probably inevitable) consequence of thought and the raw material of literature, more than as a tool for social navigation. It's the elders I mostly want to listen to, and the elders are always mostly gone: Greek and Chinese poets and philosophers; Haida and Navajo mythtellers; Baghdadi and Florentine craftsmen polishing their fine syllabic inlays centuries ago. Where their voices have survived, it is because they took their own dictation or someone did it for them. Sitting down to read them, we are free to move as slowly as we please – and to travel at that speed through all the worlds they enfold. Paper is two-dimensional space, but as soon as language dances on the paper, it becomes a form of time.

For better or for worse, this book was written to be spoken, largely in homage to poets and thinkers in cultures where writing didn't or doesn't exist. Partly for that reason, I've left all thirteen sections in their spoken and localized form, as thirteen separate talks, not thirteen essays. I could certainly have turned them into placeless, dateless prose, but I know how often oral poems and stories have been edited that way, and how little has been gained, and how much lost, as a result.

If writing is like swimming, reading is like wading. Not all of us have outgrown it. That is why, when texts are quoted in this book, the originals are almost always given. If the original isn't in English, there is always a translation (and wherever it might help, if the original is in another script, there is also a romanization). Readers who don't want to take their shoes off can of course leap over these originals. Perhaps they can also enjoy them as pictures of language, to be looked at rather than read. As pictures of language go, they're pretty good. Inside the pictures, though, are the sounds of human speech – and inside those, if they're worth quoting, are traces of meanings not wholly invented by us. That's a creek worth walking up.

Heriot Ridge · Quadra Island · February 2006

THE POLYHISTORICAL MIND

I

Years ago, on a visit to England, I was introduced to the recently retired head of a prestigious girls' school. The discussion turned to the subject of language, as postmodern conversations often do. I was asked what languages I spoke. I replied, in all honesty, that I spoke none well but that I read a bit of Haida and Navajo. "What are those?" the headmistress asked, and I said they were Native American languages. This terminology was unclear to her, and I eventually explained that they were languages spoken by what she might call Red Indians. "Oh!" she said. "Did they have languages?"

I thought I should weep, that the articulate, forceful, well-mannered and profoundly ignorant woman before me had been what is called an educator all her adult life, and I thought I should rejoice that she was retired. I also thought that if she could not spend time with Native Americans themselves, she might at least spend more time with scholars and less with colonial stereotypes.

But what would the scholars have told her?

Any anthropologist, of course – and ideally any intelligent high-school student – could report to her that the world has been thoroughly searched for people without language, and the only people ever found who answer to that description are infants and a few individuals suffering serious injury

---

Third Ashley Lecture, Trent University, Peterborough, Ontario
9 March 1994

15

or disease. Adult human beings lacking the mental organ of language are as rare as human beings lacking a tongue in the physical sense.

But how much more would the scholars have told her, even if she had asked?

Suppose, to make things easy, she had turned to the standard imperial reference, the Encyclopædia Britannica, which was shelved on the wall behind her in the room where we were speaking? I know, because I looked myself in secret later on, that if she had consulted that authority, a well-respected scholar would have told her this:

Indian languages have of course no literature, as this term is ordinarily understood. But American Indian groups do possess oral folk cultures, the anonymous creations of many generations....

Most, and probably all, American Indian languages are doomed to extinction.... One does not therefore study Indian tongues for their practical usefulness, or, since they are unwritten, to gain a better understanding of a great literary tradition. But these languages, like all others, are valuable to the science of language.... They provide, in fact, a laboratory....[1]

The author of these words, Harry Hoijer, studied with one of the few undoubted geniuses ever to work in the field of linguistics, Edward Sapir. But Hoijer's statements prove that he had not learned what Sapir attempted to teach. These pronouncements, imbued with the authority of the Britannica, are not good science, not good scholarship, not good history. They are not good prophecy either. They are nothing, in fact, except the thoughtless repetition of old assumptions: unexamined, uninformed, untrue, and, I suspect, highly destructive. The scholar, in this case, like the schoolteacher, is blinded by his books, blinded by his skill with reading and writing.

The poems of the Haida poets Skaay and Ghandl prove that there is something deeply wrong with Hoijer's view. Skaay and Ghandl were oral poets, unable to read or write, but they are anonymous only to those who will not take the trouble to learn their names and to recognize their talents. They were bearers of a great intellectual and literary tradition – and because John Swanton, a good and quiet linguist, transcribed hundreds of pages of their poems, they continue even now to serve as bearers of that tradition, though their culture is much changed, their villages are empty, and they themselves are dead. All human languages are doomed sooner or later to extinction. So are all species, not excluding ours. In the meantime, the language of Ghandl and Skaay – because of the wisdom and skill with which they spoke it, and the care with which John Swanton wrote it down – is no more doomed to extinction than Homer's language, or Shakespeare's, or Isaiah's.

Skaay – who belonged to the Haida lineage called Qquuna Qiighawaay – and Ghandl – who belonged to the Qayahl Llaanas – are, I admit, unusual cases. They are two of the finest oral poets I know of, in any language, on any continent. But it would not be hard to call up here and now the ghosts of a couple of hundred other mythtellers, exemplifying the great traditions embodied in a hundred other Native American languages. It would not be hard, but to do any kind of justice to the names and the traditions of these artists would mean giving hundreds of lectures and writing hundreds of books. That is a task for a hundred others to take on.

II

In 1934 an English immigrant to British Columbia compiled an anthology of stories he had culled from the mythology of the Haida and other coastal peoples, and rewritten for popular sale to English colonial readers. "These stories," says their editor, "existed among the Coast Peoples, not embellished by fine or sonorous language, but told in such a way that their simple minds understood and appreciated them."[2] Thirty years later the Warden of Wadham College, emeritus Professor of Poetry in the University of Oxford, undertook to write about the oral literature of hunter-gatherers worldwide. He was learned in Latin, Greek and Russian, but not in any of the languages this wider study involved. He felt certain nonetheless that in the cultures he had ventured to describe, myths

are usually told in prose tales of a very simple kind with none of the elegance or artifice of song, no doubt because this presents less dangers [sic] *in a sphere where errors must be avoided and precision and correctness are paramount.*[3]

The Oxford don is less discourteous in his language than the colonist, but he is not one millimeter closer to the facts.

It is easier to sympathize with the grim view expressed by Jean-Paul Sartre in 1947. It was not, after all, colonial pride nor a pretension to omniscience which led him to conclude that "literature's only chance is the chance of Europe."[4] Happily, this has not turned out to be the case. But in his summary of the usefulness of literature, Sartre touches on the character of oral as well as literate culture and reaches far beyond the boundaries of his favorite continent:

S'il devait se tourner en pure propagande ou en pur divertissement, la société retomberait dans la bauge de l'immédiat, c'est-à-dire dans la vie sans mémoire des hyménoptères et des gastéropodes. Bien sûr, tout cela n'est pas si important: le monde peut fort bien se passer de la littérature. Mais il peut se passer de l'homme encore mieux.[5]

If [literature] should turn into pure propaganda or pure entertainment,
society will slip back into the sty of the immediate – which is to say,
the memoryless existence of hymenoptera and gastropods. None of
this is so important, to be sure. The world can get by nicely without
literature. But without human beings it can get by better yet.

If the same headmistress were to ask that same encyclopedia
for basic information on the literatures of Canada, she'd be told
that there are two, English and French. She would be told that
Charles G.D. Roberts, Bliss Carman, Archibald Lampman and
Duncan Campbell Scott "wrote the best poetry composed in
Canada before 1920." Roberts, she'd be told, is memorable for
his "nationalistic optimism"; Carman is "a popular poet, even
outside Canada" for his "pagan aestheticism and ... bohemian
vagabondage"; Lampman important for his "natural description and ... social comment." But it is Scott, she would be told,
who gives voice to "the remote and vast northern wilderness
where the Indian lived, a region and a people that Scott knew
intimately during his long career in the Department of Indian
Affairs."[6] How can a work of reference go so wrong?

III

Human beings have been migrating widely over North America
at least since the last ice age. Some of these movements – like
the migration of the Navajo and Apache south from the Yukon
to New Mexico and Arizona – can be dated fairly closely; others are harder to fix. But it is not hard to distinguish between
these earlier Native American migrations and the colonization
of North America by Europeans. The difference is cultural, not
racial. It is the difference between, on the one hand, families of
hunters learning their way through the landscape step by step,

and on the other hand, boatload after boatload of refugees uprooted from a sedentary life in one land, crossing the great ocean to another they know nothing whatever about.

The first kind of movement encourages learning, alertness, adaptation, and it generally allows the kind of *time* this adaptation requires. The second kind of movement is abrupt. It involves the imposition of remembered patterns, or idealized versions of remembered patterns, even where they will not fit. Often it involves the building of large-scale artificial realities. In one of Ghandl's narrative poems, a man marries a goose. She is unhappy living with him on the earth, and he is unhappy with her in the sky, but neither tries to rearrange that other world. Europeans arriving in North America routinely attempted instead to remake the place in the altered image of home. The maps are still replete with names like Nouvelle France, New England, Nova Scotia, British Columbia, New York. That habitual refusal to accept the actual world continues to this day. It is responsible for Disney World, the West Edmonton Mall, and for the bridge that will soon reduce Prince Edward Island to one more faceless piece of the mainland.[7]

The old star maps made by the astronomers of Alexandria and Baghdad show the sky as a congregation of constellations – recognizable clusters of visible stars – that sometimes overlap and otherwise have gaps between them. Those old maps leak like a Haida house. They are full of fictions, full of stories, but the sweet wind of reality blows through the cracks. Neoclassical astronomers replaced the old star maps with others in which every scrap of sky is accounted for and claimed. No overlaps or cracks or blanks allowed. Europeans colonized the sky in that sense in the early eighteenth century, long before they had spacecraft. At the hands of neoclassical geographers, the earth, which once had room on it for gypsies, hunter-gatherers and herders, and for wolves and bear and caribou and passenger pigeons and cranes, was all accounted for too. Lines were drawn on maps and on the ground, with no free space between them. What didn't fit into the system didn't exist, and if it tried to exist, it might soon find that legislators and schoolteachers and missionaries and farmers marched against it.

The map of Canada, on which Ontario can't stop until Manitoba begins, and Manitoba can't stop until Saskatchewan or Hudson's Bay or the Territories begin, is a fiction of that kind: an accountant's dream and not a picture of reality. But that map continues to be used as a tool to change reality, to try to make it fit the hallucination of perfect managerial control.

This simple and familiar map is making the task of accepting and acknowledging aboriginal self-government much more difficult than it might be otherwise. It does not help us in understanding the real shape of Canadian literature either.

IV

Astronomers worked on their leakproof map of the sky until 1945, by which time it had very little use. The step from neoclassical science to modern science involved learning to live with and appreciate open-ended taxonomies instead. The periodic table used by chemists, the binomial nomenclature and synoptic keys of biologists, and the ever zanier and more wonderful mythworlds of particle physicists and contemporary astronomers, are examples. Each of these lists of categories and types is something like a tree. Because its purpose is to grow, it is always *incomplete* – like the list of sentences or sentence patterns possible in the English language.

Anthropology, if I'm not mistaken, went through a similar shift, and Franz Boas is its Mendeléyev or Linnaeus. He envisioned, it seems to me, something like a periodic table of cultures, which always had room for newly discovered (or newly created) elements, and which did not claim that the more elaborate atoms were necessarily better than the others. Uranium is not better than oxygen, according to a chemist, even though its atomic weight is greater and its spectrographic portrait more complex. And the culture of the German Empire or the Weimar Republic, according to Boas, is not better than the culture of Haida Gwaii, even if German towns and warships are larger than Haida villages and canoes, and even if they require more elaborate political organization and greater accumulations of capital to create.

Boas had dueling scars on his face from defending his honor as a Jew against opinionated Prussians in the country where he was born. He was also, in Alfred Kroeber's words, "honored, on Hitler's accession, by having his books publicly burned."[8] He spent his entire adult life amassing and publicizing evidence that race is not a factor in human intelligence, and that intellect and wisdom cannot be judged by skin color, blood type or head shape, nor by complexity or weight of material culture.[9] Fools can ride in limousines, and Sokrates and Gandhi can walk naked, or the other way around. And Ghandl of the Qayahl Llaanas can make a poem as complex and as beautiful as a string quartet by Mozart, or the other way around.

Yet if Boas – who was born in 1858 – were with us today, he would have his work to do all over again. On every street in North America, and in every university, he would meet people who fervently want to believe that a human being's genetic pedigree will tell us how that human being thinks and what it knows.

We often speak of being related by blood and of knowing things in the bone. These are, or they can be, beautiful metaphors. And in my line of work, the metaphor is an essential and serious tool, not a decorative device. But every metaphor has its bounds. In Haida, a person who takes things literally is called *skundal*. If I ask such a person to eat crow or to bury the hatchet or cut the crap, I had better be prepared to see the metaphor exhaustively acted out.

If I tell myself that my Haida and Navajo teachers have inborn knowledge that other people lack, I had better know that I'm speaking in metaphor. Otherwise, I am committing the same intellectual error as a colonist in the Transvaal who tells himself that Europeans possess inherent abilities that black Africans lack. That mistake can get much uglier yet – as when the Serb militiaman rapes a Muslim woman and tells her that the child she bears will be a Serb. We do not have the same *crime* in these three cases, but we do have the same intellectual error: that is, the confusion of culture and nature. We have real human beings trapped in demented metaphors.

In London there is a sperm bank, serving the immensely multiracial, multicultural community that has gathered in that old imperial capital. It receives requests, on a daily basis, for Muslim sperm, for Christian sperm, for sperm that belongs to particular nationalities, and for sperm that belongs to particular sects: Isma'ili, Sunni, Shi'a, Protestant, Anglican. Frequently, it receives requests for sperm that comes from a particular locality – Devon or Cornwall, or a certain region in Asia. Sometimes it receives requests for sperm that speaks a particular language, and the most commonly requested language, I am told, is English. Some of these requesters, according to information they supply, have university degrees. It seems that they were promised an education and given a decoration instead. Or that their teachers could not find time, in a busy curriculum, to touch on the basic difference between what nature will do for us and what we must do for ourselves and for each other: the difference, that is, between nature and culture.

There is an old Greek story of a woman by the name of Semele. Zeus fell in love with her and told her she could have anything she wished. She said she wanted to see her lover as he really was, and Zeus said, "Semele, ask for anything but that." She insisted. And Zeus, who keeps his word, came to her then, bright as a lightning flash, blinding her and burning her to a crisp.

Evidently it is also very difficult for many of us to accept the raw and pure humanity of other human beings – and easier to focus on the masks they wear – even when we think of ourselves and of them in the most vulnerable, naked, fragile form, as a single pair of mating cells.

What my teachers know that other people don't is in their minds and in their cultures, not in their genes. If their cultures die, the knowledge that lives in them dies too, no matter how many children they bear, or how well fed those children are, or whether or not they have the vote.

v

I would like to go back now, for a moment, to the map of Canada.

A literary map of this country would be first of all a map of languages, several layers deep. On the base layers, there would be no sign at all of English and French. At least sixty-five, perhaps as many as eighty, different languages, of at least ten different major families, were spoken in this country when Jacques Cartier arrived. Each and every one of them had a history and a literature. It is with them, or what remains of them, that the study of Canadian literature must start. So the question is, what does remain?

I have been chided once or twice for using the phrase "the Haida holocaust." To me the term seems apt. The Haida lost more than ninety per cent of their population in less than a century. In Haida Gwaii the epidemics that brought this about are still, as they should be, a sensitive subject. Any suggestion that others have suffered as much – even comparisons to the experience of the Jews – can cause offense. But this is not at all an isolated case. In 1492, there were perhaps ten million people in the area we know now as the USA and Canada. By 1900, the census figures tell us, the total aboriginal population in this same vast stretch of country was much less than half a million.[10] Decimated is too mild a word. While the colonial population had risen steeply in both countries, the total indigenous population had shrunk by a factor of twenty-five or thirty.[11] Disease had a lot to do with it – smallpox, measles, cholera, diphtheria, scarlet fever. These were abetted, of course, by repeated eviction and forced relocation, and by deliberate diseducation, massive destruction of resources and, in consequence, outright starvation. Declared or not, a war was going on. And its most effective weapons, whether or not anyone ever intended to use them as such, were biological.

Improbable as it may seem, after that much death and destruction, some fifty indigenous languages are still spoken in Canada.[12] The number is shrinking now, faster than in the past, while aboriginal populations are rapidly rising. It is shrinking because of increased pressure, both social and commercial, to speak the colonial tongue. One of my teachers, Ch'óonehte' Má, who died in Whitehorse in 1991, was the last fluent speaker of a language called Tagish. Her grandchildren speak English. Her death alters the map.

It is quite possible to treat what is left behind from all this carnage as a kind of sacred boneyard that no one should go near. But stories and poems are not bones. They are the products of the mind. They are the one kind of sperm that *can* speak a language; they are generated by men and women alike; and they will speak their languages to anyone – male or female, African, Asian, European or Native American – who listens.

I am convinced, myself, that those stories and poems are often of great practical value as well as artistic merit. They are the legacy, after all, of peoples who knew how to live in this land for thousands of years without wrecking it. I do not see a super-abundance of such knowledge and intelligence around me now.

It may be that we as a species will soon learn again what we once generally knew – which is, how to live in the world on the world's terms. But for now, the trees, the rivers, and the sea-run fish are going the way of the buffalo, and if that bleak march continues, humans themselves will soon be next.

If we do want to learn how to live in the world, I think that the study of Native American literature is one of the best and most efficient ways to do just that. It is, after all, a literature of ideas. The ideas are expressed in images, not in abstract language, yet the thought is often dense and profound. And the fundamental subject of this thought, this intellectual tradition, is the relationship between human beings and the rest of the world. I think that is a necessary study, just as important as physics and forestry, chemistry and oceanography. But the study of these literatures has to be conducted, like the study of anything else, by paying respect to the sources, not through reading somebody else's opinion of somebody else's description of what an aboriginal oral poet meant or said. Most of the books in this field are a deep embarrassment. They are nothing more than paraphrases and summaries made at three and four removes from the sources. Whether or not that is cultural appropriation is for someone else to say. It is certainly cultural dilution, of a kind no artist or scholar should condone.

There are, as I said, enough major Native American literatures in the record to give any student who wants it a broad and deep acquaintance with precolonial art and thought.

This is true even if we trim the subject down using the non-aboriginal border between Canada and the USA. There is enough aboriginal oral literature – salvaged in paper form through the collaboration of poets like Skaay of the Qquuna Qiighawaay and anthropologists like John Swanton – to fill an undergraduate and graduate curriculum in the subject. And enough useful work to do – editing and elucidating texts, seeking interpretations, seeking historical facts – to occupy thousands of candidates for graduate degrees.

VI

Thirty years ago, when I first stumbled into the world of the university, I imagined it to be what its name suggested: a place where everything that existed was a bona fide subject of study, and where perspectives could range freely between the global and the microscopic. I began my studies in the sciences, and there the presumption of universality did indeed seem to apply – passably in theory, if poorly in fact. When I slid sideways into the humanities, I did not see at first that the terms of reference had changed, but of course they had. History, philosophy, literature and the arts were fields shaped much more strictly by sectarian or partisan ideas than chemistry, biology or physics.

Universities have changed, of course, in thirty years. They seem to me more fearful and beleaguered than they were, but they also seem more conscious and considerate of cultural diversity. Still, if you read the list of courses offered in history and philosophy at any North American university, and the lists of literature and language courses offered, you will see that the universality of the university is a very distant goal.

Teachers of literature and the arts know that works of the imagination, which lie at the center of what they do, possess in themselves a degree of immunity to the sectarian teachings I have mentioned. The imagination needs ideas and facts, which are the nutrients it feeds on. But until greed or hatred or dishonesty distorts it, the imagination is whole. It keeps making things that are real and complete. And the more specific and localized they are, the more real and complete they often seem to be. So works of art and works of literature are forever making a mockery of the partisan chronologies and hierarchies into which historians often try to place them.

Every culture, like a language, is an endless set of possibilities that works with finite means. That is to say, it can and will transcend itself. Until we touch that self-transcending capability of language, we haven't learned to speak it – because we haven't yet let *it* speak *us*. And until we touch the self-transcending character of a work of art or literature, we are condemned to function as tourists, seeing the other as the picturesque.

When we hear stories one at a time, we're still in a sense trapped in the bus with the tourists. A single story might reseed itself, like a tree – a monoecious tree, like a pine or a spruce. (Other stories, I think, are dioecious, like willows: they need another companionable story with which to mate.) But even an orchard of trees, all the same species, is not the same as a forest. A coherent *system* of storytelling is like a system of science or mathematics. And like a forest, it is more than the sum of its parts. So long as it remains alive, a literature is a system of storytelling, not just a collection of stories or myths. It is a system that can be used to regulate and to record transactions with reality.

We've inherited an educational system with many defects and limitations, but it too is a culture and can reach beyond itself. Within this culture of cultures which we call the university, comparative literature is now a respected discipline. Thanks chiefly to the labors of Northrop Frye, it is also a discipline in which Canadian perspectives have played a formative role. The indigenous literatures of Canada, and of this continent, have nevertheless been systematically ignored. This is not because they are oral. We teach the Odyssey, the Iliad, the Beowulf, and any number of shorter works that are orally composed. And it is not, as I have mentioned, from lack of material. There are works of aboriginal North American oral literature which any jury of scholars, if forced to examine the evidence, would appraise as works of literary genius. But most of these works were transcribed and published a lifetime ago, as ethnographic or linguistic data, not as the poetry they are.

Native American visual art used to be – and frequently still is – collected and exhibited as proof of strangeness, not attainment. It used to be put, along with the dinosaur bones and geodes and stuffed buffaloes, in museums of *natural* history. The museums of *cultural* history were reserved for the work of urbanized Europeans and urbanized Asians, and for those who accepted the primacy of these official traditions. The literary heritage of our species has been segregated and categorized on very similar terms.

Because I know, now, a little bit – certainly no more than that – about the artistic and intellectual achievements of Native American oral poets, I am embarrassed and disturbed to see them still shut out of the academy – or worse, perhaps, ghettoized within it. Few people, I think, earn a university degree in any branch of European Studies or Asian Studies without acquiring some rudimentary knowledge of a European or Asian language. Students of African Studies are also routinely expected to learn an African language. But how many universities ask even their doctoral students in American Studies or in Canadian Studies to learn an indigenous North American language? Not one.

It is true that our universities now teach the work of Leslie

Silko, Scott Momaday, James Welch, Thomas King and others of Native American ancestry who write novels and poems in English. These are four very fine writers, whose works I admire. But we are lying to ourselves if we pretend that teaching these writers can satisfy the university's duty to teach the indigenous literature, art, and intellectual history of the North American continent. When we teach Greek literature, we do not limit the offerings to novels conveniently written in English by Greeks.

It is also true that we now invite aboriginal mythtellers into the schools. You will notice that we do it far more often if they've written books, and we usually ask them to speak in English or French when they get there. It would be far better, I think, if we asked them always to speak in an aboriginal language, and asked them to bring a translator if one were required – because anything the schools and universities can do that adds everyday practical value and dignity to the knowledge of aboriginal languages is for the good. In Haida Gwaii, many young men and some women now grow up to be carvers. If they are good, they can make an excellent living by practicing this art and working from within the Haida tradition. There are no such practical incentives for learning the Haida language. It will not get you much of a job. And Haida poetry, like English poetry, is not an easy commodity to sell in the contemporary world.

Why does it matter? It matters because a language is a lifeform, like a species of plant or animal. Once extinct, it is gone forever. And as each one dies, the intellectual gene pool of the human species shrinks. The big, discontinuous brain to which we all in our way contribute, and on which we all depend, loses a part of itself that it cannot rebuild.

It is true, of course, that languages, like plant and animal species, are dying all the time. But in a healthy forest or lake or ocean or grassland, constant replacement also occurs. In a healthy system there will be long-term change and there will be seasonal variations, but neither the total number of species nor the overall biomass nor the aggregate richness of the gene pool will suffer steep and steady decline. In the global forest of language, over the past three centuries, chronic depletion is precisely what we have seen. The number of living languages has been continuously shrinking. So has the intellectual gene pool – the word hoard and grammar hoard and story hoard of the earth. As for the intellectual biomass, I do not claim to know. We could measure it, I think, as the total number of stories per year that are told, adjusted for vividness, length, complexity, and ecological attention. Unadjusted, it is probably increasing, like the harvest of Christmas trees and nutritionless potatoes and the production of sliced white bread.

A story is an assemblage, you could say, of intellectual chromosomes. Each time a story is told and heard, something like fertilization occurs. But real perpetuation and renewal, as we know, are not achieved by fertilization alone. Gestation and birth and upbringing and maturation are also parts of the process. The accumulation of wisdom is part of the process, not performed by individuals so much as by whole ecologies. Stories need those too.

Translation, of course, is a hurdle. But it can be crossed, unlike the painted wall of paraphrase or the blank wall of silence and denial. The labor and pleasure of crossing it should be shared, I think, as widely as possible. But it shouldn't be thrust on the storytellers themselves.

Mythtellers tell their stories to those who are listening. They also tell their stories to themselves. That is hard to do in a foreign language. When you ask a mythteller to tell you a story in your language rather than hers, the mythteller must talk only to you, not to herself. And then something is missing.

I'm not suggesting the foundation of more departments of native studies, such as several North American universities already have. I am proposing that to teach Canadian or American literature, history, philosophy, and art in an honest way, some part of the faculty in each of *these* departments will have to become conversant with aboriginal languages. Any individual scholar who wishes to should be free, of course, to concentrate on the writings of the colonists or on the postcolonial period, and to specialize in the work of any colonial writer. But when the entire profession chooses that path – without giving the other so much as a thought – then the profession erects and sustains a *language bar* as dangerous and difficult to cross as the color bar, whose place in colonial history we know, or ought to know, so well.

There are scholars who hold that Canada is the name of a human construct, empty of meaning until the dream of Confederation. Canadian writers and critics, on the other hand, have been saying for many years, with almost perfect unanimity, that Canadian literature speaks from the land, that its allegiance is to *place*. If we believe any of that, doesn't it follow that our literature, and our literary history, has to begin with the voices that spoke from this place first and have spoken from it longest and appear to know its deepest layers best? But to admit that this is so would make things inconvenient. The professors of literature, the school teachers, librarians, and newspaper editors, all proud of their grasp of current issues, would suddenly need to go back to school and learn to construe a basic Haida or Ojibwa or Chipewyan sentence.

The United States of America is indeed a human construct. We can tell that by its name. But America or Canada might, like France or Ireland or Tibet, be the name of a place. And Canadian might be the right name for any person who is in any deep sense connected to that place. (English requires us to call US citizens Americans. Spanish lets us differentiate between *americano* and *estadounidense* ["United-Statesian"] – a sometimes necessary and useful distinction to make.)

Canada is a country much reshaped by immigration. I'm an immigrant here too. Still, this is not a world invented out of nothing in 1867 or 1534. Nor was the USA invented out of nothing in 1776 or 1492. Language and literature both know this. They will tell you if you ask. Both literature and language are human universals, as natural to us as feathers are to birds. We extend them and elaborate them, yes – but as Aristotle knew, poetics is rightly a branch of biology. Neither literature nor language is entirely man-made. Countries aren't entirely made by human beings either.

VII

In polyphonic music, several voices sing or play at once. They sometimes say very similar things in several different ways; they sometimes contradict each other. Each voice has its own melodic line, its own simultaneous path through musical space. Dissonance can occur; it may even be sought, though it is rarely expected to last. Some voices may say more than others, but no one voice is allowed to dominate the whole. Shakespeare can tell two or three stories at once. So can some oral poets I have met. Polyphony is not a distinctively European phenomenon, either in literature or in music. And something approximating visual polyphony – simultaneous multiple visual identity – happens so frequently in Haida sculpture that it almost seems routine.

The principles of polyphonic structure have been very important to me in my own writing for years, and it may seem more than a little egocentric for me to suggest that the entirety of Canadian literature and intellectual history should join in this pursuit. But I hold no patent on polyphony. And the motet is something like the forest: a supple, flexible, trim and self-policing form with room for many voices. In its earlier days, it was one of the forms that passed freely through the wall between pagan peasant cultures and the church.

Immigrants to Canada tell many different stories now, as they always have. But the great waves of colonial migration that came in earlier years put one story far above the others and told it every day or every week throughout the year. It is a story obsessed with its own beginning and end. Creation, garden of Eden, discovery of knowledge, descent into sin, redemption through torture and death and resurrection, and one last act: a final judgement yet to come.

In pagan stories around the world, there is usually no original sin; human beings as a species are not guilty. Neither are they perfect, and there is no final judgement. There is death and resurrection or reincarnation, but it happens every day, through making love, bearing children, telling stories, killing animals, eating their flesh, wearing their clothes, and leaving animals enough, and fish enough, and trees enough, that they will be here next year and the next and the next without end. There is, I think, an implicit understanding in these stories that you *must* eat of the fruit of the tree of knowledge, a little every day, and that you *can* eat from the fruit day after day, but what you mustn't do is cut down the tree or sell the ground on which it grows.

One story is not enough. One history is not enough. One literature, in a country such as this, is not enough. Nor two. But the world I meet in the television set and in the store has evolved no system for dealing with multiple stories except to turn them into commodities. That divorces them from the land, and it divorces them from us. Money, in the narrow sense in which we understand it now, is species-specific. We need a more meaningful currency – one acceptable to some of the other creatures with whom we share the planet.

VIII

Jan Zwicky, reading an earlier draft of this lecture, asked what I think is a very important question. If we conceive Canadian literature in this polyphonic and multicultural way, as simultaneously aboriginal, colonial, and postcolonial, it is a literature that is deeply fissured. In how many other world literatures would we confront an epochal split like that?

It seems to me that if we are speaking of literatures *as we might intelligently study them* rather than literatures as we *do* usually study them, then the answer is *quite a few.* The literatures of all the Americas, and of Australia and New Zealand, certainly qualify. The literatures of Africa, India, Oceania, and those of Siberia and Tibet, Indonesia and the Philippines, qualify as well. With that, we've already covered most of the globe.

What happens if we look a bit more closely at the favored and famous literatures of imperial Europe and Asia? Is there such an epochal split hidden in Latin and Greek tradition? There is evidence that such a split once existed, even if we can't confront it squarely anymore. All we get is linguistic silt, like the little discovery that θάλασσα [thálassa], the Greek word for *sea*, isn't really Greek at all. Greek was an inland language, brought to the coast by invaders. We can't quite come to grips with the contradictions this implies, because we don't have records of the pre-invasion literatures of Greece, nor of the pre-invasion literatures of the invaders. There is a polyphonic residue, in the rich polytheism of Homer and Hesiod, but only one Greek language and one Greek literature left to read.

In British literature, such an epochal split is palpable, however, to anyone who studies Welsh or Gaelic. The literature of

Spain embraces not just Spanish but also Basque, Catalan, Gali-
cian, Hebrew, and Arabic components. Italian literature used to
include Etruscan and several other strands, now altogether lost.
The literature of what we now call Russia properly includes
the oral literatures of the Buryat, the Chukchi, the Komi, the
Tatars, the Tuvinians, and many other peoples who speak non-
Slavic and indeed non-Indo-European languages. The literature
of Japan, with its layers of Ainu epic, the Kojiki and Nihongi,
and the highly Sinified lyric and prose narrative that have succeeded them, is another bundle of deeply divergent traditions.

Even in China itself, after several millennia of sustained and
often savage but never wholly successful attempts at imposing
centralized control, many traces of heterogeneity remain. The
diplomatic line is that Chinese is one language with a number
of regional dialects. In fact, as any reputable linguist will happily inform you, Chinese is a family of at least eight different
living languages. Many specialists count thirteen. In addition
to Mandarin (the language of Beijing), there is Wú (spoken
widely in Zhejiang and Jiangsu), Yuè (Cantonese, the language
of Guangzhou), Northern Min (the major language of Fujian),
Southern Min (the language heard most often in Taiwan), Gàn
(spoken in Jiangxi), Xiang (spoken in Hunan), Hakka (spoken in Guangdong). But there are also, in Taiwan and on the
mainland, dozens of other living indigenous languages and
literatures that may, if you insist, be geographically Chinese
but are linguistically and historically something else. One of
these languages, Tibetan, has a long and highly developed written tradition as well as a substantial oral literature. There are
others with scripts of their own, and more that are effectively
unwritten. The literatures exist, though they are hidden.

Written Chinese consists, to a large extent, of symbols for
meanings rather than sounds. It does have phonetic components, but most of these are archaic and therefore imprecise

in relation even to classical speech. This makes the script far more difficult to learn than the script of English, Tibetan, or Arabic, but it makes it more portable. Maimonides could write Hebrew in Arabic script, but the Hebrew he wrote in this way can only be read in Hebrew, just as English written in Latin letters can only be read in some version of English. The most we can do in such a case – reading Shakespeare or Yeats aloud, for example – is fiddle a bit with the dialect. What is written in Mandarin, however, can be read in Wú or Yuè – or in Japanese or Vietnamese or Korean. When you pierce the veil of Chinese writing (and of equally formal performance arts, such as Chinese opera) and enter the storytellers' world, you discover, again, tremendous multiplicity and the richness of regional difference. That richness doesn't appear to be much threatened by the unusually homogeneous Chinese script. What threatens it is industrial and commercial homogenization, relentlessly standardized education, and conformist politics.

Perhaps, then, harmonically pure literatures are rare and rather freakish. Perhaps they are the legacies of a few expansive empires whose standardization campaigns succeeded too well. Or perhaps they are mostly figments of imagination: bowdlerized versions of cultural history masking a richer and livelier cultural reality. It seems to me that world literature is really rather holographic. The multilayered, multistranded character of the whole is echoed locally almost everywhere you look. And China is not the only place in the world where that richness and variety are now under serious threat.

NOTES

1 Encyc. Brit., 14th ed. (1973), vol. 1: 729. This is the edition "dedicated by permission to the heads of the two [sic] English-speaking peoples, Richard Milhous Nixon ... and Her Majesty Queen Elizabeth the Second."

2 George H. Griffin, *Legends of the Evergreen Coast* (Vancouver: Clarke & Stuart, 1934): [8]. In Griffin's versions, the stories are not only "embellished"; they are "modified in such a way as not to offend good taste" (p 137).

3 C.M. Bowra, *Primitive Song* (London: Weidenfeld & Nicholson, 1962): 236.

4 Rien ne nous assure que la littérature soit immortelle; sa chance, aujourd'hui, son unique chance, c'est la chance de l'Europe, du socialisme, de la démocratie, de la paix. – Jean-Paul Sartre, *Qu'est-ce que la littérature?* (Paris: Gallimard, 1948): 356.

5 *Qu'est-ce que la littérature?*, pp 356–7.

6 Encyc. Brit., 14th ed. (1973), vol. 4: 762. For a more thoughtful view of Scott, see Stan Dragland, *Floating Voice: Duncan Campbell Scott and the Literature of Treaty 9* (Concord, Ontario: Anansi, 1994).

7 The Confederation Bridge was opened for traffic in June 1997. As bridge proponents hoped and others feared, chain stores and vastly increased tourist traffic followed.

8 Alfred L. Kroeber et al, *Franz Boas* (Menasha, Wisconsin: American Anthropological Association, 1943): 20. In the same work (p 18) Kroeber, who should know, casts doubt on the familiar story of the dueling scars. But Boas himself mentions both the duels and the wounds in letters he wrote before his 21st birthday. See Clyde Kluckhohn & Olaf Prufer, "Influences During the Formative Years," in *The Anthropology of Franz Boas*, edited by Walter Goldschmidt (Menasha, Wisconsin: American Anthropological Association, 1959): 8.

9 Boas was also, incidentally, one of the first North American educators to encourage the full participation of women in the learned professions. That is the reason why students such as Margaret Mead, Gene Weltfish, Ruth Bunzel, and Ruth Benedict prospered under his leadership just as fully as

Alfred Kroeber and John Swanton. His friend Paul Rivet, who was with him when he died, reported his last words: "Il ne faut pas se lasser de répéter que le racisme est une monstreuse erreur ou un impudent mensonge...." (Paul Rivet, "Franz Boas," *Renaissance* I.2, New York, 1943: 313).

10 The estimates, especially for earlier years, are many and vary widely. For a convenient summary, see Russell Thornton, *American Indian Holocaust and Survival: A Population History since 1492* (Norman: U of Oklahoma Press, 1987). Two other important studies are William M. Denevan, *The Native Population of the Americas in 1492* (Madison: U of Wisconsin Press, 1992) and J.W. Verano & D.H. Ubelaker, *Disease and Demography in the Americas* (Washington, DC: Smithsonian Institution, 1992).

11 This in turn raises one of the grisliest questions in demographics. To reduce a population from ten million to, say, 350,000 at one blow, you have to slaughter 9.65 million. But how many must be killed in order to produce a steady decline from ten million to 350,000 over a span of 400 years? So many variables now come into play that a simple answer is impossible, but it appears that the answer is more – perhaps much more – than the simple difference of 9.65 million.

12 For a list and an assessment of the status of these languages – like all such assessments, open to quibbling and already out of date – see M. Dale Kinkade, "The Decline of Native Languages in Canada," pp 157–76 in *Endangered Languages*, edited by R.H. Robins & E.M. Uhlenbeck (Oxford: Berg, 1991).

THE PERSISTENCE OF POETRY

AND THE DESTRUCTION OF

THE WORLD

What it pleases us to call the New World is in fact a very old world – just as old, at any rate, as Asia, Europe, and Africa. It is part of the ancient continent of Pangaea, born from the same geological matrix as Europe. Its rivers and forests, and its ecology and geology, were thoroughly developed long before Columbus. And it has been inhabited by thinking, speaking, knowing human beings for several thousand years.

But an inhabited world, with its own philosophical, artistic, scientific, and literary traditions, is not what the European conquerors and colonists wanted to find. It is therefore not what they saw. They saw instead an empty world, free and ripe for the taking. They saw a gift of God meant for no one but themselves.

This deliberate hallucination is still with us, like the star of a Christmas without end.

The European colonists' arrival in the New World marks the escalation of a war that had been fought in Europe and Asia for more than two millennia and continues even now. It is the war between those who think they belong to the world and those who think that the world belongs to them. It is the war between the pagans, who know they are surrounded and

---

Universidad de La Laguna, Tenerife
8 May 1996 [translated from Spanish]

outnumbered by the gods, and all the devotees of the number one – one empire, one history, one market, or one God – and who nowadays insist on the preeminence of everyone for himself: the smallest number one of all.

It is no accident that prophets of monotheism, including Plato and Mohammed, have often banished the poets. These prophets understand that the poet is a pagan and polytheist by nature. In a certain sense, even Dante, Milton, San Juan de la Cruz, Teresa of Ávila, Gerard Manley Hopkins, and T. S. Eliot are pagans. Without admitting it, they seem to understand, like the peoples of the Altiplano of Bolivia and Peru, and like many Native Canadians, that it is best to interpret Christianity as one more form of paganism.

But Mohammed and Plato are poets too in their way, monotheistic and tedious at times, but very much livelier and more pluralistic at others.

The great danger is single-mindedness: reducing things to one perspective, one idea, one overriding rule.

A polytheistic understanding of the world survived in Europe even in the time of the conquistadors, though it was then forced to take a wordless form. Music gave it refuge. It is found in polyphonic music, which is the music of multiple, simultaneous and independent voices. The churches of Europe overflowed with music of this kind in the fifteenth, sixteenth and seventeenth centuries. It did not change the course of history, but it preserved an essential perception of the plurality of being. It preserved the essential, faithful heresy that reality is not of just one mind.

European music of more recent centuries is, for the most part, homophonic. It is the music of one voice that speaks in the name of all and of many voices that answer as one voice.

In the meantime, the conquest continues – in South America, North America, Asia, Australia, and in Europe too.

It continues in Bosnia and Hercegovina, where a tradition of oral epic poetry survived from Homer's time until even a few months ago. Now, at this moment, the villages in which those poets lived are rubble and mass graves.

From Alaska to Tierra del Fuego, and from Ireland to Japan, the forests fall and subdivisions replace them. The homes of the gods are supplanted by the houses and garages of human beings. It is hard work, this eviction of the gods and of all the cultures that acknowledge their existence. We keep at it even so.

The Haida poet Skaay refers to human beings as *xhaaydla xitiit ghidaay*: "plain, ordinary surface birds." Creatures with more power – killer whales, loons, grebes, sea lions, seals – know how to dive. They pierce the surface, the *xhaaydla* it is called in Haida. If we go with them – if, that is, we are invited to go with them – we enter the world of the myths. We come back speaking poetry.

Two thousand kilometers south of the country of the poet Skaay, in the Ruby Mountains, the country of the Paiute, now part of the state of Nevada, there are pines of the species *Pinus aristata*, bristlecone pines. These trees live longer than any other creatures on the earth. The oldest individuals – not much taller than I am – are 5,000 years of age or more. A few years ago, a person who called himself a scientist found in these mountains a pine that might, he thought, be the oldest of all. He cut it down to count its rings. He killed what may indeed have been the oldest living being in the world, to convert it into a statistic. Then he published his report, without the least apology, in a scientific journal.[1]

This is not science. It is one more thoughtless manifestation of the conquest, one more step in reducing the world to human terms.

The American novelist William Faulkner, when he received

the Nobel Prize, concluded his address, by saying, "Mankind will not only survive, he will prevail." I am an admirer of Faulkner, but I think that his prediction is logically impossible. I think that if humanity survives, it can only be because it does *not* prevail, and that if we insist, like Ozymandias, on prevailing, we will surely not survive.

I have been listening to the world for barely half a century. I do not have the wisdom even of a young tree of an ordinary kind. Nevertheless, I have been listening – with eyes, ears, mind, feet, fingertips – and what I hear is poetry.

What does this poetry say? It says that what-is *is*: that the real is real, and that it is alive. It speaks the grammar of being. It sings the polyphonic structure of meaning itself.

In the great ceiling of the Sistine Chapel there are readers rather than writers. The prophets and sibyls scrutinize their folios and scrolls. Nothing is written there that we can read. The great pages in their laps and in their hands reflect what happens as if they were mirrors. In front of these blank mirrors the blind prophets are listening. There is only one writer, Jehosaphat the scribe, tucked away in the corner with his scrap of paper, listening to those who really listen.

The theme of the ceiling is the poetry of the world, not the glory of the poet.

It is true that the face of Michelangelo is there in the midst of the chapel's big back wall. It is rendered, this self-portrait, as a face still attached to a human hide freshly peeled from someone else's living body. The sculptor is subsumed in his own tale. The listener listens to himself. In the midst of his own vision, the visionary can be seen. But he is peeled. In the midst of that most sculptural of paintings, the image of the sculptor is reduced to two dimensions.

When I was a youngster in school, someone asked me, "If a tree falls in the forest with no one there to hear it, does it make a sound or not?" The question is demented. If a tree falls in the forest, all the other trees are there to hear it. But if a man cuts down the forest and then cries that he has no food, no firewood, no shade, and that his mind can get no traction, who is going to hear him?

Poetry is the language of being: the breath, the voice, the song, the speech of being. It does not need us. We are the ones in need of it. If we haven't learned to hear it, we will also never speak it.

Beings eat one another. This is the fundamental business of the world. It is the whole, not any of its parts, that must prevail, and this whole is always changing. There is no indispensable species, and no indispensable culture. Especially not a culture that dreams of eating without being eaten, and that offers the gods not even the guts or the crumbs.

When he sees his own people destroying the world, what is the poet to say? *Stop*? Or more politely, *Please stop, please*?

All the poets of all times can only say one thing. They can say that what-is is. When he sees his people destroying the world, the poet can say, "we're destroying the world." He can say it in narrative or lyric or dramatic or meditative form, tragic or ironic form, short form or long form, in verse or prose. But he cannot lie, as a poet, and offer himself as the savior. He can believe or not believe that salvation is possible. He can believe in one God or in many gods or in none. He can believe or not believe in belief. But he cannot finally say anything more than the world has told him.

When he sees that, in absolute terms, we human beings are now too numerous – in addition to the fact that we seem too powerful as a species – what is the poet going to do? Pull the trigger? Sing a song of praise to Herod or to Hitler? It is hard to say it to other humans, and humans, of course, are loathe to believe it, but this is the fact: human beings have built a world in which humans need to die more and faster than they do. Yet even in this condition, murder is not the answer.

Long ago, in a book of poems protesting the war in Vietnam, I read a simple statement that stays with me. I have not in thirty years been able to find the book again, and I am told that the lines I remember are really quoted from a speech by Martin Luther King. I remember seeing them in a poem, but perhaps the book in which I saw them was published only in my dreams. The lines as I remember them, in any case, are these:

> When one is guided by conscience only,
> there is no other side
> to which one can cross.

There is no other earth to cross to either. There are no new worlds. Paradise will not be our asylum, and our hell will not be anywhere other than here. The world is one, at the same time that it is plural, inherently plural, like the mind. The proof of this plurality is the persistence of poetry in our time. It is extraordinary but true, in the present day, that poetry survives in the voices of humans, just as it does in the voices of all the other species in the world.

NOTE

1 The first-person account of this event is in Donald R. Currey, "An Ancient Bristlecone Pine Stand in Eastern Nevada," *Ecology* 46.4 (Durham, North Carolina, 1965): 564–6. Galen Rowell retells the story well in *High and Wild* (San Francisco: Sierra Club, 1979): 99–105.

THE VOCATION OF BEING,

THE TEXT OF THE WHOLE

I

I've been asked to deal with two subjects, *text* and *vocation*, and therein lies a problem. The making of texts appears to be a central part of my vocation – but everything those texts are able to say depends on the silence they contain. *Text* and *vocation* are, as a consequence, two subjects I am instinctively silent *about* – not out of modesty but out of plain self-preservation. If the invitation to talk about these subjects had come from anything other than a university, where we all know we are free to make fools of ourselves in the interests of our own and one another's education, I would certainly have turned the offer down. But the terms of this particular invitation tempted me to think that I could learn something – and learning, after all, is the original vocation.

The conditions of the assignment have prodded me, of course, to think especially about the relation of text and vocation to the humanities and the sciences. Those are domains which, in my own mental universe, or university, cannot be divided from each other, as they have recently been here.[1]

Peculiar things are sometimes done with texts in universities these days, so let me warn you (or reassure you) that I don't intend to demonstrate my meatcutting skills by working over any particular text. I only want to say a thing or two about the nature of text in general and about the kinds of texts that find

University of Victoria, British Columbia
22 January 1998

their way, or sometimes fail to find their way, into university classrooms.

Texts are things I make and things I read, digest, metabolize. They're also things I frequently interpret, in the very specific sense of giving them their typographic form. But most of all, texts are things I listen to. There are some very real and significant differences between oral and written literature, but I believe that all good writing has an oral root. All writing that is good to read sounds good when read aloud, because its goodness lies in part in its *humanity*. The humanity of a piece of writing is partly intellectual, of course, but it is also partly physical, like the humanity of a shoe or a shirt or a shovel. It fits the human body. A good shovel fits the hand and foot, and a good sentence fits the voice, because that is the part of the body we normally use to handle sentences.

The voice has an anatomy, like the arm, the heart, the foot. The voice is made of breath. A sentence or a paragraph that pays no attention to the reach and rhythm of the voice is uncomfortable or painful, like a shoe that doesn't fit the human foot or a glove on the wrong hand. But a sentence that *does* fit the anatomy of voice and breath will touch, through them, some other rhythms of the body: those of the heart and hands and feet, and of the memory and mind. The limbs – the arms and legs – in Greek, are μέλοι [*méloi*]. That is the root of the word *melody* in English.

The mind has an anatomy as well, and every sentence, paragraph, or stanza has to be *humane* in that respect. The syntax of the sentence, and the pattern of its images, will touch the mind directly. Those aspects of the sentence have to fit the mind's anatomy, just the way the handle of a shovel has to fit the hand.

Part of my hope when I work as a poet is to make a text that sounds the way it thinks. And when I work as a typographer, my aim is to make a text that looks the way it sounds. If it

47

looks the way it sounds and sounds the way it thinks, and if it thinks soundly – that is, honestly and clearly – something promising has started. Once it starts to speak and sing, I want to know how far it likes to walk, and how much it can carry, and how beautifully it dances.

A text that is physically well written or well printed can of course be an extremely satisfying piece of abstract art. A piece of late fifteenth- or early sixteenth-century French or Italian printing – something from the press of Aldus Manutius or Simon de Colines or Nicolas Jenson, for example, is a lovely thing to handle and to see, in perfect silence. So is a piece of calligraphy by Huáng Tíngjiān (黃庭堅) or Ono no Michikaze (小野の道風). But now we have entered the realm of pages or characters rather than texts. A sentence that enters the body through the eye is taking the long road, not a shortcut. It has to travel through the ear as well to do its proper work. A sentence that begins in spoken language has to travel through the ear to fulfill its vocation as a sentence.

II

Vocation means, of course, a call. Diplomas are written, vocations are spoken. To find a vocation means to be summoned: called to exceed your qualifications, whatever they may be; called to explore and to fulfill your capabilities. Those who have vocations inhabit a world where doing and being are one and the same because continuous learning unites them. I have learned, as a frequent visitor to universities, that the university itself is often such a world, for its students as much as for its faculty – and that one of the greater challenges of life in North America today is not so much to *find* as to *maintain* one's vocation after leaving university.

All the outside world seems to offer nowadays is a job – if it even offers that. But a job is not a vocation. A vocation won't fit within the confines of a job. And the wealth that vocations generate is not the kind of wealth you can measure in money. A vocation is work instead of a job. Hunting, fishing, farming, cooking, healing, nursing, mothering, fathering, painting, writing, teaching, composing, performing, watching the sky, talking to plants, talking to animals.... All these ancient and recent vocations – some of them much older than the species *Homo sapiens*, and some of them much younger – are facets or forms or corollaries of the one fundamental vocation, which is *learning* – and maintaining and refining and protecting and sharing whatever we can of what we have learned. Some of these ancient vocations have impressive modern names – agriculture, medicine, astronomy, botany, zoology, pedagogy and so on. And all of these domains are now encrusted with institutions. Institutions – including universities, when managers get hold of them – have a strange way of smothering and muffling vocations and reducing them to fragments. Those fragments of vocations are called jobs.

In the beginning, a vocation isn't much. Just perhaps a nagging interest that blossoms as habitual attention. It matures into continuous, compassionate, active, multivalent curiosity. Curiosity like that has a peculiar side effect. It produces, over time, a sense of intellectual responsibility. And that produces in its turn a nonconforming and nonconfining sense of identity. In other words, it is whole. A job is always a fragment. Vocation is whole.

A Douglas-fir's vocation is to be a Douglas-fir. A trout's vocation is to be a trout. The vocation of every human is to be a human being – and that would be the full text of this lecture if humans were summoned into being on the same terms as the Doug-fir or the trout. If humans had no driving need to manufacture stories, clothes, and houses, and if humans

49

turned their offspring loose in the form of fertilized eggs or seeds, then the task of *being human* would be out of our control. The genes would be in charge. But we as human beings take delivery of ourselves in a state of natural and perpetual incompleteness, for which culture is the one imperfect cure. That built-in incompleteness is the biological price and the foundation of free will. We are born questions. Culture is the thin but sometimes lovely web of answers we keep spinning for ourselves. Yet the questions are still there – and when we start to hear them clearly, what we hear is our vocation. A vocation is a call, but the call is not a command; it is a question.

III

There are over 4,000 living species of mammals and almost 9,000 living species of birds. That is a tiny fraction – less than a tenth of one per cent – of the total number of living animal species, but virtually all of those 13,000 species of mammals and birds have something intriguing in common. They train their young. They actively define and shape their species. They have two interlocking kinds of heredity: genetic and exogenetic. They inherit from the previous generation not only through the genes but through the senses and the brain, by learning skills and facts and songs and patterns of behavior. They then continue learning. And they teach skills and facts and songs and patterns of behavior to the younger generation in their turn.

Culture is exogenetic heredity, nothing less and nothing more. It is everything we transmit from generation to generation by nongenetic means.

Taking a narrow view, we can say that everything required to practice the vocation of trout or mosquito or Douglas-fir or black-eyed Susan is transmitted through the genes. It has to be, because these and millions of other species abandon their young as eggs or spores or seeds. But to practice the vocation of winter wren or black-tailed deer or black bear, or the vocation of human being, a standard share in the species' genetic bankroll is simply not enough. An education is required. Culture is not a luxury. It is life-support.

That, to repeat, is the narrow view. In the broader view, it is obvious that even for the trout or Douglas-fir, its genetic endowment alone is inadequate. The trout needs a trout stream. The Doug-fir needs a forest floor. All of us – animals, plants, bacteria and fungi – need the community we create for one another and the earth that underlies it and the sun that keeps it warm. The community we create for one another is, of course, the ecosystem. That is culture in the large sense. Culture in this large sense is identical with nature. It is nature *seen from the inside*. From the standpoint of any given species, this culture in the large sense – the environment – is exogenetic too. It is genetically produced and genetically maintained, but not by any single species. On its own, no species can create a situation that enables it to live, much less to thrive.

If there is anything unusual in the culture of human beings, compared with the culture of other animals, it is this: the degree to which we draw not only parents but grandparents and ancestors into the educational process. The native nations of North America claim, quite justifiably, to be more cultured than colonial societies, because of the strong relationships they form between children and grandparents, and the respect they pay in general to their elders. Colonial societies, like those of the old world, though they pack their elders off to retirement communities and rest homes, claim to be more cultured than everyone else because of their obsession with old books and historical records, which extend the thread of exogenetic heredity still further.

Human culture has, we like to think, become unusually complex. We pose more questions and produce more answers, right or wrong or good or bad, than any other species: shoes, hats, tools, boats, houses, gardens, ovens, kilns, roads, cities, epic poems, printed books, sonatas, violins, electron microscopes, rosaries and so on. But all those *things* are expendable if need be. The essentials aren't the artifacts themselves. The essentials are the foraging and navigating skills, and the techniques and understanding of materials that are needed to make the artifacts – the shoes, hats, tools, boats and so on – on demand. This knowledge is embodied in the structures of the mind, and the structures of the mind are embodied in the artifacts. The mind is part of the body, the body is part of the world, and the world is part of the mind. The artifacts move around that circle as long as they are used.

The archaeological dig is a good place to begin the study of culture. It also helps explain why *vocation* has two basic connotations: one of the spirit and one of the hand. Vocational schools train carpenters and cooks, yet we are apt to say the singer and the surgeon and the scholar have vocations. These are two halves of one meaning. The space between them is filled with all the kinds of fragmentary work that isn't vocational: all those aberrations and illusions known as paying jobs. Intellectual and manual vocations have many other things in common. The institution of apprenticeship is one. Out of that grows allegiance to the craft, based in the practical realization that the facts, whatever they are, are not inert; they are the native tongue of meaning.

Another thing that intellectual and manual vocations have in common is the danger of misuse, the danger of betrayal by historical and personal ambitions. Vocation is fascination, not ambition; it is work emancipated from time: a dialogue with being, not a program of predation and control. Freedom from time means not just freedom from the clock but freedom from agendas of apocalypse and freedom from the hunger to make history. History isn't made; it is discovered. Historical agendas and ambitions – the appetites for conquest and for profit and for power – often masquerade as real vocations. And true vocation brings a consciousness of power, which sometimes spells the end of the vocation out of which it grew. The soldier and the statesman and the priest, the lawyer and the trader and the scholar, even the physician, work in the shadow of this danger. Piety is twisted into missionary zeal, defensive skill is pumped up into armed aggression, the search for knowledge withers into hunger for authority.

Beauty, Immanuel Kant says, is something we perceive as the trace of a certain kind of intention, more or less synonymous with play:

Schönheit ist Form der Zweckmäßigkeit eines Gegenstandes, sofern sie, ohne Vorstellung eines Zwecks, an ihm wahrgenommen wird.[2]

That means, beauty is perceived as the quality of *innocent intent*: the quality of purpose *without any end in mind*. In forms which have that quality, Kant says, nature and culture function as one. And that is close – very close, it seems to me – to the essence of vocation.

You may hear an echo of that notion in something Northrop Frye said once about the study and teaching of literature, which was his own vocation:

No one who believes that he teaches the best subject matter in the world is going to worry very much about the goals of teaching.... There can really be no goal where taking the journey itself is the best thing to be done.[3]

You may hear that echo once again, in something else Frye said about his calling – something that bears very closely on the nature of vocation and on the vocation of the university itself:

The English teacher's ideal is the exact opposite of "effective commu-nication," or learning to become audible in the market place. What he has to teach is the verbal expression of truth, beauty and wisdom: in short, the disinterested use of words.[4]

The *school* may indeed exist for the purpose of adjusting the student to society. But the *teacher* exists for the purpose of frustrating that adjustment. Why? Because vocation is bet-ter than adjustment, and the two are not the same. Vocation is articulate; adjustment hums along. But why, in a healthy society, should vocation be a form of maladjustment? Because society is never healthy in that sense. Health in society *means* that maladjustment can be fruitful.

IV

The vocation of every human, I've been saying, is to be a hu-man being. When we succeed in that vocation, what we make and do is typically *humane*. And a text, even a sentence, in order to function, has to be humane. It has to be humane in a very physiological sense. The mind is no less physiological than the body.

The word *humanism* was oddly misunderstood by a num-ber of twentieth-century writers. Many of them defined it, wrongly, as the view that human beings are or ought to be the center of the universe. It is as if they traced the etymology of "humanism" back to David Hume. In fact the root appears to be **dhghem*, an archaic Indo-European word for *earth*. Latin *humanus* is related to English *humus* and Greek χθόνιος, as in *chthonic*. A human is an earthling. These and other shreds of linguistic evidence suggest that Indo-Europeans and Native Americans once thought about such matters in similar terms. In Navajo, humans are called *nihokáá dine'é*, "earth-surface people." In Haida, they are *xhaaydla xhaaydaghaay*, "surface people," or in the language of classical Haida poetry, *xhaaydla xhitiit ghidaay*, "ordinary surface birds." Not the center of the universe, but shallow-rooted denizens – and absolute dependents – of the world.

Humanism is not quite a philosophy in the conventional sense of the word. It is the name of a form of expression, sensuous and reticent both at the same time. It is the name of a pagan tradition of thought, alive but not unchallenged in Periclean Athens, revived to some degree in Augustan Rome, and powerfully revived once again in the north of Italy during the Renaissance. It is, like the Jewish tradition, highly literate. It has had to be, for precisely the same reason: because of persecution. Yet, in its way, it is nearly mum – because it is the custom in the humanist tradition that rich philosophical ideas are expressed in art and poetry: in images and myths, far more than in expository or analytical language. What occurs in these images and myths is what occurs in every developed mythic tradition. That is, a distillation and condensation of time and space. Ancients and moderns, Christians and pagans, gods and humans, sinners and saints commingle in similar form and at similar size. The implicit assumption is not that humans and gods are equally powerful. The assumption is that gods and humans are equally *interesting*, despite the inequity of power, because they inhabit a single world and are bound by a single fate. There is one intellectual ecosystem for all, because there is one earth on which to live.

The product of the humanist tradition is the study of the humanities. And as Charles Frankel said a few days before his murder, in 1979,

The humanities are that form of knowledge in which the knower is revealed. All knowledge becomes humanistic when this effect takes place, when we are asked to contemplate not only a proposition but the proposer, when we hear the human voice behind what is being said.[5]

If all knowledge is or can be humanistic, where do we begin? The education that you need depends on the life that you foresee, and that depends on the world you inherit. Education can be, and it has been, a force for the destruction of culture as much as for its maintenance and creation. This is worth remembering. There were, for example, in recent time, a number of residential schools for aboriginal children here on the West Coast. At Mission, Chilliwack, Alberni, Ahousat, Alert Bay, Kitimat, Port Simpson, Metlakatla, Sitka, and at Carcross in the Yukon, for example, children from all the native nations of the coast were taught to be apprentice Europeans instead of indigenous North Americans.

Much of the instruction in these schools was vocational, in the shrunken sense of the word. Girls were taught to cook and sew in the English manner – to make dresses, tablecloths and curtains in the current English style. Boys were taught European farming and gardening, carpentry and tinsmithing. Personal hygiene was also – as we know from school records and advertisements – a subject very popular with supervisors and staff. But half the day, as a rule, was spent on more elevated subjects: European history and geography, English literature, arithmetic and bookkeeping. Often there were art classes, invariably based on nineteenth-century European landscape and figure drawing. Students were regularly punished for speaking their own languages, and for drawing or carving in aboriginal style. When they returned to their bands or villages, they were of course completely unequipped to live in what had been their world. Some of them drifted into the cannery towns and cities looking for work. Others picked up and continued their real education from the point at which the school had interrupted it.

What if those students had been offered a *humanist* education instead of assimilationist training? Would that have meant teaching them Latin and Greek, and the Doric and Ionic and Corinthian architectural orders, or showing them reproductions of the works of Michelangelo and Titian?

I think not. Not unless they freely chose to specialize in European Studies.

I think that a humanist education, in those schools, would have included language, first of all: meaning the students' indigenous languages and other neighboring tongues. It would have included tribal history, local geography, astronomy, oceanography, zoology and botany. And above all, it would have included what always lies at the center of a humanist education: mythology. Not Latin and Greek mythology. Not the mythology you need to read the plays of Shakespeare or the poems of Keats and Shelley, but classical Northwest Coast mythology. If those students had been in a real humanist school, they would have been reading and editing and correcting the very texts that their own parents and grandparents had recently dictated to Franz Boas and John Swanton and Edward Sapir: the linguists and ethnologists who were the first humanist scholars to come to this coast from the outside.

In other words, if those students had been offered an education in *the humanities*, it would have been, more or less, a bookish version of the very education they could have had in oral form at home – provided the missionaries and fur traders and gold miners and lumbermen and colonists had left their homes intact and left the land that they depended on as fruitful as it was.

There is a lesson in that, it seems to me, for the universities – which have become, in some ways, big residential schools for the world, and which have in their hands the power to sustain and enlarge and deepen and, especially, to *restore* the cultural life of the communities they serve. They also have the power, like the residential schools, to do enormous cultural damage.

The goal of those schools was to transform hundreds of distinct indigenous societies into a single alternative, and thereby to replace a sustainable condition of cultural prosperity with a regime of increasing material wealth and political cohesion. The cultural prosperity of North America before the colonization arose from the fact that human cultures were sustained within the larger culture which is nature as a whole. But to those who ran the schools, the integration of humans with their natural environment was not just undesirable, it was evil; it was satanic. The schools therefore taught the subjugation of nature as a duty.

The biosphere is a self-policing system. Plainly it can tolerate human participation. Human management is something else again. But the unsustainability of a human-centered system posed no problem for those who ran the residential schools. If they were faithful to their creed, they expected the age of human mastery to give way in its turn to the universal kingdom of God.

Take God out of the equation and you have the modern public university as its political masters conceive it. It is an institution that aims at a secular millennium: a global state of limitless material prosperity managed and controlled by human beings. Most of those elected to public office in the present day appear to actively believe in or passively consent to such a vision. But many who work inside the university, and some who come to study there, know that the human millennium is unsustainable. The steadily increasing cultural poverty and material sterility which the search for that millennium has brought are only a foretaste of what it will actually cost.

Even reluctant observers find it obvious by now that in a finite and overexploited world, endlessly increasing material wealth for an endlessly increasing number of humans is a suicidal dream. That leaves us in the short term with two choices: to continue insisting that humans come first, though we know that only a few of those humans will ever enjoy the delusion, or to relinquish the ideal of a global ecology owned and controlled by human beings. In the long run, of course, the self-policing biosphere will edit any choice we make, and its list of alternatives is shorter.

v

It has been argued in the meantime that the university is, or that it ought to be, just an intellectual or educational marketplace. The market, after all, is also an ecology; it too is self-policing, we are told, and instruction should be offered, like guns and butter, strictly in terms of supply and demand. When society at large or the students in particular want Haida instead of English and ethics instead of genetics, Haida and ethics is what they will have.

Universities have never, so far as I know, been truly immune to the law of supply and demand, nor do they need to be. But we are living now in an era that has taught that law some complex flips and twists. Commerce, not so many years ago, was a profession of sometimes grudging, sometimes willing public service. It was the distribution and supply of what it pleases us to call material *goods*. That sort of commerce still exists – the corner store is not entirely extinct, nor is the camel train. But commerce on the whole has changed from a profession of public service to a profession of public predation. Its function now is not to meet demands but to create them, and to strengthen those demands, turning them into addictions, which cause material goods to turn into drugs.

In fact, only some of these commodities are material, like cigarettes and soda pop and T-shirts and potato chips and beer. The newer staples of the market are images instead. I won't dwell here on the power of advertising, market manipulation, and the concoction of empty commodities. I simply remind you that furnishing people with what they really need or *genuinely* want, or what might do them any good, is not the primary aim of modern commerce.

The study of markets often begins with the basic analysis and classification of goods. There are capital goods and perishable goods, for example. An equally simple distinction exists between goods that act like food and goods that act like drugs. Food, in this analysis, is anything that tends to promote the independence and autonomy of the purchaser. Drugs are anything that tends to promote the buyer's dependence instead. In this respect, a shirt or a jacket is food. But if the *style* of the garment is a separate salable element, it is probably a drug. Lottery tickets, by this definition, are drugs. Videotapes and television programs could be either, but in practice they are usually drugs.

Perhaps it is worth asking – with these definitions in mind – to what extent the university serves food and to what extent it pushes drugs. Threats of salvation and damnation, by this definition, are not food; they are drugs. I suggest to you therefore that during the time when the universities of Europe were under the strict hand of the church, in addition to serving food, they were also very actively peddling drugs. Islamic universities, of course, have done the same. With these long and glaring exceptions, I believe we can say that the university has been fundamentally in the business of serving food. The Athenian Academy had served intellectual food, so far as we know, for over 900 years before Justinian closed it. In fact, the university is the place, or aspires to be the place, that renders everything wholesome and nutritious. In the university, even the study of the history of the Crusades and the Inquisition, the Stalinist terror and the genocidal madness of the Third Reich, is rendered educational. The history of madness is transmuted into sanity, the history of poison into food. The university can turn even *style* into a food, where modern commerce turns it, for reasons of profit, into a drug.

It is curious that universities have undertaken to model themselves increasingly on the marketplace at the very moment when the marketplace has changed from a colorful public square, which sells primarily food, into a strobe-lit global shopping mall selling as little food as possible, because of course the profit is greater in drugs.

Serving food in this broad sense is a vocation. Making a profit is not – but it has become a religion instead.

Like all evangelical faiths, modern business claims to bring great blessings to believers. Here and there a piece of evidence appears to prove the claim. We do now have in Canada – in a few select locations – better grocery stores than ever before. Better, at least, than anything since the colonization closed down the enormous grocery store that was the land itself. These new alternative grocery stores – the ones that sell nothing but food, and that tend to sell the best food they can get – are run by university graduates. That is an interesting development. A generation ago, people with university educations didn't go into the grocery business. Selling groceries was not a vocation; it was a job. The conversion of the market into a system for dealing in drugs has *transformed* the grocery business into a serious vocation. Some people who might, a generation or two ago, have entered medicine or law – not for the money, but for the vocation of public service – have in the past ten years gone into the grocery business instead. It may seem a trifle odd to suggest that the university could model itself on a grocery store – a small, revolutionary grocery store – but it is worth a thought. Such a grocery store begins, like any department of classics or anthropology or physics or mathematics, with the fundamental assumption that what it offers is real in itself and good in itself, and that no force should be allowed to make it less so.

VI

The cheerful term *postcolonial*, which I often hear on campuses these days, might suggest that the age of destruction is over. In fact, the colonization is still at fever pitch. The great transformation of gold into lead and of forests into shopping malls continues. Some analogous transformations can be seen in the university itself. One of the reagents used for this purpose is the acid of postmodernism: the thesis that nothing has meaning because everything is language. It works especially well in parallel with the acid of unrestrained commerce: that nothing has meaning because everything is for sale. Repeated exposure to these ideological acids produces human beings who cannot wonder at the world because they are not at all sure the world exists, though they can wonder all the more at social power and reputation. When you take the world away from a human being, something less than a human being is left. That is the inverse of education.

To me it is clear that things have meaning because they *are* meaning, and that language has meaning – or *can* have meaning – because it can speak, poorly but truly, of some of the things that language is not. For me, these facts have a practical outcome: because things have meaning and I want them to continue to have meaning, not everything is for sale. In a healthy economy, only the surplus and the precipitate are for sale, because those are the only things in actual need of recirculation.

Language listens to the world. I listen with it. What I hear when I listen is a question, which is listening itself. The question often changes form: from silence to breathing to speaking to music to voices to visions to silence again. But that is my vocation. The trail it leaves, more often than not, is a text. Real texts are the products of vocation, not the other way around. That is almost all there is to writing.

NOTES

1 In 1997, the University of Victoria dissolved its Faculty of Arts and Sciences, replacing it with two separate entities, a faculty of science and a faculty of the humanities. The newly created Faculty of the Humanities convened a series of invitational lectures to address specific aspects of the question "What are the humanities?" This was one lecture in the series.

2 *Critik der Urtheilskraft* (1799): §17.

3 Northrop Frye, *On Education* (Markham, Ontario: Fitzhenry & Whiteside, 1988): 11.

4 *On Education*, p 26.

5 Charles Frankel, "Why the Humanities?" In *The Humanist as Citizen*, edited by John Agresto & Peter Riesenberg (n.p. [Washington, DC]: National Humanities Center, 1981): 3–15.

NATIVE AMERICAN ORAL LITERATURES AND THE UNITY OF THE HUMANITIES

I

I was two years old and far away when Garnett Sedgewick died, so I never met the man. I know him only through his writing, which, so far as I can tell, he put in second place behind his teaching for nearly the whole of his life. The writing he allowed himself to do is full of shrewd love for his subject, attentive respect for his readers, and impish delight in the language. That, I imagine, is the kind of teacher he was. And I think there is no finer way of honoring the teachers of the past than by enriching the traditions they have taught. In the field of literature, we can do that by writing good books and by telling good stories, and we can do it by learning to read and learning to listen to stories and books that already exist and whose worth has been wrongly denied or forgotten.

This is not, in North America, an incidental problem. There are not, in North America, just a few forgotten works in a few overlooked or marginal traditions. There are a hundred major North American literatures still waiting for recognition.

In the visual arts, the richness and importance of the Native American heritage is no longer much of a secret. Most people who visit the Museum of Anthropology here at the University of British Columbia, for example, now realize at once that it

Garnett Sedgewick Memorial Lecture, University of British Columbia, Vancouver
5 March 1998

is in fact a museum of art. Many who visit it recognize that it is the most important museum of art in this region of the country. Some of them even see that this museum, which displays thousands of works made by Native American artists, and one painting by the great immigrant painter Jack Shadbolt, gives something like a statistically balanced sample of Canadian art history.

The importance of the corresponding literary heritage is known to relatively few. Literature is invisible. It cannot be exhibited to tourists – and many North Americans, it seems, are tourists in the land where they were born. To most of the population of the United States and Canada – including most of the writers, most of the readers, and most of the teachers of literature – the most fundamental literary facts about the land where we are living are unknown.

Some of the most painful of those facts can be expressed in simple numbers. The human population of North America north of the Rio Grande – what is now the USA and Canada – at the end of the fifteenth century has been very cautiously and conservatively estimated at seven to ten million. One to two million of those would have been here in Canada. This total may have been much higher; it cannot have been much lower. But at the end of the nineteenth century, if the census figures are vaguely correct, the total aboriginal population was about 100,000 in Canada and 250,000 in the United States. This means that over a space of four centuries, while the colonial population of North America rose from zero to several million, the total indigenous population shrank by a minimum of ninety-five per cent.

I don't want to sponsor a competition to resolve the terrible question of who has suffered most in human history and who are the runners up. I only want to register a fact: one holocaust museum is not enough. Native American oral literatures are full of dramatic and narrative subtleties, full of complex metaphors, and full of hilarious jokes. But their history, like the literary history of Yiddish and of Hebrew, and like the history of many African literatures, is also steeped in anguish. It is no accident that the central work of Iroquoian literature in the eighteenth and nineteenth centuries was the Ritual of Condolence, nor that the grand opening movement of the greatest extant work of Haida oral literature begins with a promise of perpetual sustenance on earth, based on a reciprocal relation between human beings and the creatures of the sea, and sweeps all that aside, after 1,700 lines, in a vision of mass destruction, brought about by strangers who derive their power from an old man in the sky. The language of the story, and its structures, are entirely indigenous; the savagery of the climax is likely to be a gift of the colonization. The author of that poem – that immensely complex, immensely beautiful, immensely sad piece of narrative music – was a man known as Skaay of the Qquuna Qiighawaay. He was one of the survivors of the smallpox and measles epidemics that swept through Haida Gwaii in the nineteenth century. In 1800, his group of Haida villages – Qquuna, Hlkkyaa, Qqaadasghu and Ttanuu – had a population of close to a thousand. In 1897, when the last survivors moved out to Skidegate, there were a total of sixty-eight.

Four hundred years ago, about three hundred indigenous languages were spoken in the region now mapped as the USA and Canada. By 1900, that number had shrunk by about a third, to around two hundred languages. It is down now to a little more than half: about 170 languages. But the number of speakers, for all but a small handful of those languages, has fallen by more than ninety-five per cent and is continuing to fall. Of those three hundred indigenous languages, only about thirty are spoken now by children.[1]

"The life of the mind" is not only a reassuring and comfortable metaphor; it is a plain though intangible fact. Yet the life of the mind, like the life of the forest, only exists in an interactive and polymorphous form. Your life may be yours alone, but unless a lot of other things are living, neither am I and neither are you. This is true for the individual, true for the species, and true for the mind. It is also true in a slightly different way for languages and forests. Languages and forests, unlike you and me, contain within themselves multiplicity enough for propagation and evolution. I do not think that means we can afford to throw them away. It takes a lot more than some trees to make a living forest, and a lot more than some languages to make a living mind, but languages loom large among the creatures whose lively interaction adds up to the life of the mind. One language, like one tree, is also not enough.

A language consists of a symbol set, a grammar and a medium. The medium can be either a mouthful of air or a handful of silence. In the case of American Sign Language, the medium is gesture – manual, facial, and bracchial gesture. In the case of almost every other language that is native to North America, the medium is sound – oral, laryngeal, and nasal sound. The symbols pass, in either case, through the representational medium with a certain amount of drag, and if nothing goes wrong, the disturbance this creates is noticeably beautiful – just as with any natural process. Humans are designed to be delighted by the workings of their languages, just as they're designed to like the way the flowers and the trees grow.

In addition to becoming good to hear or good to look at, those linguistic symbols link up into chains that obey and embody the rules of grammar. These chains are big linguistic proteins. Their function is to make sense, and that is why we call them sentences. They form still larger units in their turn.

A poem or a story is in one sense just a larger kind of sentence: another level of structure, three or four or twenty tiers up from the level of the ordinary sentence. The *Iliad* is a big sentence. *Paradise Lost* or *The Sound and the Fury* or *Green Grass, Running Water* is a big sentence. Any competent speaker with the requisite patience and knowledge could in theory utter any of these sentences. In practice, only one person can utter them, and only one person ever has, though many professional speakers may have uttered sentences resembling the *Iliad*, and others have read and perhaps recited them after the fact.

That, for me, is the point at which linguistics, the study of language, bursts into flower. Linguistics becomes the study of literature at the point where there is only one speaker for every complete unit of speech. There is only one speaker, yet sense continues to be made. That, incidentally, is why literatures can be killed so much more easily than languages. Literatures are languages in which the number of speakers for every real and complete unit of utterance can only have two values: zero or one.

Every normal, healthy human being, once past the stage of infancy, speaks and contributes to a language. And every normal, healthy human language – no exceptions – speaks and nourishes a literature. It is harder, most of the time, for human beings to restrain themselves from telling stories than it is for them to keep from shedding tears. Perhaps that is why human beings keep on going, even when anyone can see they ought to stop and weep.

Most literature is oral, and all literature is oral at its root. In most written traditions, the oldest works of literature we have are examples of oral transcription. The *Iliad* and *Odyssey* are instances. So are the *Beowulf* and the *Seafarer*, the *Nibelungenlied*, the *Poema del Cid*, the old *Rāmāyana* from India, the *Kojiki* from Japan, the *Shī Jīng* from China, the *Táin Bó Cúailnge* from Ireland. Once in a while we are lucky enough to know, or think we know, the author's name – Homer, Hieda no Are, Vālmīki, for example. More often, we know nothing. But this anonymity isn't inherent in oral tradition. It is a sign of literate pride: a reminder that over and over again, literate cultures have taken what oral traditions could offer and then have turned their backs and walked away. Whenever you enter a living oral tradition, you discover that the storytellers there, the mythtellers there, the poets there, have names, the same as authors everywhere. Poets in oral traditions, like poets in literate traditions, are individuals with individual styles, tastes, abilities, and interests. Whether we learn their names or not, no two are interchangeable. No two are ever the same.

The mechanization of language – through the radio, the television, the tape recorder, the computer, as well as the alphabet and the book – reduces the scope of oral literature, just as the mechanization of travel reduces the distance that people will walk, and reduces the value and pleasure of walking. But walking doesn't stop altogether when the buckboard or the limousine arrives. Dancing doesn't stop. And talking doesn't stop when the printing press arrives. Nor does oral literature. What stop, after a time, are the great achievements of oral literature: the Iliads and Odysseys, the Seafarers and Finn Cycles. The mechanization of language dissolves the conditions under which such works can be composed, and the conditions in which it is convenient to appreciate and enjoy them.

There are substantial living traditions of oral poetry still in many corners of the world, including the Americas. And there was such a tradition in Bosnia until the recent war. If that is gone, as apparently it is, what is lost is the last direct and lineal descendant of the Homeric epic tradition. That may be a greater loss than all the buildings, all the bridges, all the paintings, all the churches, all the other material structures destroyed during 2,000 years of European wars. But so far as I'm aware, the deaths of the oral epic poets of Bosnia, almost all of whom were Muslims, did not once make the evening news in North America during the siege of Sarajevo and the long, methodical massacre outside. There is not much money in oral literature, and not much political power or glamour, but there is sometimes an immense amount of intelligence, resting on the earth, where, in the age of industrial warfare and recreational genocide, it is awfully easy to lose.

When oral poems are transcribed, writers often try to edit and revise them. People with no direct experience of an accomplished oral tradition often think that oral poetry *has* to be revised, finished, polished by literate men and women in order to reach the higher standards of writing. That is simply not the case. The technology does not determine the quality. There are crude and clumsy works of oral literature, just as there is clumsy, incompetent writing. And there are works of purely oral poetry that are every bit as sophisticated, intricate, refined, highly accomplished as the work of any writer you can name: Dante, Shakespeare, Sophokles, García Lorca, Flaubert, Margaret Atwood, Thomas King. The greatest poets and novelists in the literate traditions turn out, most of the time, to be precisely those who are closest to oral tradition, not those who have left it behind. Great writing is tested and revised by oral standards far more than the other way around.

II

In Mexico, indigenous efforts to capture oral literature in pictographic form began more than a thousand years ago. Alphabetic script – brought by the Europeans – was put to use for the same purpose in the 1540s. The tradition remained, and still remains, primarily oral, but there are also written texts from central Mexico equivalent in age to the poems of Thomas Wyatt and Ronsard.

Here in the north, there are written texts in Native American languages from as early as 1595, but all the early texts from the USA and Canada are religious propaganda: catechisms, Bibles and the like. This is writing used as an instrument of cultural attack, not cultural defense – and that is a crucial distinction in literature.

Those attacks provoked defense, sometimes employing the same weapon. Iroquoian oral historians say that indigenous texts were written in Mohawk and Onondaga as early as 1750. But these were manuscript books, and like many other manuscripts they have perished in floods and in fires. For our knowledge of early Native American writing, we are still dependent on oral tradition.

It is worth remembering that when writing was introduced to Europe, nearly 3,000 years ago, it was used for purely political and mercantile purposes. Later, people saw that social changes – possibly brought on by the use of writing – had put their oral literatures at risk. It was then that they started to write their poetry down. Healthy oral cultures neither need writing nor want it, as a rule. This is true here and now in North America among the deaf community. The deaf form a literate community, reading and writing in English, French, Spanish or any other languages they please, but they are united among themselves by an oral – more correctly, a manual – language, ASL or American Sign Language. Some years ago a team at the Salk Institute created an excellent script for ASL. It was greeted with disdain by most fluent speakers of the language, who understood the value and the power of a functioning nonliterate culture. There is the same resistance to writing among the otherwise literate speakers of many dialects – Joual and Milanese for example. In many aboriginal communities, writing is viewed with similar disdain. Writing, which some of us regard as a badge of social power, is really a badge of social disintegration. It is not without its value, of course, but also not without its cost.

European linguists started to transcribe oral texts in northern North America only toward the end of the nineteenth century. The history from that point to the present is primarily a history of lucky intersections between generous and gifted Native American oral poets and patient, skillful scribes. I want to spend the next few minutes touching on some of the highlights of this history. There are, as we all know, plenty of ugly moments in the chronicle of interaction between Europeans and Native Americans. The instances I want to mention here are of a different kind: instances in which the Europeans came to learn and not to teach. The fruits of those encounters make further learning possible for every human being.

III

The French missionary Émile Petitot was born in 1838. In his early twenties he arrived, Bible in hand, on the shores of Great Slave Lake. He had come to teach, and to pursue the cultural assault, but he had also come to listen. He began taking lessons in Chipewyan from a blind elder known as Ekunélyel, "Caribou Louse," and in 1863, he transcribed a series of stories told by his teacher. In the next ten years, Petitot transcribed many texts in Chipewyan, Gwichin, Dogrib, Slavey and Cree.

In 1870, at Fort Good Hope on the Mackenzie River, a woman named Lizette K'atchodi, Big Rabbit Woman, sang him some songs and told him some stories in Slavey. K'atchodi was a practicing shaman, but she showed little fear of the missionary, and he showed little fear of her. They were, I think, intrigued by one another's powers. So far as I can tell, she was the first Native Canadian woman recorded in her own language.[2] Petitot's transcriptions are imperfect, to be sure, but there is enough in those texts to confirm Big Rabbit Woman's status as a crucial figure in literary history. I don't have the faintest idea why the historians neglect her, nor why there is no modern edition of her work, and no acceptable English translation.

In 1886, when Lizette K'atchodi was dead and Émile Petitot was safely back in France, Franz Boas made the first of many visits to the Northwest Coast. In 1890, on his fourth trip, he visited the mouth of the Columbia, at the border between Oregon and Washington. He had heard about a language called Chinook: not the pidgin language Chinook Jargon, used primarily in trade, but a true Chinookan language better called Shoalwater Chinook. He was looking for someone who could speak it. People told him to go up the coast to what is now Willapa Bay. There in the village of Nutsxwułsóq – since renamed Bay Center, Washington – he met one of the greatest American poets who ever lived. The poet's name was Q'eltí. He was born in 1832, and he spoke four languages: Shoalwater Chinook, which he had learned from his father; Kathlamet, which he learned from his mother; Chehalis, a Salishan language which he learned from his wife; and Chinook Jargon too, which he had learned, as many people in the region did in those days, to keep in touch and stay alive. He had been baptized as an adult and given an English name, Charles Cultee, but English is a language he did not speak.

For three summers – 1890, 1891 and 1894 – he dictated narrative poems to Boas in three of these languages, and then translated the texts and explained the grammar in the fourth, which was one language he and Boas shared: the Chinook Trade Jargon.

Q'eltí, who died in 1897, is the author of two books: *Chinook Texts* (1894) and the posthumous *Kathlamet Texts* (1901). They are two of the finest books ever published in America. Q'eltí belongs on the shelf of essential American poets alongside Emily Dickinson, Wallace Stevens, Robinson Jeffers and Sylvia Plath. But Q'eltí didn't write his poems; he spoke them – and he didn't speak in English. So in a state that has taken some pride in its poets – Theodore Roethke, Bill Stafford, Carolyn Kizer, Richard Hugo, David Wagoner and others – Q'eltí remains almost entirely unknown. I have never seen him mentioned even in the largest of American literary histories. Yet his unmarked grave is easy to find if you talk to older people in the village. And he is a poet well worth learning two languages to read – just as one would willingly learn Spanish to read García Lorca or German to read Rilke.

There are no native speakers of Shoalwater Chinook or Kathlamet still alive, but Dell Hymes, who is a poet as well as a linguist, and who is one of the best scholars of Native American oral literature who ever lived, has spent more time on those languages than any of the rest of us. I have a dream that some day he will edit and translate an edition of Q'eltí's complete works – so that the life of that particularly graceful mind can be more widely shared.

Hymes was not the first scholar to study Q'eltí's poems. The first, after Boas himself, was John Swanton, who started to study with Boas in the same year Q'eltí died. In 1900, Swanton completed his doctoral thesis on Q'eltí's verbs, and three months later he arrived here in Vancouver, took a boat to Victoria, and another boat north to the mouth of the Skeena. He arrived in the Haida village of Hlghagilda – Skidegate Mission, the Europeans called it – on Wednesday, 26 September 1900. Twelve days later he met the Haida poet I mentioned earlier: Skaay of the Qquuna Qiighawaay.

Skaay explained to Swanton what was going to happen. He explained that he would tell a cycle of five stories that came in a certain order, and then another story known as Xhuuya Qaagangas, "Raven Traveling." Swanton and his Haida colleague Henry Moody spent the next three weeks, working six days a week, taking dictation from Skaay. They started at 30 pages a day and worked their way up to 45. When we edit the results, we find the five-part cycle, just as Skaay described it in advance. It is a narrative poem about 5,500 lines long. Xhuuya Qaagangas is short by comparison: only about 1,400 lines. These are the two largest, and in my view also the two greatest, extant works of Haida literature. And they are two of the greatest works of literature in any Canadian language, whether indigenous or imported.

Skaay could not read or write, and he spoke nothing except Haida and perhaps a bit of Tsimshian. He knew that Swanton was taking dictation, and he could see that from the marks he made on the paper, Swanton could approximate the sounds of Haida speech. Skaay had seen the missionaries using writing too, but in his world poetry remained entirely oral. Not every great artist is so pure.

François Mandeville was born about 1878. That makes him roughly fifty years younger than Skaay and Q'elti, and maybe sixty years younger than K'atchodi. He was also born in a different world: into a family of interpreters at Fort Resolution, on Great Slave Lake. He was fluent from childhood in Chipewyan and French. While he was still a young man, he learned English and went to work for the Hudson's Bay Company. He learned Dogrib from his wife. Then he moved to Hay River, and there he learned Slavey. He ran several different trading posts in the Slavey country and then moved to Arctic Red River, where he learned Gwichin. After that he moved to Rae, where his wife was born, and for the next four years he spoke mostly Dogrib. In 1921 he left the HBC, and in 1925 he retired to Fort Chipewyan, in northern Alberta. That was his home for most of the rest of his life – though in 1940 he visited Wood Buffalo, where he also learned some Cree.

Mandeville lived for the most part in an oral world, like K'atchodi, Skaay and Q'eltí, but in the early 1900s he taught himself to read and write Chipewyan in syllabics and French in Latin script. He used those skills for keeping records at his trading posts. He also listened, all his life, to the stories told by his elders and friends, and in the 1920s, he came to be known as one of the best mythtellers in the Chipewyan country.

In 1928, when Mandeville was fifty years old and living in Alberta, a visitor arrived: Li Fang-kuei (Lǐ Fānggui, 季方桂), who had just finished his doctoral work in linguistics with Edward Sapir. Li asked if Mandeville was willing to tell stories. Mandeville agreed, and the two men worked together six days a week for six weeks. Mandeville knew how writing could be used, and he prepared, every evening, for the next day's work. He didn't write the stories down, but he did make notes about stories he wanted to tell, the order in which he wanted to tell them, and the episodes he wanted to include. He used Li in much the same way that Q'eltí used Boas and Skaay used Swanton: as a scribe who would record and edit anything the storyteller chose. Mandeville knew there was nothing to read in Chipewyan apart from the awkward translations of blatantly alien scriptures. He knew that he was creating the first indigenous Chipewyan book, and he went about it carefully.

François Mandeville died in 1952, and Li Fang-kuei did not get around to publishing those texts until 1976, nearly fifty years after they were spoken. (He would not, it seems, have done it even then, if Ronald Scollon hadn't come along to do the editing and finish the translation.) They were published in Taipei, where there are not many Chipewyan speakers, but *Chipewyan Texts* is one of the great Canadian books. Like the work of

Kʼatchodi, Skaay and Qʼeltí, it needs reediting and retranslating, but there is no doubt whatsoever of its literary quality.

The last poet I want to mention is Anna Nelson Harry, a speaker of Eyak, who was born in 1906 and died in 1982. She had her first brush with a linguist in 1933, when Kaj Birket-Smith and Frederica de Laguna came to Cordova, Alaska, near the mouth of the Copper River, and talked to her and her husband Galushia. The two ethnologists noticed that Anna was the one who knew the stories, though her husband always told them to the guests. Anna answered the visitors' questions about the Eyak language and the facts of Eyak life, but she wouldn't tell a story to outsiders. When the visitors were there, it was her husband – who didn't do it well and often needed her prompting – who always did the telling.

Thirty years later she agreed to tell her stories to the linguist Michael Krauss – but conditions then were different. Galushia was dead; Anna was living in the Tlingit community of Yakutat with her Tlingit-speaking second husband; Krauss was young enough to be her grandson and was passionately interested in Eyak; and Anna was keenly aware that she was one of the last three or four fluent speakers of Eyak still alive. Most importantly, perhaps, she could whisper as quietly as she pleased – and that was often very quietly indeed – because Krauss wasn't taking dictation by hand. He used a tape-recorder instead.

Anna Harry spoke to that recording machine in 1963, 1965 and 1972. In 1982, the year in which she died, Michael Krauss published a superbly edited and superbly translated transcript of those tapes. It includes, once again, some of the finest poetry published in North America, in any language.

I've mentioned a few, but I know of at least two hundred fifty, possibly three hundred, cases of this kind: three hundred Native American oral poets in desperate need of editors, translators, biographers, readers, and once those basic needs are met, even in need of some literary critics.

IV

A few years ago I found myself in the American south, lecturing on the work of Anna Nelson Harry and the Zuni poet Nick Tumaka. The audience was a highly eclectic group, and at the end of one lecture, a young woman asked me very suspiciously, "Why are you so interested in this stuff?"

"What's in it for you?" I guess is what she meant. Or maybe, "What are you trying to steal now?" I confess that I was baffled by this question. All I could do that day, and all I can do now, is ask another question back. How is it possible *not* to be so interested in this stuff? What's in it for me is what's in it for you and for everyone else. The subject of classical Native American literature is nothing more or less than the nature of the world. It is a literature concerned with fundamental questions. At its best, it is as nourishing and beautiful and wise as any poetry that exists.

After all the theft, all the destruction, all the persecution suffered by native peoples in North America, it is no surprise that some of the survivors are resentful and suspicious. But you cannot steal someone else's language in the same way you can steal someone's land. Languages, like happiness, are easy to destroy and not difficult to share, but they are virtually impossible to expropriate and keep.

The importance of this fact is far from academic. If, for example, Mayan languages and culture were taught right now in Mexican schools – not to Mayan children only but to all Mexican children – the massacres in Chiapas would stop. I do not know, myself, of any other way to stop them.

78

V

In 1935, when no Canadian literature was taught at the University of British Columbia, Garnett Sedgewick issued a simple challenge: "Show me the Canadian literature that is worth teaching, and we'll have a course." Things are different now, but not quite as different as they may at first appear. Margaret Atwood, Thomas King, Marie-Claire Blais and many others have written their fine books, and there is plenty of Canlit in the syllabus as well as in the bookstore. But the work that no one showed to Sedgewick in 1935 is still waiting to be shown. There was as much, or maybe more, Canadian literature worth teaching then than there is now, and plenty of it then was in a form that Sedgewick could have learned to see. It was, for the most part, oral literature, recently captured in writing. It wasn't in English or French, but it was all in Canadian languages: Inuktitut, Haida, Gwichin, Chipewyan, Dogrib, Slavey, Nootka, Nitinaht, Nisgha, Tsimshian, Onondaga, Mohawk, Kwakwala, Nuxalk, Kutenai, Maliseet, Ojibwa, Blackfoot, Cree. The people who could have shown it to Sedgewick were not professors of literature. Some were translators, who always had at least two names because they lived in at least two worlds: people like Q'ix̌itasu' (George Hunt) and Gwüsk̲'aayn (William Beynon) and Hiixuqqin'is (Alex Thomas). Others were linguists: Edward Sapir, Morris Swadesh, John Swanton, Leonard Bloomfield, Li Fang-kuei and Mary Haas. Their students and successors are still with us: quite ready and quite able to do what Garnett Sedgewick asked.

NOTES

1 Widely varying numbers are given for the past and present language population of North America. A degree of imprecision is inescapable, because
   some linguists classify as languages what others hear as dialects. Larger
   variations in the numbers stem from differing definitions of North America. Simpletons like me prefer to draw the southern boundary through the
   Isthmus of Panama. Ethnographers often draw it along a complicated line
   through central Mexico (near the latitude of Tuxpan and Tampico) and frequently extend the northern boundary beyond the Bering Strait. Between
   the Bering Strait and the Panama Canal, about 270 native languages now
   survive, from a precolonial total of something like 500. In "ethnographic
   North America," some 200 now survive from a precolonial total closer
   to 350. The lower figures given in this lecture are for Canada, Alaska, and
   the continental USA alone.

2 This appeared to be the case in 1998, but in 2003 Peter Sanger discovered,
   in the archives of Acadia University, Wolfville, Nova Scotia, the Micmac
   transcript of a story that Susan Barss of Cape Breton dictated to Silas Tertius
   Rand in 1847 on Prince Edward Island. This may soon be published.

THE AUDIBLE LIGHT IN THE EYES

I

The whole of France, according to Camus, is a place where human time and nature's time have mingled past division. And according to a calendar that mingles nature's time with man-made time like a glass of wine or a vase of flowers, today is summer solstice in the year 2000: a good day to be in Paris.

One hundred years ago this month, in a land where the peaceful mingling of time had been violently upset, a young man by the name of John Reed Swanton was beginning his career, defending his doctoral thesis at Harvard. It was a study of the grammar of two closely related languages: Kathlamet and Shoalwater Chinook, whose last fluent speaker had been dead since 1897. Linguistics was not taught at Harvard in those days – Roman Jakobson was only four years old – but after taking two degrees at Harvard, Swanton had begun linguistic work with Franz Boas in New York. A student doing this today would be expected to transfer to Columbia, where Boas was on staff. A century ago, *alma mater* had a meaning it has lost. He had done his graduate course work in New York, and no one at Harvard could evaluate his doctoral research, but Swanton had become a Harvard man, and on the strength of Boas's recommendation, Harvard gave him his doctorate as well.

Three months later – Tuesday, 25 September 1900 – Swanton stepped ashore in the Haida country, off the coast

---

Collège de France, Paris
21 June 2000

of British Columbia. In his pocket was a five-page letter of instructions that Boas had written the previous June. Before him was a world where smallpox and missionary pressure had exercised their powerful effects. The skeletons of ancient Haida structures were still standing in the ghost towns. In the two inhabited villages, all the traditional houses and nearly all the monumental sculpture had already been destroyed. Yet as soon as Swanton asked to hear stories in Haida, the world he was seeking reappeared. Just beneath the surface, a rich tradition of Haida oral literature lay secretly alive.

Swanton's Haida teachers saw at once how his talents could be used. They told him what they wanted written down and declined to tell him what they didn't – and Swanton eagerly went along, ignoring Boas's instructions. He took dictation and language lessons six days a week for a year and spent another two years editing the texts he had transcribed. These texts include the following:

1 a myth cycle of epic length (close to eight hours long in oral form; in printed form about 5,500 lines) dictated in October 1900 by the poet Skaay of the Qquuna Qiighawaay;

2 the longest and by far the most complex version of the Raven Cycle ever recorded on the Northwest Coast, about two hours long, again dictated by the poet Skaay;

3 a village history of great literary stature and once again of epic length – at least six hours, and in printed form about 4,000 lines – dictated in December 1900 by Kilxhawgins of Ttanuu;

4 about eighty independent narratives, averaging twenty to forty minutes but ranging in length up to two hours

each, dictated for the most part by three oral poets named Ghandl, Haayas, and Kingagwaaw;

5 several thousand lines of autobiography dictated by an old warrior and trader by the name of Sghaagya; and

6 a great deal else belonging to the four main genres of Haida oral literature, which are *qqaygaang* (myth), *qqayaagaang* (lineage story), *gyaahlghalang* (history, autobiography, memoir) and *sghalaang* (song).

In short, what Swanton heard, and single-handedly transcribed, was a literature of classical dimensions and complexity and power. At the end of his first month of transcribing, Swanton likened the work he was hearing to Homeric epic,[1] and indeed the resemblance is deep although the surface similarities are few.

When they were made, Swanton's Haida texts formed the largest body of literature transcribed in any native language north of Mexico, and by far the largest literary corpus from the Northwest Coast. This has not remained the case. Boas and his colleague Q'ixitasu', working separately and together from 1886 until 1931, wrote about three times as much in Kwakwala as Swanton did in Haida in the course of that one year. Thanks to the work of other devoted scribes, working steadily for decades, there is now also more to read in Navajo, Meskwaki, Inuktitut and Cree than there is in Haida.

The eight-hour cycle that I mentioned, dictated by the Haida poet Skaay of the Qquuna Qiighawaay, nevertheless remains one of the longest and most complex works of Native American oral literature ever recorded. And embedded in Sghaagya's autobiography is a set-piece poem composed and performed as part of a peace-making venture some fifty years before Swanton wrote it down. It dates, in other words, from roughly 1850. As such, that little poem is almost certainly the oldest single piece of literature we have from the Northwest Coast. It is one of the oldest surviving actual texts in any Native Canadian language. More to the point, the major authors in Swanton's collection – Skaay, Ghandl, Haayas, Kingagwaaw and Kilxhawgins – have survived as major authors, patiently waiting for the rest of us to recognize how good they really are.

Back in Washington and New York, neither Boas nor anyone else appeared at first to see the value of this work. The most important of Swanton's manuscripts sat unpublished in Boas's office for more than thirty years and has been sitting, still unpublished, in a Philadelphia library since Boas's death in 1942. The rediscovery, retranslation, and publication of these texts as literature rather than anthropological data or folklore therefore stands as a new phase – not an entirely peaceful phase at the moment – in the generally bleak and dispiriting history of interaction between Europeans and Native Americans on the Northwest Coast.

The appreciation of Native American oral literature as literature is not, however, a new idea. Native American audiences have been appreciating the skill and wisdom of their mythtellers for centuries, no matter how slow outsiders have been to catch up. And a few of the outsiders were not so slow at that. The literary qualities of Native American literature were a central concern to Jeremiah Curtin, who was born two decades earlier than Boas, and the example Curtin set was important to Edward Sapir. But Curtin spent little time on the Northwest Coast and did his most serious work on Seneca. In a more technical sense, the study of native literatures as literature starts late in the 1950s. That is when Dell Hymes began his lifelong study of literary form in Native American oral literature. This has proven an extremely fruitful line of inquiry. Like the work of Vladimir Propp, Roman Jakobson, and Claude Lévi-Strauss, it also proves the essential seamlessness of literary studies and linguistics – a seamlessness that far too many linguists, and far too many literary critics, still ignore and some deny.

Swanton is important in this respect not just because he took a lot of texts that are literarily superb, but because a sense of literature, of poetry, of literary value, is something he and his Haida teachers shared.

I regret my own long-standing habit of referring to these texts as Swanton's texts, after the man who wrote them down. I think we ought to call them, like other works of literature, after the names of their actual authors. But Swanton's contribution was essential. He did far more than take dictation. He *asked* for stories to be told; he paid the tellers to tell them, and he paid, in every case, for a capable and fluent Haida listener, so that he as the transcriber was always in a tertiary position. He also, almost always, *let the storyteller choose* the size and scope and content of the work. The effects of this procedure are easy to see. During his year in the Haida country Swanton functioned not just as a linguist and ethnographer. He functioned as a major patron of the literary arts. No better use was ever made of the Bureau of American Ethnology's congressional appropriation or the American Museum of Natural History's budget for ethnographic research.

Along with John Swanton, the significant transcribers of classical North American oral literature include Leonard Bloomfield, Franz Boas, Ruth Bunzel, Roland Dixon, Pliny Goddard, Berard Haile, John Hewitt, Melville Jacobs, William Jones, Michael Krauss, Li Fang-kuei, Ekkehart Malotki, Douglas Parks, Paul Radin, Edward Sapir, Cornelius Uhlenbeck and Gene Weltfish: all familiar names to specialists but to the literary public quite unknown. Yet they are just as important in their way to the sustenance and propagation of culture as Carnegie or Morgan or Guggenheim or Barnes.

Four of the great transcribers published significant theoretical work and so acquired scholarly renown. These four are Boas, Radin, Bloomfield, and Sapir. But the people who told them the stories – even the best and most prolific of those who told them the stories – and who in consequence deserve the fame the most, have attained it least of all. I am thinking of mythtellers such as Kainaikwan in Blackfoot; Q'eltí in Chinook and Kathlamet; François Mandeville in Chipewyan; Kâ-kîsikâw-pîhtokêw and Sâkêwêw in Cree; Anna Nelson Harry in Eyak; Skaay, Ghandl and Kingagwaaw in Haida; Hetsmiixhwn in Hanis and Miluk; Sam Brown and Mrs Molasses in Hupa; Bill Ray in Kato; Kootye in Kawaiko; Pahlnapí in Kutenai; Hánts'ibuyim in Maidu; Chiishch'ilíts'ósí and Charlie Mitchell in Navajo; Saayaacchapis and Qiixxa in Nootka; Kaagigeepinäsi and Midaasuganj in Ojibwa; Ctaahaaritkari' in Pawnee; Gwìsgwashaán in Takelma; Seidayaa and Tsiixwáa in Tlingit; Nick Tumaka and Leo Zuñi in Zuni. In an honest and nonpartisan study of North American literature, these and other indigenous authors would be given a prominent place. Yet their names are only now beginning to appear in a few encyclopedias of literature and bibliographical catalogues.[2]

Enlightened North Americans who advocate equality for persons of all races and all creeds are often far less liberal, or far less self-aware, in their attitudes toward language. Literature is taught, in the Americas, in much the way that pizza, wine, and cheddar cheese are sold: as something foreign at its root, now also made with skill and pride in the New World. Poets and mythtellers – even the greatest among them – working in the languages indigenous to Canada, the USA, and all the nations to the south, have, in colonial circles, generally been regarded as perfectly irrelevant to the culture and identity of the countries in which they were born.

Yet there are all those texts to read. There is all that proof that literature, great literature, belongs to the Americas as fully as salmon, tomatoes, corn, and squash.

The patron saint of all this text collecting is of course Franz Boas. Like many saints, he proves to be a highly complex character with secular as well as sacred interests. I would like to spend a moment considering the impact made upon his work by two men less well known. One of these was a Frenchman. The other was one of the greatest Native American oral poets ever recorded.

The first substantial anthology of Native North American texts was gathered by Émile Petitot, a native of Dijon, and published in 1888 in Alençon. Most of the texts are Athapaskan – Chipewyan, Dogrib, Slavey, and Gwichin – but there is a supplement in Cree, all with parallel French translation. The book was subsidized by a well-to-do philologist, the Comte de Charencey, who was dissatisfied with Petitot's first treatment of these stories: a bowdlerized and prettified translation published in Paris in 1886 as part of a library of popular literature, and as such still in print.

Boas rarely mentions these two books, but I think they had considerable impact on his thinking. Directly after the first and more popular version of Petitot's anthology was published, Boas started working on a popular collection of his own: *Indianische Sagen von der Nord-Pacifischen Küste Amerikas*. Most of the work for this anthology was completed by the fall of 1889, and all of it by summer 1890, though the full text was not issued until 1895. In the meantime, two important events had occurred. First was the publication of the more rigorous version of Petitot's anthology, with full aboriginal texts and much more literal translations. The second was Boas's meeting, in the summer of 1890, with a 58-year-old oral poet named Q'eltí. The jubilant letters Boas wrote his wife and parents to commemorate that meeting show that Boas sensed, early on, what later and more careful study would confirm.[3] In years of pestering Native Americans for stories, Q'eltí was the first great mythteller, the first real poet, the first substantial *man of oral letters* that Boas had ever met.

Culture, of course, is not genetic. Ethnological identity has to be learned, where biological identity does not, but it has to be learned from those who possess it. Like Skaay, Q'eltí was not only a poet; he was a library: a living means for the reproduction of his own civilization.

Boas had done serious transcription work before, with the two Tsimshian mythtellers and singers he called Old Matthias and Mrs Morison, but he recognized Q'eltí as an artist of a different order. Accordingly, Boas rearranged his travel plans and spent three seasons with Q'eltí, in 1890, 1891, and 1894. These were some of the most fruitful years of Boas's life. Q'eltí's two books, Chinook Texts (1894) and Kathlamet Texts (1901), are the pride of the harvest. They were the first indigenous texts of genuine substance published by Boas – the first proof he could really do the job – and they are the first substantial printed books by a single Native North American author.

Another result was less direct. In 1896, under Boas's direction, John Swanton had started doctoral work on Lakhota. Then, brooding on the brilliance of the stories told him by Q'eltí, and on the imminent extinction of his languages, Boas overruled his student's decision. And so Q'eltí became not only the first Native American author to have his own book; he also became, if anyone cares, the first Native American author to serve, albeit surreptitiously, as the subject of a doctoral dissertation: Swanton's "Morphology of the Chinook Verb."

Swanton never met Q'eltí, but that poet's literary skill is the underlying reason why Boas leaned on Swanton to set aside his study of Lakhota and work on Chinook and Kathlamet instead. Swanton learned his sense of Native American literary form and literary value from Q'eltí. He spoke about this sense of form and value very little, but his actions leave no doubt that he possessed it. That was the sense he put to work when he arrived in Haida Gwaii, where he sat with fanatical patience at the feet of the best mythtellers he met. It was the sense he put to work again a few years later, defending his transcriptions against everyone's attempts, including Boas's, to cut them down to preconceived dimensions.

The way to prove what I have said about these texts would be to offer some examples, but listening to myths takes time, and listening for style in a foreign tongue or through the veil of translation takes a lot of time. In printed form, this time turns into space. A thousand pages, I have discovered, is barely sufficient to lay out the evidence.[4] What I would like to do instead, in the time and space we have, is attempt a short demonstration of certain familiar features of mythtelling. These are features often found in the masterworks of Native American literature, but I will show them to you here in a different form, relying on mythtellers who work in a different medium and belong to a different tradition.

II

Figure I (overleaf) is an instance of mythtelling. The medium is oil on canvas instead of spoken words, and the mythteller – Diego Rodríguez de Silva y Velázquez – is a figure known by name to millions of admirers of European art. In almost every other respect, this work can be directly and closely compared with accomplished instances of mythtelling transcribed in North America by linguists like John Swanton. The painting was made in Seville about 1618. It is known now as *The Kitchen Maid and the Supper at Emmaus*, and it hangs in the National Gallery of Ireland.

1 Diego Rodríguez de Silva y Velázquez. *The Kitchen Maid and the Supper at Emmaus.* c. 1618. Oil on canvas, 55 × 118 cm. National Gallery of Ireland, Dublin.

2 Detail of figure 1: the myth scene.

3 Diego Velázquez. *Christ in the House of Martha and Mary.* c. 1618. Oil on canvas, 60 × 103 cm. National Gallery, London.

4 Detail of figure 1: the dishes.

Most of the things in the painting are actually not part of the myth. They are part of the mythteller's mental and physical world. But because they are here in the company of the myth, the myth affects them. That is a feature typical not only of Velázquez's early paintings but also of narrative poems told in Haida by Skaay and Ghandl, Kingagwaaw and Haayas. Myth illuminates the quotidian, and vice versa.

The myth in this case is the story of the dead Christ rising from the grave, walking toward Emmaus, meeting some old friends along the way and joining them for dinner, where belatedly he is recognized. The myth *per se* is stated only in the upper left corner of the canvas (figures 1 & 2, page 90). Yet the light cast by the myth permeates everything around it: everything within the frame of the painting, and everyone outside that frame who comes up to the painting and allows it to keep saying what it says. This is another feature typical of many of the finest Haida stories Swanton heard. The myth illuminates the life and times of those *outside* the frame as well as those within it.

For this to happen, it is necessary to enter the world of the story, but not to violate the frame. For the myth to do its work, the hearer or the reader or the viewer of the myth must learn the language of ideas in which the myth performs its function – but that is not to say one must sign on. The beneficiary of myth need not marry into any ethnic group or subscribe to any religion. Velázquez's painting can and does work its magic on non-Christians, the plays of Sophocles work magic on non-Greeks, and the narrative poems of Skaay and Ghandl can have plenty of meaning for those who are not Haida.

Figure 3 (page 91) is another painting made by the same painter, in the same place, at nearly the same time: *Christ in the House of Martha and Mary*, now in the National Gallery, London. The surface structure (to borrow Chomsky's term) is much the same in these two paintings, though symmetrically inverted. There is a background scene confined to one far corner, and a foreground scene located in a kitchen. But I am not sure that in this case there is any fundamental separation between the realms, as there is in the earlier painting. The women in this kitchen may be myth creatures just as fully as those in the farther room.

Like works of Haida oral literature, these paintings disobey one of the central tenets of modernism, that form and content ought to be the same. Form is something more (or something less) than an extension of content in mythology just as it is in human language. Forms exist in their own right, like cups and bowls and sentence structures. Forms exist as independently as chairs, in which anyone may sit unless restrained by social prejudice or custom.

Incidentally, there is food in the second painting. There are fishes, boiled eggs, a broken bulb of garlic, a capsicum pepper. In the *Supper at Emmaus*, there is no food at all apart from garlic – but that is a painting in which the central character no longer needs to eat; and where food is no longer required, purification may well be needed instead. The central character in the *Supper at Emmaus* is painted with a few quick strokes and tucked away in a back corner, but his story fills the frame. This kind of atmospheric effect and symbolic detail is typical, once again, of well-told works of Haida oral literature.

One of the former owners of the *Supper at Emmaus* – we do not know who it was – had the myth painted out. The alteration was forgotten and remained undetected until 1933, when the painting was cleaned. So for much of its life, this piece of mythtelling lay in obscurity, misunderstood. In that respect again, it resembles some of the finest works of Native American oral literature. There may be some authority, however, for the alteration. Figure 5 (overleaf) is another mythless version of

5 Diego Velázquez. *Kitchen Scene*. c. 1620. Oil on canvas, 56 x 104 cm.
[Robert Waller Memorial Fund, 1935.380.] The Art Institute of Chicago.

6 Diego Velázquez. *Old Woman Cooking Eggs*. c. 1618. Oil on canvas, 99 x 117 cm.
National Gallery of Scotland, Edinburgh.

the painting, now in Chicago. It was made, some experts claim, by Velázquez himself.

It seems to me that the mythic dimension is crucial to the *Supper at Emmaus*, but there is also plenty to be learned from the quotidian details. Notice if you will the basket and its towel, the upright pitcher, the mortar and pestle, the inverted stack of dishes (figure 4, page 91). In Velázquez's original painting, those dishes are lit by the myth. But they didn't come from the myth. They came from the mythteller's circumstance. They came, in all probability, from Velázquez's mother's kitchen.

Another work by the same painter, also dated 1618, is known as the *Old Woman Cooking Eggs* (figure 6). It is in Edinburgh now, in the National Gallery of Scotland, though it was painted in Seville, where Velázquez was born and where he lived until 1621. There is the same basket, the same towel. There is the mortar and pestle. There is the pitcher. The story, however, is gone, replaced by another in which eggs have a very different connotation. Myths are stories, and stories, like music, like painting, like language itself, are full of repetitions. Forms are repeated, phrases and rhythms and images are repeated, but content may change.

Figure 7 (overleaf) is yet another painting made in the same years: *Two Young Men at Table*, now in the Wellington Museum, London. There is the same inverted stack of dishes, and the same mortar and pestle, here also upside down. This kind of imagistic echo, this recycling of luminous detail, is frequent in poetry worldwide. Haida narrative poetry is no exception.

Stories can be inverted just as easily as kitchen utensils and bowls. In Velázquez's version of the *Supper at Emmaus*, the kitchen maid is in the foreground, Christ and his disciples in the back. But when Rembrandt painted the same scene, in Leiden about 1630, he reversed them (figure 8, overleaf). Here the myth is right up front. The serving maid is in the

7 Diego Velázquez. *Two Young Men at Table*. c. 1619. Oil on canvas, 65 x 104 cm.
Wellington Museum, London.

8 Rembrandt van Rijn. *Pilgrims at Emmaus*. c. 1628. Oil on paper over panel,
39 x 42 cm. Institut de France, Musée Jacquemart-André, Paris.

background, opening her oven. This painting is in Paris, where it hangs in the Musée Jacquemart-André. The paraphernalia in this painting isn't reused, so far as I recall, in other works by Rembrandt, but there are qualities of light and color here that belong to him alone. Art historians and amateurs alike perceive them as the Dutch painter's signature. In Haida literature as well, we find inversions of this kind, and equally personal, identifying touches.

Such inversions are explored in some detail in one of the most imaginative works of twentieth-century scholarship, Claude Lévi-Strauss's *Mythologiques*. But it is important, I think, to remember that they occur in the domain of the individual just as much as in the domain of the cultural type. We encounter such inversions when comparing the works of individual Haida mythtellers, or of individual European painters, just as we do when comparing themes and forms across great spatial and temporal distances.

III

Close attention to individual artists and their works is a well-established practice in European studies, and the museum collections are built with that approach in view. Native American art has rarely been collected, catalogued, or displayed in the same way. But when we look at Native American art more closely, and pay it the same attention and respect to that we routinely pay to works from Europe, we always find that Native American artists are individuals too. I will try to demonstrate this fact in a token way through a single pair of illustrations.

Figure 9 (page 100) is a stone dish carved in low relief by the Haida artist Daxhiigang (1839–1920). It was made, I believe, around 1880, and is now in the Field Museum of

Natural History, Chicago. The material is argillite, a soft black
stone much used by Haida carvers in the nineteenth century,
but very seldom used for works that were intended to remain
within the community. The theme is a much-loved episode
in the story of the Raven. Skaay put this episode in the final
movement of his poem *Xhuuya Qaagaangas* (*Raven Traveling*)
when he dictated it to Swanton in October 1900. In that performance, it goes like this:

Gyaanhaw sta lla qaaydang, wansuuga.
Ll qqagighans gutxhanhaw
jaasing lla xadangxidang, wansuuga.
Gyaanhaw jaaghang qquhlgha jaasing lla qqaawdas.
Gyaanhaw sta lla tluuqaaydang, wansuuga.   5

Taana qankkugya lla ttsaa'anhlingas
gyaan qqadang lla isdas.
Kittaw ising lla isdas.

Gyaanhaw ll qaadla qqayghudyas
        gutgwiixhan guttagahliyasi.
Gyaanhaw llaghan aaxhana ghyalgaay dluu   10
ll aadagaghihls.
Gyaanhaw lla dangat styaalang, wansuuga.

Gyaan ttlaayttlaay ising lla ttsaa'anhlingas
gyaan lla dangat ising lla gittaxidas.
Llaghan aaxhana ghyalgaay dluu   15
lla ising haaying xitxidaginggwangas.
Gyaanhaw giina wadluuxhan ghaduu lla ghitsgyas.

Gyaan gyalgas naangha lla qqalingas
gyaan ttaangghaa lla tsaadlnadas.

Gyaan, «Agang aa qqadangaadang ttaas   20
gaystlgangan hla,» han lla lla suudas.

Gyaan lla dangat lla tluuqaaydasi.
Llaghan aaxhanaghilaay dluu
haying qajing lla qqaynaangas.

Gyaanhaw nang yuuwan at nang xajuu lla kitxhaghadlgas   25
gyaan dangat lla stiihlsi.
Gyaanhaw ll isghaawas
gyaan jaaghang ghan lla ghaghuyins
gyaan gii nang lla ttl guusgidas.

Gyaan jaasing gi ising nang lla istas.   30
Gyaan Siiwas sghayhlas.
Gyaan han lla suudas,
«Haw skkyaan dang gyaagha qagana aldasghasga.»

THEN he left the place, they say.
And as he was leaving,
he picked up his sister, they say.
He left his sister with his wife.
Then, they say, he set off by canoe.   5

He asked the Junco to serve as his steersman
and took him aboard.
He also took a spear.

The things he had come for were sprawled on the reef
        over top of each other.
As soon as they drew alongside,   10
the Junco went mad.
He brought the Junco back, they say.

99

9 Daxhiigang (Charlie Edenshaw). *The Raven and His Bracket Fungus Steersman* (1).
c. 1882. Argillite plate, 35 cm diameter (broken and badly mended).
Field Museum, Chicago. [Top view only.]

Then he asked the Steller's Jay to be his steersman,
and they headed out together.
As soon as they drew alongside,   15
the Jay started shaking and flapping his wings.
Whoever tried to do it failed.

Then he painted a face on a piece of fungus from a tree trunk
and seated it in the stern.
"Look alive there, and backpaddle   20
as soon as we come alongside," he said.

10 Daxhiigang. *The Raven and His Bracket Fungus Steersman* (2). c. 1892. Argillite plate, 32 cm diameter (heavily chipped). National Museum of Ireland, Dublin. [Top view above; side view below.]

> Then he headed out with him.
> When they drew alongside,
> the fungus just nodded his head.
>
> The one we speak of speared a large one and a small one,   25
> and he brought the two of them home.
> He went ashore there

> *and called his wife to come*
> *and put one of them on her.*
>
> *Then he put the other on Siiwas, his sister.*   30
> *She started to cry,*
> *and he said to her,*
> *"Yours will be safe, my darling."*[5]

Skaay never says point-blank what the Raven and his bracket fungus steersman are hunting. His Haida audience knew as well as he that the quarry was a crucial part of feminine anatomy, without which the Raven's wife and sister were clearly incomplete. Skaay was not the least bit bashful in such matters, nor was he hiding his light under a missionary bushel – but he did possess an ancient virtue: hunterly reserve. To name the quarry plainly in the poem might have spoiled the hunt. It would also have been pointless, like carving the quarry's image naturalistically in the midst of a formline sculpture.

The old Haida villages were filled with public painting and sculpture. Housepoles, memorial and mortuary poles, masks, rattles, frontlets, storage boxes, serving bowls, canoes and other objects were dense repositories of images. *The Raven and His Bracket Fungus Steersman* is a subject not found on any of these works, but it was a favorite theme of Daxhiigang's, and he carved it in argillite at least three times. The Field Museum's plate is the earliest extant example. Another, which remained for many years in private hands, is now in the Seattle Art Museum. The latest version known, made about 1892, is in the National Museum of Ireland (figure 10, page 101). These three plates were made for export, yet each is intelligible only from within Haida intellectual culture, for that is where Daxhiigang's graphic language has its roots and where the story itself is most perceptively and enthusiastically told.

There is a real sense, then, in which these works are international. They were made in and for a world with a cultural outside and a cultural inside – but one in which the outside and the inside did not exclude each other. Beyond that, of course, they tell us something about the individual artist who made them. They tell us how Daxhiigang's sense of form, and his sense of the Raven's character, changed over the space of a decade or so, while his sense of spatial organization stayed pretty much the same.

If we had several transcriptions of Skaay's poem *Raven Traveling*, made over the space of a decade or more, we could compare them in the same way. We do not have that luxury in his case, nor in the case of any other Haida author. But during the single month of October 1900, as he dictated some 7,000 lines of Haida narrative poetry to Swanton, Skaay returned many times to certain themes. We can watch him reuse certain phrases and ideas, in much the way that the young Diego Velázquez reused a stack of dishes and a jug. We can also watch him vary the arrangement of components, changing the pace from one occasion to the next, and focusing on certain aspects here, other aspects there.

IV

Every skilled performance of a myth, it seems to me, whether the medium is oil paint or words or something else, is usually speaking to at least four themes at once. It will speak to us about the human species, about the local culture, and about the individual telling the myth, all the while that it pursues its ostensible subject. The fact that myths are timeless stories, capable of traveling the globe, does not in any way prevent them from exploring local conditions nor from expressing individual emotions. The mythtellers Swanton met in Haida

Gwaii a century ago used shared and inherited stories to speak not only of timeless concerns but also of deeply personal matters, including the deaths of their wives and the loss of their villages.

Along with these four kinds or planes of information, I think there is usually a fifth, which is there because myths are not just stories; they are narrative hypotheses, personified theorems that address the very nature of the world. Myths are not like landscape paintings, which are merely *about nature* or nature's position vis-à-vis the human domain. Myths are really about *the nature of nature*. They are, for all their marvelous concreteness, also wonderfully abstract. They are vehicles of art and of science too, giving voice and heritable form to human perceptions and possibilities, and at the same time investigating facts and principles of form that extend beyond our species.

This brings us, if you will, to another inversion, another transformation in which content is divided but maintained while its form undergoes a drastic change.

In mythtelling cultures, theorems that address the nature of the world are expressed in personified form. A grammatical statement made with personified elements is what we call a story. Where the languages of myth are displaced by those of mathematics, a different assumption is made. Even where we all know better, both the constants and the variables are treated as if they were dead. A grammatical statement made with depersonified, depersonalized elements is known by and large as an equation. We find them in music, abstract painting, and academic prose as well as in mathematics. These are the denatured forms of myths, in principle no better and in principle no worse. Tradition matters in both cases. But in both cases, who is doing the telling, and how, matters every bit as much.

Nearly forty years ago, in the overture to the first volume of Mythologiques, Lévi-Strauss expressed the essence of his undertaking in a simple, lucid sentence: *Nous ne prétendons … pas montrer comment les hommes pensent dans les mythes mais comment les mythes se pensent dans les hommes, et à leur insu.* "We don't pretend to show how people think in myths, but how myths think themselves in people, and without their even knowing this occurs." That sentence has lingered in my brain since the day long ago when I first read it. I think that it expresses Franz Boas's aim too, though Boas himself was never quite sufficiently articulate to put it in those terms.

In my own studies of Native American literature, I have turned more and more in the other direction, to dwell on the contributions of individuals. This, it seems to me, is what Swanton also wanted at the start of his career, though again, he never said it plainly. It is something that Edward Sapir and Leonard Bloomfield also valued highly, and Sapir is the one who stated it most clearly.

But these are not in the end alternatives. There are no individual artists without a tradition, and there are no artistic traditions that don't depend for their existence on the work of individuals. *The ways myths think themselves in people* are intimately linked, *à leur insu*, with *the ways people think themselves in myths*. And the study of each enriches the study of the other.

NOTES

1 Swanton's statement on this subject – contained in a letter to Charles Newcombe – is published in A Story as Sharp as a Knife (1999/2000 – see note 4 below): 175.

2 W.H. New's Encyclopedia of Literature in Canada (U of Toronto Press, 2002), which pays considerable respect to aboriginal literatures, is much the best example I have seen of this new attitude.

3 These are published in The Ethnography of Franz Boas: Letters and Diaries of Franz Boas Written on the Northwest Coast from 1886 to 1931, edited by Ronald P. Rohner (U of Chicago Press, 1969): 121–2.

4 In the trilogy Masterworks of the Classical Haida Mythtellers (Vancouver: Douglas & McIntyre; Lincoln: U of Nebraska Press). The three volumes are: Bringhurst, A Story as Sharp as a Knife (1999/2000); Ghandl of the Qayahl Llaanas, Nine Visits to the Mythworld (2000); and Skaay of the Qquuna Qiighawaay, Being in Being (2001).

5 See Skaay, Being in Being, pp 335–6.

THE VOICE IN THE MIRROR

I

There are, it seems, two kinds of calendars. One, I like to think, is under the patronage of Henry David Thoreau. Some days it seems as if the other is under the patronage of everybody else.

One of these calendars is founded on recurrent real events – morning and evening, summer and winter, full moon and new moon, solstice and equinox. The other kind of calendar deals in weeks and weekends, decades, centuries, millennia, and other quite illusory units of time. That mode of clock-watching may have begun as administrative or clerical time. It seems to have mutated into journalistic time, which has more to do with television schedules and marketing techniques than with the cycles of art history, the reigns of kings and queens, or the terms of electoral office.

Millennium and century aren't natural units at all, but there is one thing in their favor: they are longer than a normal human lifespan and therefore do not threaten, like the soundbite and the timeclock, to cut our lives and thoughts to bits. It seems to me that one can learn to love the recurring shape of the year as one can learn to love a mountain range, a valley or a river – and maybe one can feel the same affection for a century that one can feel for an old highway or a barn, a house, a city street, or maybe even for a book.

I have been asked, at any rate, to pronounce a sort of epi-

American Printing History Association, Rochester Institute of Technology
20 October 2000

1 Vittore Carpaccio, St Augustine in His Study. Oil on canvas, 140 x 210 cm. c.1503. Scuola di San Giorgio degli Schiavoni, Venice.

taph for the late and not entirely lamented twentieth century, and for the twentieth-century book. I will do this in a round-about way, because of my devious nature and because I am convinced that, to have any grasp of what our own eventful century has been, we need a sense of what it was not. I sub-scribe, in other words, to the old, familiar idea that a little excursion into the past is the best way to give depth, perspec-tive, and a triangulated location to an otherwise seemingly isolated and two-dimensional present.

We might begin, like many intruders before us, by visiting the study of a sixteenth-century scholar, reflecting on the dif-ferences between his world and our own, and on the threads that still connect them.

Much in this room (figure 1) should look familiar: the clutter of books, the private shrines of treasured objects, the presence of a house pet, even perhaps the pose of the scholar

2 Vittore Carpaccio, *St Augustine in His Study*. Ink on paper, 28 x 43 cm. c.1502. British Museum, London (Cat. 1934-12-8-1).

himself – though he is plainly out of date: he writes with a pen instead of a keyboard and gets his news by looking out the window instead of consulting the internet.

The painting was made in 1503 by Vittore Carpaccio, who was then in his early forties and as good as he was ever going to get. It hangs to this day in the same building (though not the original room) for which it was made: the Scuola di San Giorgio degli Schiavoni in Venice.

Color photography and electric light – two of the standard components of twentieth-century life – make it possible for us to be here in a lecture hall, looking at a large-scale image of the painting projected through a lens from a tiny scrap of celluloid. Digital lithography, a slightly later technology, enables us to move to a room of our own choosing carrying a tiny reproduction in a book. On most scholars' desks, here at the end of the twentieth century, sits a computer that makes such feedback loops of time and space seem simple and routine. Five centuries and five thousand miles collapse at the touch of a key, the click of a mouse, or the flip of a switch.

It may occur to you that this is one important difference between the sixteenth century and the twentieth. I think, however, that this painting has all the sophistication of a microchip. It is oil on canvas, 140 × 210 cm, and it is one – the middle one – of a set of three canvases linked together, not by coaxial cable or infrared but by threads of narrative, in a highly complex circuit. By itself – and even more as part of the series – the painting performs, or allows us to perform, a set of operations tying space and time in knots.

The cycle of three paintings is devoted to the life of St Jerome, who was born, I am told, near Ljubljana, in Slovenia, about 355 CE and died in Bethlehem about the year 420. The figure in this painting is not, however, St Jerome. This is St Augustine, Jerome's contemporary and friend, who died a decade later. There was a story, current in Europe in the fifteenth and sixteenth centuries, concerning the relation of these saints. At the moment of Jerome's death, according to that story, Augustine was writing him a letter. And Augustine, at that moment, felt a presence, heard a voice and saw a light – not a figure, just a light – which was the spirit of St Jerome.

So this is a painting of Jerome in which Jerome cannot be seen. Because Augustine cannot see his friend Jerome, neither can we – but we can see Augustine, hearing the voice and seeing the light.

We can also see his Maltese terrier, who also sees the light, and casts a shadow to confirm it. Dogs, of course, are every bit as sensitive to spirits or to presences as saints are. And to prove that painters are, at the height of their powers, just as sensitive as dogs, there is Carpaccio's signature, just beneath the shadow of the pen that Augustine is holding in his hand.

The event that is portrayed here, you may say, can never have occurred. But if it had occurred or did occur, it would have been or was in the year 420, more or less, in northeastern Algeria, where Augustine spent much of his life. Carpaccio has set it in sixteenth-century Venice instead.

Hanging near the desk – and right beside the vision – is an armillary sphere. This confirms Carpaccio's (and by inference, Augustine's) awareness of secular reality, the roundness of the globe, the movements of the sun and moon and planets. That sphere was a very modern device in 1503. It's only fair to guess that if Carpaccio repainted this work now, he might include a cell phone and a laptop. But even as it stands, I think the painting has no trouble keeping up.

The clutter of books belongs to the sixteenth century too – but since this is 1503, we ought to think that most of them are fifteenth-century books. Aldus's edition of the *Aeneid*, set in Francesco Griffo's new italic, might be somewhere on that desk. Somewhere on the shelf on the opposite wall should be a copy of Augustine's own *De Civitate Dei*, printed at Venice in 1470 by Johannes and Wendelin van Speyer.

In the alcove at the back (figure 3, overleaf), beneath the astrolabes, is a rotary lectern: another favorite Renaissance device, although Augustine and Jerome, in the fourth and fifth centuries, could certainly have used one. Its function is avowedly humanist and secular, like the function of the astrolabes and armillary sphere. It is, in effect, the prototype of everyone's favorite software: a device for comparing variant texts; that is, for keeping several documents open at once.

This is a painting about light, spirits, and voices. It's also a painting about lucidity: about the satisfaction of accurate observations, accurate measurements, good hearing, clear sight, and dependable texts. These things occur, in Carpaccio's world, where the sacred and secular meet.

3 Detail from figure 1.

That is why, underneath the table, down below the armillary sphere, two works of music are propped open. One is a sacred work, the other a secular piece, and both are painted so precisely that it's possible to sing them from the painted image of the score.[1]

The matching drawing (figure 2, page 109), now in the British Museum, is in Carpaccio's hand. It appears to be the actual master drawing, perhaps the one submitted for approval to his patrons and used in laying out the canvas. The drawn room, being smaller, is less cluttered than the painted one. Fewer books are piled and scattered about; there are no astrolabes in the alcove; there is no armillary sphere – though a large, empty circle is marking the sphere's place. Perhaps the sphere was the first and foremost of a set of late additions: something Carpaccio planned to add but didn't render in detail because it wasn't present; he had to go elsewhere to draw it from life.

I think this is a real room, known both to Carpaccio and to those who commissioned the painting. I think that because of the precision of the drawing, and because of something else which I'll explain in a few moments. But whether the room is fictional or real, the painting has many layers. It is as modern, in that respect, as Eliot's *Waste Land*, Joyce's *Ulysses*, and other seminal twentieth-century works.

At the bottom of the painting, underneath the desk, resting against the pedestal, is an emblem that belongs to Cardinal Bessarion. And the face in the painting may well be Bessarion's face. That is to say, this may be Bessarion in St Augustine's shoes – but that is only fair. These, remember, are shoes that St Augustine, through Carpaccio, has borrowed from a Renaissance Venetian, such as Bessarion himself.

Bessarion was a literary man, and I think he understood his bookshelves and his desk in much the same way that Carpaccio did his canvas: as something like a focal plane where past and present could meet. Like Carpaccio, he also left a legacy that functions now as a link between his century and our own.

In the Eastern and Western churches alike, Bessarion was a kind of prodigy, promoted ahead of everyone else. In the secular world, he was revered as an authority on Plato and was busy as a diplomat. He was born at Trabzon in northeastern Turkey, probably in 1408, and while still in his twenties was appointed a Greek Orthodox archbishop. At the age of thirty he came to Italy, working in vain on a project to unite the Western and Eastern churches, and in the West was made a cardinal for his efforts. In fact, he was nearly elected Pope after the death of Eugenius IV. He was an avid collector of manuscripts, and in 1468 he donated most of his library to the church of San Marco at Venice. This donation was the seed of the Biblioteca di San Marco. The library building which stands on the Piazza San Marco today was built expressly to house Bessarion's books.

The first consignment of those books arrived in Venice in April 1469: thirty cases on the backs of fifteen mules. There were three more consignments before Bessarion's death, at Ravenna in 1472. The books, however, stayed in their cases for sixty years, picked through and occasionally borrowed by privileged insiders but inaccessible to most – including Aldus Manutius, who could, of course, have put them to good use. Things began to change in 1530, when one of Aldus's authors, Pietro Bembo, was appointed librarian of San Marco. He had the books unpacked and shelved by 1531. Yet they were not moved into their own building until the late 1560s – a hundred years after delivery.

The face and dress of the man in Carpaccio's painting differ in many respects from those of the man in his drawing. They differ nearly as much from those in Joos van Wassenhove's portrait of Bessarion, painted about 1473 for Federigo of Urbino and now in the Louvre. But there is no reason to think that Joos's painting and Carpaccio's should match, even if both are really meant to represent Bessarion. Neither artist, so far as we know, had ever laid eyes on the man he was painting.

Bessarion is the Latin form of Greek Βασσάριον, diminutive of βασσάρα. It means "little fox." It was probably the Little Fox himself who chose the name; he took it at his ordination in Constantinople in 1423. But the use of this diminutive goes back at least another two millennia, to Herodotos' list of North African flora and fauna. Herodotos uses the name not for a fox but for the creature known in English as a fennec. Fennecs (which belong to the same family as dogs and foxes) make good pets, and I have tried more than once to convince myself that the long-tailed animal in Carpaccio's drawing is a fennec: a suitable pet for Augustine and an allusion to Bessarion both at once. The problem is, the ears are much too small. What Carpaccio has drawn looks more like a bushy-tailed weasel and may be just an oddly rendered cat. I do not know why a

Maltese terrier has replaced it in the painting, and I hope the day will come when I find out. In any case, Augustine's house pet serves to counterbalance, in its small way, the much more famous quadruped kept by his friend Jerome.

The painting of Augustine writing to Jerome is, as I've mentioned, one of three. The series as a whole seems more concerned with the saint's death than with his life, but in the first canvas (figure 4, overleaf) Jerome is very much alive: an elderly and peaceful-looking man whose equally peaceful African lion is causing a considerable fuss. This painting is set in Venice, in a fairly secluded but easily recognizable spot: the gardens off the Campo Ugo Foscolo and the Salizzada delle Gatte, in the sestiere del Castello. The pinkish building in the background is the Scuola di San Giorgio degli Schiavoni: the very institution which commissioned and still holds the paintings we are looking at.

The Schiavoni are the Slovenians, and the Scuola degli Schiavoni is the Slovenian Guild or Slovenian Club, a fraternity established in 1451 by Slovenians in Venice. You could think of it as something like the Lions Club or Rotary or Elks Club in a modern American city, though it had an ethnic basis and something very close to a political agenda. It engaged not just in public service work but also in an effort to launch a new crusade against the Turks. A lot of expatriate Slovenians and Croatians lived in Venice in the fifteenth century, and the area east and north of Piazza San Marco was their quarter – what Venetians call their *sixth*, their *sestiere* – of the city.

The Slovenians of Venice were not a wealthy group. They met for thirty years in San Giovanni, a church that belonged to the Knights of Malta. It too is in this painting (figure 4): that brownish building on the right, with the big wooden porch. In 1480 the Slovenian Guild built a house of its own. Twenty years later they commissioned these paintings from Carpaccio

4 Vittore Carpaccio, *St Jerome with His Lion*. Oil on canvas, 144 × 208 cm. c.1502. Scuola di San Giorgio degli Schiavoni, Venice.

5 Detail from figure 4.

– whose reputation then was largely based on his portrayals of St George slaying the dragon. In Carpaccio's treatments of that theme, the emphasis is not on the rescued maiden but on the skill and triumph of the knight. But in the paintings of Augustine and Jerome, the Guild of Slovenians got something more complex, intellectual, and artful than a dragon slayer with shining armor and lance.

The building in which the painting hangs appears in the painting itself. That is one of the reasons why I think Augustine's study is also a real room. We are in that building, looking at this painting. And when we step outside, we can expect to see Jerome, leading a lion into the garden, and some frightened monks attempting to escape.

There are other things of interest in the painting – pheasants, reindeer, men in Oriental dress. In the background (figure 5), two monks are racing up the stairs. Their scapulars are rhyming with the horns of the reindeer who is headed the other way.

This kind of formal rhyme or homology was important to Carpaccio, to Dürer, and to other Renaissance painters. It was equally important to their earliest known predecessors, who painted the great murals of Chauvet and Lascaux. Things that we know to be different, and might suppose to have nothing in common, are vividly linked by the simplest possible trick: by matching and mirroring colors or shapes. The mechanics of metaphor are excruciatingly simple, like binary math, and can nevertheless give wonderfully subtle and complex results.

The same process is intrinsic to the history of the Greek and Latin alphabets, the syllabic scripts of India, and to Chinese logographic script. Similarities are seized upon to make component elements which echo and reflect each other. This is how we get from isolated pictographic images to the self-sustaining textures of real alphabets and scripts. All scripts are self-reflective systems built from a limited number of elements: the basic strokes and radicals of Han Chinese, or the equally basic components – stems and bowls and hooks and dots – of Greek and Latin letters.

Felice Feliciano, Luca de Pacioli, and other letterform analysts of Carpaccio's time and place loved formal order every bit as much as Carpaccio did himself. Perhaps they loved it more; perhaps too much. Theoreticians and designers are exposed, more than the rest of us, to the temptations of mathematical and logical exactness. Working painters and calligraphers – no matter how devoted to clarity and precision – discover that the echoes and reflections they create cannot and must not be precise. They learn that the imperfections in the metaphor are what allow the metaphor to work.

Carpaccio was pleased with his little gesture – this echo of scapulars and horns. We can be certain he enjoyed rhyming the symbols of male chastity with the symbols of male vigor, because he put that little backhand metaphor right in the center of his painting. The stairway, which the monks are running up, aligns with the diagonal from the top left to the lower right corner of the painting and is (not mathematically but visually) just halfway across.

I'd like to call attention to one further detail. Those monks are running in fright from the peaceful lion that is walking here in sixteenth-century Venice with St Jerome, a man who died eleven centuries before. They are running up the stairs at the center of the painting, into the building where the painting itself is hung. Surely, when they get inside the building, they will climb, for safety, back inside the painting whence they came. But when they get there they will find, inside that painting, the same lion that was stalking them outside. There is no rest for the innocent any more than for the wicked. That is how civilization works. You can move from the pan into the fire or onto the plate, but there you find the very images you fled from. There is no escape from lions in either history or art – especially not in Venice, whose emblem after all is the winged lion of St Mark. Those monks are trapped in the circle of fate no less than any postmodern reader or writer. If Jerome is at peace, that is because he has been on a vision quest, where he has come to an understanding with the lion and all he represents. The only other undisturbed figures in the painting are those who are fully absorbed in their talk or their work.

It also interests me that, here in this first painting, the books are firmly closed, except for one that has fallen to the ground. They are girdle books, wrapped in their built-in bags, flapping from the belts of fleeing monks. In the middle painting of the three – which is the one we looked at first – many books are neatly shelved and many others are in use. They seem almost to form a culture of their own. Some are asleep, some are awake, and several are apparently engaged in conversation with each other.

The last of the three paintings (figure 6, overleaf) shows the funeral of Jerome. Here I only see two books, and both are opened wide, though surely no one needs to read them. All those gathered in this scene must know by heart the service for the dead.

History and legend are agreed that Jerome's death occurred in Bethlehem, yet Carpaccio, again, has made the buildings reassuringly Italian. Precisely in the center of this painting, mirroring the stairway with its monks, there is a well: a shaft leading down instead of a stair leading up. But the stairs do not lead to salvation, and the shaft does not lead to the realm of the damned. It is the source of the water of life, there in the midst of the vision of death. Between us and the well is a palm, the liturgical calendar's symbol of triumph – and tied to the palm is another tame animal, just as perplexing to me as

6 Vittore Carpaccio, *Death of St Jerome*. Oil on canvas, 144 x 208 cm. c. 1502. Scuola di San Giorgio degli Schiavoni, Venice.

the one in Carpaccio's drawing. In art as in the alphabet, even where symbols or symbol-decipherers falter, the sweetness of imperfect parallels persists.

The fact that Jerome was born in Slovenia might be reason enough in itself for the Slovenian Guild to adopt him – but so far as I can see, these paintings never allude to the Slavic connection. They are much more concerned with the portable heritage – stories, ideas, books – and in a subtler way with the guild's political future. What the Guild of Slovenians and Cardinal Bessarion shared – and what brought them into contact when the cardinal lived in Venice – was their practical and hardcore opposition to Islam. Both were in favor of reviving the crusades, but for them this was not an ambition with roots in religious doctrine alone. Bessarion and the Slovenians both regarded the conquest of Palestine – where Jerome had breathed his last – as a step toward the reconquest of their homelands: Slovenia and Greece.

These are some but not all of the ways we can look at Carpaccio's paintings. The readings pile up, like the books in the study, where many are open at once, and many more are waiting to be opened in good time. But I think it is good that Augustine is raising his head from his papers and books – looking beyond the circus of symbols, the frame of the painting, the page of the letter, the circle of life and death. The reassuring thing, for me, about this scene is that whatever the human is sensing, the dog can sense it too. Dogs, if you like, are a test for distinguishing Neoclassical from Renaissance ideas, as they are for testing real against imagined ghosts and bears. In Renaissance thought, as in Renaissance letterforms, the artificial and the natural repeatedly – though, of course, always imperfectly – coincide.

Writing means making abstract marks into a more or less continuous string of recognizable elements, deciphered by a process known as reading. It involves keeping the nose to the page, if not the grindstone. But in that gesture of *looking up* from writing and from reading is everything that makes reading and writing what they are. The meaning of that gesture is *seeing and speaking* what is written, *hearing and seeing* what is read. Hearing, seeing, and speaking are natural acts, in a way that reading and writing are not. Looking up from the page is what brings them together.

In the early days of the alphabet, letters often lived outside, where they could get fresh air and light. In the long reign of manuscript and print, they have mostly lived indoors, and in the short reign of the keyboard and the microchip, letters have mostly lived in an airless world fully divorced from forest, mountain, garden, earth.

From time to time – in imagination or in fact – letterforms

7 Giovanni Bellini, *St Francis in the Desert*. Oil on canvas, 124 x 142 cm. c.1480. The Frick Collection, New York.

and books have been taken back outdoors. This happened often in northern Italy toward the end of the fifteenth century and early in the sixteenth. It happens for instance in Giovanni Bellini's *St Francis in the Desert* (figure 7), which was painted in Venice about 1480 and is now at the Frick. And it happens, tongue-in-cheek, in the National Gallery's *Magdalen* (figure 8), which was made around 1520, probably in Parma, by Antonio da Correggio. Fresh air and exercise are good for books and letters, just as they are for us.

In general, after the Renaissance, the book went back indoors – and yet, in every century, it seems, some people learn to make interiors hospitable to light and air. Pieter Janssens's

8 Antonio Allegri da Correggio, *The Magdalen*. Oil on canvas, 38 × 30 cm. c. 1519. National Gallery, London.

reading woman (figure 9, overleaf), painted in the Netherlands toward the end of the seventeenth century, may not be a saint, but she is having an experience of some kind through her book. With luck, her world is being enlarged, her life enriched. She could be reading letters cut in her own time by Christoffel van Dijck: letters surely made indoors, but letters which

9 Pieter Elinga Janssens, *Woman Reading*. Oil on canvas, 75 x 63 cm. c.1700. Alte Pinakotek, Munich.

are graceful, energetic, and peaceful enough that through their very forms, they open up the shutters and let light into the room.

From the point of view of a typographic historian, one of the major facts about the twentieth century is that, during this period, some books and letters were brought back into the

10 Pablo Picasso, *La Grande baigneuse au livre* [*Big Woman at the Beach with Book*].
Oil and pastel on canvas, 130 × 97 cm. 1937. Musée Picasso, Paris.

open air. The sanserif woman whom Picasso called *La Grande baigneuse au livre* (figure 10, page 125), painted in 1937, is an emblem of this fact. She could be reading something in Gill Sans, though I suspect, myself, that she was waiting, in 1937, for a type that didn't yet exist: a type that many people tried to make before the century was out.

St Augustine and his dog are inside looking out; the *grande baigneuse* is outside looking inward. He is writing; she is reading. She may be reading something other than a letter from the saint, and to the best of my knowledge, no one has yet painted St Augustine writing to Picasso's mistress. Nonetheless, the two are linked, both by the inward world of writing and by the outward world of light.

The last illustration I want to show you (figure 11) is nowhere near as rich and interesting as the painting with which we began. Yet in its unassuming way, each of these modest little marks shares something with Carpaccio's much larger and more complex imaginary portrait. These are twentieth-century letterforms, each with its own historical and geographical references built in. Each is therefore many things at once: a piece of idealized writing, a miniaturized historical allusion, a quite sophisticated piece of computer programming, and yet a legible and useful little sign which its users can quite rightly take for granted. Each is a twentieth-century artifact, yet each embodies a legacy reaching back to the dawn of writing.

All we need to do to annihilate their worth is to cut that historical thread. This is true of letters; it is just as true of books. We keep on making new designs and images, and writing down new texts – and yet, however new they claim to be, their usefulness depends upon the strength of their connection to two things: first, the world beyond our species, which is to say, the nonhuman environment; second, the world beyond our time, which is to say the future and the past. The former,

11 Four variations on the letter "a" (Sanvito, Centaur, Bembo, Frutiger) and four on 月 yuè, "moon" (楷 Kǎi, 宋 Sòng, 明 Míng, 黑 Hēi; or kai, sōchō, minchō, goshikku).

simply put, is the test of what is true; the latter is the test of how we know.

II

Language has a lot of charming properties, but the one I value most is its enduring insufficiency. I haven't the slightest chance of fully translating Carpaccio's paintings into words – no more than he has any chance of exhausting a good story by putting it into a painting. Failures of this kind, it seems to me, can be far more productive than any apparent success. Writing and painting are fruitful tasks because they lead us out so easily and far beyond our reach.

Talking about talking, writing about writing, and painting about painting are more incestuous kinds of activity – and incest raises the worrisome specter of a success that is absolute. I would like to say a few words about words, but I think that I would stand a better chance of fruitful failure if I could show you a few pictures of these words instead. I would like in particular to offer you a picture of what is meant by *language* itself.

Language is different from writing. Both must be learned, but every human society shelters and nurtures a language, which all its full-fledged members are expected to acquire. Writing is an optional technology which most human beings and most human cultures have done happily without.

Using language is as natural to humans as walking and running and picking things up. It is well to remember, however, that one species' nature is another species' artifice. Flying, not walking, is what comes naturally to bats. This does not make bats superior or inferior, nor closer to or farther away from the angels, nor does it mean that they possess immortal souls. It only means that they are bats. Martin Heidegger claimed that our abilities with language give members of the species Homo *sapiens* privileged metaphysical status, but this merely repeats at a grander level the error Heidegger made when he claimed that the two languages most inherently disposed to speak the truth were by coincidence two of the three or four languages he read, namely German and classical Greek.

Most of the words we use to talk about language – including the word *language* itself – seem to rest on the assumption that language comes out of the mouth. Words like *speech*, and words like *linguist* and *phonology* and *phonetics* are all part of this conspiracy. But these assumptions about language, like Heidegger's assumptions about value, are worth a closer look.

Well along in the twentieth century, linguists finally began to study sign languages closely – and so began to understand that *linguistics*, despite its etymology, has to reach out way beyond the mouth. *Speech* is just a special case of *gesture*: a half-hidden kind of gesture, producing an audible trace. Language begins when the mind hitches a ride on signals transmitted by the body and another mind receives (through the aid of another body, as a rule) at least some of what is sent.

Inaudible languages – ASL or American Sign Language, for instance – are, you could say, written rather than spoken, but they are normally written on air and not on paper. Or they are spoken, you could say, but spoken in silence, with the hands, arms, shoulders, head, and face.

There are now some dozens, if not hundreds, of publications on the *phonology, phonetics* and *prosody* of ASL and other silent languages. There are learned discussions of *syllables* and *sonority*, and even of *vowels* and *consonants*, in sign languages. These terms, apparently, are metaphors. But where does the metaphor reside? In the application of these terms to ASL – or in their original usage? When we study the phonology and prosody of an oral language, are we "literally" studying something to do with speech – or is speech itself, like literality, a metaphor for something else?

I am fond, myself, of concrete things and terms and notions – hand and mouth and shoe and foot, for instance. But if I undertake the study of comparative anatomy, I am faced at once with fascinating parallels connecting my own bones, muscles, nerves and veins with those of dogs, whales, chickadees and lizards. What words can I use to express the identity of the whale's pectoral flippers, the dog's forepaws and forelegs, and my own arms and hands? In the Haida language, this is not a problem. One word (the Haida word *stl*) is used for all. English, by contrast, is hyperspecific. So the metaphor in this case is transparent and self-evident in Haida, but in English we have to write it out: *forepaw = flipper = hand*. Because it coincides with a fundamental theorem of Darwinian biology, many English speakers will classify that metaphor as scientific fact. It is no less potent or poetic a metaphor for that. In Haida, where the equation is tautological, it attracts no particular attention either as poetry or as science; it qualifies instead as common sense. Language is like blowing snow. It hides some things, exposes others. Metaphor is one way of scratching through or leaping over language to get a little closer to the underlying truth.

Writing, like speech – to return to an earlier metaphor – is a special case of gesture. It begins as a universal act – a simple movement of an equally simple tool on which the mind hitches a ride. Through steady use, it grows increasingly refined, stylized and specialized: anything *but* universal.

When we enter into language – oral or manual, audible or silent – or when language enters into us – we make recognizable, meaningful gestures and register the gestures made by others. Perceiving these gestures involves a kind of mental reenactment which is part – a crucial part – of understanding. If I speak a word – the Arabic word مغرب *maǧrib* or the Haida word *qquuna*, let us say – containing a phoneme that is not in your own repertoire, you hear that phoneme indistinctly, though I pronounce it clearly. It will remain indistinct until you learn to reproduce it – until it becomes part of your own physical, proprioceptive experience. Once the phoneme and its uses *are* a part of your experience, you begin to hear it even when it's missing or is not distinctly pronounced.

When prefabricated letters entered Europe, in the fifteenth century, every person skilled at reading was also skilled at the physical making of letters. So long as every letter was handmade, no one really learned to read without also really learning how to write. The prefabricated letters of the printers were modeled on the letters of the scribes, so reading a printed page was not altogether different from reading a page of manuscript. It involved a mental reenactment of the *writing* of the letters.

Over time, the psychophysical tie between readers and texts grew weaker. The letterforms used by the printers of books and the manuscript hands of the readers of books diverged. Yet until the twentieth century, readers remained, at least in a tentative sense, writers.

Then the pen was replaced by the keyboard. Then prefabrication came home. Now people "write" (as we still say) by pressing keys with the tips of their fingers. The touch may be graceful or clumsy, violent or gentle, earnest or hesitant. The result will be the same ten-point Times Roman or Helvetica or Courier, or whatever is installed in the machine. This changes the process of writing, of course, but it also changes reading. For those with no experience of the actual making of letters, reading is not psychophysical, it is abstract. The proliferation of the personal computer has led a lot of people to learn to type, but with the shift from pen to keyboard, reading has become more and more purely a spectator sport.

Letterpress printing became an important business in Venice while Carpaccio was a child, but reading was still rooted in the manuscript tradition. The mental act of apprehending written forms still had a physical dimension, almost like a handshake. Printing made the psychophysical relation between letterforms and readers a bit more artificial but also gave it depth. Letterpress, after all, is a three-dimensional process, a sculptural process, leaving a subtly three-dimensional mark. You can walk around the text as you turn the page.

Think back now, if you will, to Carpaccio's three paintings. Think of the physical bond he creates by placing the figures of myth – Augustine, Jerome, the lion – into a two-dimensional image of a real and familiar three-dimensional space. Optical perspective, still a fresh technique in Carpaccio's time, gives depth to these images as well. It places the story in physically thinkable, livable space.

That space is vital to the mind. It is space in which to read and think and look and be oneself. Why? Because *language* arises in *groups*, but *mind* arises in *space* and in *solitude*. Until it gets entangled in the mind, language just repeats like a stuck record. After it gets entangled in the mind, it sometimes starts to talk.

I hold, like Eric Gill, that letters are things, not pictures of things. I beg to remind you, however, that what you find on the font of a photosetting machine is the photographic image of a letter, and what you set with photosetting equipment is not in truth a letter but a picture of a letter. More precisely: a picture of a drawing of a letter. What you find on a digital font is likewise not a letter but a Bézier or cubic-spline description of a letter. What you set with your computer and print with a laser printer is a digital simulation of a letter. What you find in a California job case is also not a letter but a sort, which is a sculpture of a letter. What you print with a Vandercook or an Albion is the imprint of a sculpture of a letter. Where is the letter itself? This is the mind-body problem of the philosophers writ small.

Letters, like words, are things – but letters, like words, and like language itself, are also metaphors, and metaphors, I think, stand in much the same relation to the mind as proteins and amino acids to the body. All the more reason to give them convincing and tangible forms: forms with which our bodies, minds, and memories can really interact.

The original book is, of course, the world itself. People in all cultures read that book. Especially people without writing. Especially hunter-gatherers, who study the great book day after day, night after night. People who have writing make their own books – little models of the world – and often study those instead, as if their little books were somehow more correct or more important than the book in whose immense, detailed pages we all live. In the twentieth century, replete with comforts such as central heating and air conditioning, and awash in printed books and magazines, films, cassettes and compact discs and nonstop broadcasts on TV, a lot of people ceased to read the original book. In the course of the same century, most people came to live in cities, under constant artificial sound and light. Many now have never seen the night sky, the grasslands in the spring, the hardwood forests in the fall, the taiga or the tundra or the desert or the mountains, except as pictures on TV or printed images in magazines or illustrated books. When people raised this way read books, their reading is untested in a way. It hasn't been calibrated against the original book.

Yet people keep on hankering to write and publish books. It seems to be the way we are. People keep on wanting to make love in spite of overpopulation and wanting to write books in spite of overpublication.

What else can we say for the twentieth century? It was, like every century on record, a time when things got better and a time when things got worse.

It was a time when linguists fanned out over North America, taking dictation in some three hundred indigenous languages, from Inuktitut in the Arctic to Kuna on the Isthmus of Panama, while others did the same in South America, Asia, Africa, Oceania, and in the several corners of Europe where a true oral literature survived.

Through the joint efforts of mythtellers and linguists, in the space of a single century, hundreds of whole literatures acquired written form. The number of recorded literatures increased perhaps a hundredfold, and many oral masterworks acquired, through the metaphor of writing, the ability to multiply and travel round the world. Many of these works are still in manuscript, and those that have been printed have mostly been ignored, but the world's body of written, preservable literature has been magnificently broadened and deepened as well. The picture of humanity preserved in written text is now a much more complex jewel than it was in 1900.

Those linguists, however, were working against time in cultures that were being, or had already been, systematically destroyed. Many of the languages that were first written down in the twentieth century were driven to extinction in the course of the same century. The number of written literatures has risen quite dramatically, but the number of living languages has just as dramatically shrunk – and keeps on shrinking. The museum full of stuffed and mounted stories is now huge, but the forest where languages nest and literatures breed has been mercilessly cut.

Events in the big city bear a curious resemblance to events on the reservation. Trade publishing in the twentieth century blossomed under the hands of entrepreneurs such as Knopf and Gallimard and Springer and Mondadori, and yet, under the pressure of corporate cannibalism, before the century had ended, the trade standards set by these firms had generally collapsed.

In the twentieth century, publishers made immense numbers of good, cheap books – Penguin books and Anchor books and so on – in convenient, short-lived incarnations. But by and large, in the same century, they gave up publishing their most important books in any durably usable form. The university presses of Oxford and Cambridge, for instance, stopped sewing books. Even canonical books – even, for instance, the standard editions of the Greek texts of Aiskhylos and Sophokles, Aristotle and Plato – began to come from Oxford with the pages cut apart and stuck together again with glue. This saves as much as twenty cents per copy and reduces the life of the book by a thousand years. In the twentieth century, publishing, for many, ceased to be a form of public service and became a form of parasitism instead.

In the realm of typographic technology, ours was the century when the metaphor of the letter jumped from metal to digital form. Type escaped from the tangible body in which it had lived for five hundred years. This is the thrilling part of the story: the part that deals with exploration and conquest. On the other side, as usual, is a sorrier story of degradation and loss. It is connected, in this case, with the shift to high-speed planographic printing. In the twentieth century, books were turned, to a large extent, into typographic tenements: page after dreary page of badly spaced letters in sickly grey ink lying weakly on the surface of bleached white or bilious yellow paper frozen in a bed of brittle glue and wrapped in a gaudy color cover which cost more to design and manufacture than all the dreary pages it was able to conceal.

The book is like the table and the chair. The questions of how to design and produce these objects were answered long ago. Under the heavy pressure of commerce, many corners have been cut, and manufacturing speed and volume have increased, but no genuine improvements have been made. In a stable and healthy economy, nothing perhaps except the ornament would change. But where the foremost duty of the citizen is to mimic compound interest and consume more every year, we seem compelled not only to create but also to destroy and reinvent what is beyond us to improve.

After more than twenty years of inflationary development, digital type is in many respects as good as the metal type it displaced. It is also, of course, faster to set. That increased speed has two results, inescapably interconnected: first, an automatic increase in "economic activity"; second, an automatic reduction in value of everything that type is used to say.

The electronic book, another twentieth-century product, is still a crude device at present. But I assume that, like the gramophone and radio before it, it will soon achieve a kind of high fidelity. Perhaps in its moment of glory it will even achieve a kind of visual stereo by rediscovering the two-page spread. Along with that, we might expect some other luxuries:

electronic simulations of the textures of good paper and the subtle impression of good letterpress.

In the realm of typographic form and content, it seems to me we ought to remember the twentieth century for a genuine contribution to the handling of typographic space. The typography of prose has changed very little in the past four hundred years, except that paragraphs, on average, are now shorter than they were. But in 1897, Stéphane Mallarmé introduced something new to the typography of poetry. Both in manuscript and in print, a page of Mallarmé's *Un Coup de dés*, Pound's *Cantos*, Charles Olson's *Maximus Poems*, or Gary Snyder's *Myths and Texts* is recognizable on sight as a twentieth-century artifact. In this period poets learned, perhaps for the first time, to handle space as orators do silence. They learned to treat the space within a written text as conceptual and musical notation. Literary speech, in other words, took on a visual dimension that it never had before.

Mimicking the foreign and antique is a very old and widespread human habit, but I suspect that the twentieth century set a record for geographical and historical masquerade. Printing type and page design are offered now in assorted historical flavors, like Greek or Chinese take-out dinners. This masquerade depends for its foundation on real knowledge – largely, in fact, on the work of Stanley Morison, whose aim was something more than masquerade – but knowledge that is packaged as a costume is easier to sell than knowledge that is not.

Many of these phenomena embody, it would seem, a single principle. The dematerialization of the type font, the indulgence in historical masquerade, the switch from letterpress to planographic printing, are all in their way of a piece with the relentless diversion of funds from the structure and interior of books to the dustjacket or cover. In Aldus's time, one hundred per cent of the publisher's budget for design and manufacture went into the guts of the book. Binding was left to the purchaser. Now it is routine for a trade publisher to spend more than half the total budget for design and manufacture on the wrapper. Energy that once was invested in the body of the book is now invested in the surface. In physical terms, this means we no longer expect the book to absorb and radiate energy, but to reflect ambient energy instead.

And so it is understandable that the book is poised to move, in the coming century, from its familiar paper house to a kind of handheld movie screen. Then we can turn on our books as we turn on our radios, not to read ancient and modern texts against each other and compare them with the world beyond the window, but to catch the latest news and ads and hits.

I assure you that I see no reason to be worried by any of this. For while it does look to me like a part of our future, I expect that part to be short-lived. Wherever human beings live their own lives instead of somebody else's, stories form in their hearts and in their heads. Stories and people nourish each other. Where that occurs are the seeds of the book, some of which are certain to sprout.

Ours was a century in which people loved information – or claimed to – and collected it with unrelenting glee, building the largest libraries, library catalogs and data banks that humans have yet had. It was also the century in which more information was destroyed by human hands than in all previous centuries combined. In short, it was a century in which human beings had more power than ever before, and in which, as always before, they used that power for the best and worst of purposes.

People have hoped, of course, that the book would rescue the species. But books are the instruments only of nongenetic heredity, and only individuals, not species, learn by nongenetic means. Species only learn by genetic selection. The book is useless to the species, except through its effect on individuals, and that effect can only be short term.

And of course, the effects of the book are not always benign. The effects of the Bible and the Koran, to take two powerful examples, have not always been benign. This may be because the people reading books have not always learned to read the original book – the book we did not write and do not publish. I mean the book we live in: the only book that calibrates the mind.

That, I like to think, is why Jerome is walking in the garden with his lion, perfectly serene. And that, I like to think, is why, with all those books piled everywhere around them, Augustine and his dog are sitting with their ears cocked, looking up.

NOTE

1 Two important studies of Carpaccio's *St Augustine* appear in *The Art Bulletin* 41 (New York, December 1959). The first is Helen Roberts's study of the painting and its sources (pp 283–97); the second is Edward Lowinsky's reading of the music in the painting (pp 298–301). I am greatly indebted to them both.

POETRY AND THINKING

I

In the fall of 1930, Ludwig Wittgenstein was asked to give a title to the course he was going to teach at Cambridge University. I'm told that he grunted and brooded for a time and then muttered simply *Philosophy*. Late last year, when I was asked for a title for this lecture, I was sorely tempted simply to say *Poetry*. That, if you like, is the real title. *Poetry and Thinking*, which might sound still more grand, or still more grandiose, is only the redundant explanation. Poetry *is* thinking, real thinking. And real thinking is poetry.

Herakleitos says something that might help us get this clear: ξυνόν ἐστι πᾶσι τὸ φρονέειν: "All things think and are linked together by thinking." Parmenides answers him in verse: τὸ γὰρ αὐτὸ νοεῖν ἔστιν τε καὶ εἶναι: "To be and to have meaning are the same." These are concise definitions of poetry and brief explanations of how it has come to exist. Poetry is not manmade; it is not pretty words; it is not something hybridized by humans on the farm of human language. Poetry is a quality or aspect of existence. It is *the thinking of things*.

Language is one of the methods we use to mime and to mirror and admire it, and for that reason poetry, as mirrored in human language, has come to be taught in the English Department. They know at least as much about poetry in the Physics and Biology departments, and in the Mathematics and Music

---

Luther College, University of Regina
25 January 2001

139

departments, but there they always call it by different names. If they are really old fashioned, they might even call it Truth or Beauty. If they are really up to date, they will never use such words, and the silence they put in their place is the name they use for poetry. Those who are really up to date in the English Department now and then still mention poetry. But all they mean by poetry is *poems*. Poems are the tips of the icebergs afloat on the ocean of poetry. But poetry continues to exist, maybe even to thrive, whether or not we deny or misdefine it.

The obnoxious and contrary beings called poets have been around for quite some time – about three million years, if you think that poets are restricted to the genus Homo; maybe closer to three hundred thousand years, if you think that they're restricted to the species Homo sapiens. Poetry itself has been here a lot longer – as long, I suppose, as things have been thinking and dreaming themselves, which might be as long as things have existed, or maybe somewhat longer.

Poetry, of course, has many names in many languages. Its English name comes, as you know, from Greek, from the verb ποιέω, ποιεῖν [poiéo, poieîn] which means *to do* or *to make*. In early Greek, ποιεῖν isn't a word used for feeble-bodied creatures sitting at desks with pencil and paper; ποιεῖν is what carpenters and ironworkers do. It's the verb the Homeric poets use to talk about making a sword or a ploughshare or building a house.

Does that imply that poetry is made by human beings? That it only exists because of us? I think, myself, that making and doing are activities we share with all the other animals and plants and with plenty of other things besides. The wind on the water makes waves, the interaction of the earth and sun and moon makes tides, sun coming and going on the water and the air makes clouds, and clouds make rain, and the rain makes rivers, and the rivers feed the lakes and other rivers

and the sea from which the sun keeps making clouds, and
there is plenty of poetry in that, whether or not there are any
human beings here to say in iambic pentameter or rhyming
alexandrines that they see it and approve.

With a few notorious exceptions, all the mammals and all
the birds – that is, tens of thousands of species – train their
young. This means they take an active part in defining who
and what they really are. It means that they – I should say *we*,
we birds and mammals – have two kinds of heredity: genetic
and exogenetic. One is based securely in the body; the other
is more perilously rooted in the mind.

These two kinds of heredity are as different as the hard disk
and the RAM in your computer. The part that is written to the
genes is like the part that is written to disk. It can easily be cor-
rupted or destroyed, but it comes with a kind of insurance. It
exists in multiple copies, in the bodies of other human beings.
That's the back-up: other human beings, other members of
the same living species. The part that is not genetic is always at
risk. That's the cultural part. As soon as you turn off the power
– as soon as you pull the plug on any society, any band, any
village, any tribe, any language, any family, any group of social
animals – humans, wolves, moose, whales or whiskeyjacks,
or any other species that trains and raises its young – as soon
as you wreck its social organization, the cultural part of its
heredity is torn to smithereens.

Humans have always, evidently, had a knack for tearing
their own and each other's cultures to shreds, but we have done
it in recent times on an unprecedented scale, using everything
from microbes to missionaries, atomic bombs to residential
schools, machetes to law books. Nothing – not even religion
– has proven more effective in this regard than the gilded
weapons of advertising and commerce.

So the cultural floor is a killing floor, and it's littered with smithereens. Reach down and you might pick up some fragments of a Presocratic philosopher, a Zen master's wink preserved in amber, a story or two told by an aboriginal elder, or a sheaf of poems by one of the great poets who go by the name Anonymous. You'll have to sift through a lot of rubbish to find these treasures, but plenty of treasure is there: much more lying in the dust than you are likely to find in the superstructure. That's why every true intellectual alive in the present day is a garbage picker.

Even if humans were good to each other, cultures would break down. Cultures are mortal. If no one kills them, they die from old age, or from earthquake, floods, volcanic eruptions, or inexorable changes in the weather.

So long as the earth survives, humans can start over and build themselves a culture from the ground. But the ground is a considerable start. Every human culture is really just an extension of the underlying culture known as nature.

About 1,500 years ago, a young scholar from the east coast of China, whose name was Liú Xié (劉勰), wrote a book he called Wén xīn diāo lóng (文心雕龍), "The Literary Mind and the Carving of Dragons." In the opening chapter is a sentence I have loved and pondered for some time. The sentence says:

$$ 日 月 \cdots 山 川 \cdots 此 蓋 道 之 文 也 $$

rì yuè   shān chuān   cǐ gài dào zhī wén yě

This means, "sun and moon (日月), mountains and rivers (山川): these are really the *wén* (文) of *dào* (道)." *Wén* is the Chinese word for *pattern*, for *culture*, and for *literature* or *writing*. And *dào* is one of the few Chinese words most English speakers know, if only because they have heard of the Taoist masters Lǎo Zi and Zhuāng Zi (Lao Tzu and Chuang Tzu) and of Lǎo Zi's book the Dàodé Jīng (Tao Te Ching).

Dào (written *Tao* in the old missionary spelling, but always pronounced with a *d*) means *way* or *path* or *street* or *road*. It is not a mystical term; you see it on street signs and maps all over China and Japan. But in Chinese philosophical tradition, *dào*, the Way, suggests the natural, inevitable way. The way of hot air is to rise; the way of water is to boil when hot, freeze when cold, and run down hill when liquid; the way of the mountain goat is to climb on the cliffs and eat grass; the way of the grizzly is to eat berries and fish in the summer and to hibernate in winter. In a still more general sense, *dào* means something like *reality*, *truth* or *existence*. So what does it mean to be the *wén* of *dào*? It means to be the language and writing of being, the culture of nature, the poem of the world itself. The culture of nature is the culture all other earthly cultures are a part of: the culture of the whole which none of the parts can do without.

Sun, moon, mountains and rivers are the writing of being, the literature of what-is. Long before our species was born, the books had been written. The library was here before we were. We live in it. We can add to it, or we can try; we can also subtract from it. We can chop it down, incinerate it, strip mine it, poison it, bury it under our trash. But we didn't create it, and if we destroy it, we cannot replace it. Literature, culture, pattern aren't man-made. The culture of the Tao is not man-made, and the culture of *humans* is not man-made; it is just the human part of the culture of the whole.

When you think intensely and beautifully, something happens. That something is called poetry. If you think that way and speak at the same time, poetry gets in your mouth. If people hear you, it gets in their ears. If you think that way and write at the same time, then poetry gets written. But poetry *exists* in any case. The question is only: are you going to take part, and if so, how?

Simone Weil wrote something once in her notebook about the purpose of works of art, and the purpose of words: *Il leur appartient de témoigner à la manière d'un pommier en fleurs, à la manière des étoiles.*[1] "Their function is to testify, after the fashion of blossoming apple trees and stars." When words do what blossoming apple trees do, and what stars do, poetry is what you read or hear.

Aristotle called this process μίμησις [*mímēsis*]. This has been translated as "imitation," but *participation* would be closer. It is imitation in the culturally significant sense of the word: the sense in which children imitate their elders and apprentices their masters. Μίμησις means *learning by doing*. And words, as Weil reminds us, are not just poker chips that are used for passing judgements or passing exams. Words are the tracks left by the breath of the mind as it intersects with the breath of the lungs. Words are for shining, like apple blossoms, like stars, giving a sign that life is lived here too, that thought is happening here too, among the human beings, just as it is out there in the orchard and up there in the sky, and in the forest, in the oceans, in the mountains, where no humans are around.

Some people are led to the writing of poetry – or to painting, dance or music – on the promise that it will allow them to "express themselves." Insofar as you are a part of the older, richer, larger and more knowledgeable whole we call the world, and insofar as you are a student or apprentice of that world, expressing yourself could well be worth the time and trouble it involves. But if it is really only your *self* that you are interested in, I venture to think that performing someone else's poem – reciting it or reading it aloud – is likely better medicine than writing. Poetry, like science, is a way of finding out – by trying to state perceptively and clearly – what exists and what is going on. That is too much for the self to handle. That *is* why, when you go to work for the poem, you give yourself away. Composing a poem is a way of leaving the self behind and getting involved in something larger.

I remember reading a letter that Weil wrote from Casablanca in 1942, trying to explain why, after she'd embraced the central doctrines of Christianity, she still refused to join the church. This is what she said:

Le degré de probité intellectuelle qui est obligatoire pour moi, en raison de ma vocation propre, exige que ma pensée soit indifférente à toutes les idées sans exception.... Ainsi l'eau est indifférente aux objets qui y tombent; elle ne les pèse pas; ce sont eux qui s'y pèsent eux-mêmes après un certain temps d'oscillation.[2]

The degree of intellectual probity required of me, by reason of my own vocation, demands that my thought remain indifferent to all ideas, bar none.... Water is indifferent in this way to objects that fall into it. The water does not weigh them; it is they who weigh themselves after bobbing up and down a little while.

Poetry will weigh you too, I guess, if you give yourself to poetry. But taking the measure of the self is not the same as self expression. The reason for writing poetry is that *poetry knows more than any of us who write it.*

Poetry is what I start to hear when I concede the world's ability to manage and to understand itself. It is the language of the world: something humans overhear if they are willing to pay attention, and something that the world will teach us to speak, if we allow the world to do so. It is the *wén* of *dào*: a music that we learn to see, to feel, to hear, to smell, and then to think, and then to answer. But not to repeat. Mimesis is not repetition.

One way of answering that music is to sing. Humans, like birds, are able to make songs and pass them on. Human songs, like bird songs, are part nature and part culture: part genetic predilection, part cultural inheritance or training, part individual inflection or creation. These are the three parts of mimesis. If the proportion of individual creation in human song is greater than in birdsong, that's no cause for pride, though it may be very good cause for excitement. What it means is that nature and culture both are at greater risk from us than they are from birds.

Another way of answering the music of the world is, of course, by telling stories. This is the most ancient and widespread of all philosophical methods. But story, like song, is not a genre that humans invented. Story is an essential part of language, a basic part of speech, just like the sentence, only larger. Words make sentences, sentences make stories, and stories make up a still larger part of speech, called a mythology. These are essential tools of thinking. The story is just as indispensable to thinking as the sentence.

People have tried to tell me that language is the source and basis of poetry. I'm pretty sure that's backwards. Language is what thought and poetry *produce*. And stories are the fruit that language bears. You and I are stories told in ribonucleic acid. The Iliad is a story told in Greek. Stories are pretty ingenious at getting themselves told.

Plato, for good reason, tells his myths, his stories, through the mouth of a non-writer, Sokrates. This is a link to the older tradition of narrative philosophy, now ignored in a lot of the places where philosophy is taught. If you enter into a truly oral culture, you find that almost all philosophical works are narrative. The primary way – and maybe the *only* way – of doing sustained and serious philosophy in an oral culture is by telling stories. The works of the Haida mythteller Skaay and those of the Cree mythteller Kâ-kîsikâw-pîhtokêw are excellent examples. Sokrates, I think, would have been happy to sit at the feet of either one – not to practice debating technique but to study real philosophy, as he is supposed to have studied once with Diotima of Mantinea.

11

What mythtellers do is what scientists do. They think about the world; they try out their hypotheses and keep the ones that work and throw the other ones away. But the assumption made in myth is that everything of interest is alive, so it can act its part in a story – and in the mythtellers' world, anything and everything is potentially of interest. To play a corresponding part in the kinds of equations scientists write, things must frequently play dead. And in the scientific world, everything is potentially interesting too.

In other words, the mythteller thinks about the world by assuming that the world itself is thinking. The scientist – under the current regime at any rate – assumes that it is not.

The proposition that the world is *empty of thinking* is an interesting myth in itself: one that has proven heuristically useful as well as hugely destructive. Yet it's an odd myth – and so is any other – for a thinker to believe. Myths are *theses*, not *beliefs*. In normal, healthy cultures (which are not now easy things to find, among humans or nonhumans) myths are numerous and various enough to make their literal acceptance quite unlikely. The work of the mythteller or poet, like that of the scientist, is learning *how to think*, not deciding *what to believe*.

When scientists reject a piece of work, they frequently describe it as *bad science*. This can mean *pseudoscience* disguised as the real thing, or it can mean *flawed science*, the real thing in need of some correction. Poets and visual artists use essentially the same terminology. "Bad art" or "bad poetry" can mean either flawed work, not perhaps beyond repair, or fake work, to be rejected outright.

147

Is there such a thing as *bad mythology* in this double-barreled sense? There is indeed.

Bad mythology in the sense of *fake* mythology is almost everywhere you look in the present day. It comes in commercial forms – for example, in the claims that drinking a certain brand of soda pop, driving a certain kind of car, or wearing a certain brand of clothes will make you a different person. It also comes in social forms – the pseudomyths of racial and religious superiority, for example, routinely used as licenses for plain old selfishness and greed. "Social mythology," like its sister "social science," is remarkably prone to error.

There is plenty of *flawed* mythology too: flawed in the same way that science can be flawed. Mythtellers are artists, and artists, like scientists, mustn't get sidetracked or hurried. They have to make concise, economical statements; they have to see the *wén* in the *dào*. They also have to see the *dào* in the *wén*; they have to leave room for the facts in all their messy glory. Myth, like science (and like a bureaucracy), is flawed when it falls for its own explanations. I'll give you an example.

The Crow or Absároka people once ranged over most of eastern and central Montana and a large part of Wyoming. Beginning in 1870 they were squeezed onto a series of reservations, which afterward were quickly whittled down. By 1884, they were reduced to their present allotment, east of the Pryor Mountains, in southern Montana.

You could say, if you're determined to be cheerful, that the Crow have suffered less from the colonization than most other indigenous groups in North America. Between the early eighteenth century and the early twentieth, disease and starvation reduced their numbers by only about eighty per cent. The best estimate of their precolonial population is 8,000 to 10,000. The census of 1905 showed a total of just over 1,800. In 1930 it was under 1,700. After that, the numbers began to rise. By the

1990s, tribal enrollment was back to precolonial levels – and most adults were bilingual in English and Crow.

One of the people who lived through that difficult transition to reservation life was called Íaxíshiílichesh (Yellow-Brow). He was born about 1860 and died around 1940: not the best of times to be a native human in Montana. Early in his life the Crow were fugitives in their own land; from 1870 until his death they were missionary targets and noncitizens at best. It would be hard to get a good education under such conditions. But from his father Iípiakaatesh (Magpie) and other old men, Yellow-Brow learned a lot of traditional lore.

In 1910, Yellow-Brow's life began to intersect with the life of a young man named Robert Lowie. Íaxíshiílichesh was a mythteller, Lowie was a scientist, but the two had much in common – more perhaps than either of them knew.

Lowie was born in Vienna in 1883. At the age of ten, he moved with his family to New York City. There he spoke German at home, English at school, and won prizes for his command of Latin and Greek. At college he continued to do classics but spent all of his free time on zoology and botany, then tried chemistry, which led him into physics. After graduation, he decided to turn his status as perpetual outsider into a profession. He began to study anthropology and linguistics at Columbia with Franz Boas. He also took a job as a field researcher for the American Museum of Natural History.

So in the summer of 1906, the 23-year-old Mr Lowie, whose sense of the natural world had been formed in the grounds of Schönbrunn Palace and in Central Park, arrived by stagecoach in the Lemhi Valley, Idaho. He had much to learn, including how to speak and understand a little Shoshone, and how to saddle, ride and feed a horse. The following summer he was in Alberta and Montana, growing more comfortable in the saddle and learning bits of Blackfoot, Cree, Lakhota and Crow.

Over the next ten years, Lowie also learned some rudiments of Chipewyan, Hidatsa, Comanche, Hopi, Paiute, Ute and Washo, but it was in the Valley of the Little Bighorn, on the Crow Reservation in Montana, that he formed his deepest friendships with Native American people. He was there every summer from 1910 to 1916 and went on studying the language all the rest of his life. Lowie's last visit to the Crow was in 1931. He spent the whole of that summer taking dictation, mostly from friends he had known for twenty years. The person he listened to most was Yellow-Brow: Iaxíshiílichesh.

One of Yellow-Brow's stories recounts, in roughly forty minutes, the creation of the world. It begins quite handsomely:

> Saápa mbiliílak Isaáhkawuate
> > mbalaáxtak.
>
> Ilák, «At duk mbi táchkaat xawiík.
> Mbaasaápacham awákalituk
> > awáxpuk mbaliílituk
> > > íchii·iwáachik.
> Mbi táchkaat xawiík,» híhchiluk.[3]

> WHERE *the water and the Old Coyote came from*
> > *I don't know.*

> *"And furthermore," he said, "I'm unhappy all alone.*
> *If I saw another person,*
> > *if I spoke with someone sometimes,*
> > > *that would be alright.*
> *I'm unhappy all alone," he said, they say.*

Then Old Coyote meets *mbiíaxaakum íatkaatum duúpkashem ishtú híshikyaatuk*, "two small, red-eyed waterbirds" – eared grebes, I suspect – and a conversation begins. *Mbalalásah-taauwishi?*, Old Coyote asks: "Does it seem to you that anything exists?" *Saap dalás kootá?* "What does your heart say?" By way of answer, one of the grebes dives and stays down a very long time. He comes back with mud and vegetable matter. Out of these, Old Coyote makes the world, complete with trees and grass, coulees and rivers. Using earth for his raw material, he also makes humans, all the other kinds of waterbirds, and all the other animals – except of course for coyotes. One of those just shows up out of nowhere.

As creation proceeds, Old Coyote becomes more and more creative, and íaxíshiílichesh begins to sound more and more like Empedokles. When the trickster makes the prairie chicken, for instance, he does so by combining buffalo muscle, bear claws, coyote claws, box-elder leaves, and a hairy caterpillar. This leads to some lively dancing, and then to a lively discussion between the Old Coyote and a jealous, short-tempered bear who wants to do some dancing too.

Shiilapé, "Yellow Nose," the younger coyote, who has wandered in from nowhere, takes this opportunity to tell his elder brother how important it is for people to dislike each other. We should speak different languages, he says, to further the cause of misunderstanding.

Mbaapém mbalé ndásitak,
   mbaapém mbalélaas kawíilak,
      alíchilak alaxawiílak mbatuúchishdak,
         mbaam mbeelítbak íiwatbasíchiwak.

If one day we're happy,
   the next day we're not,
      if good and bad are stirred together,
         then we'll like what we can do for one another.

Flirting is also important, Shiilapé says – but right after that, Shiilapé's artful flirting with dangerous ideas is brought to a halt and the myth gets into trouble. Old Coyote insists on describing, at too great a length and with too little humor, some of the ways in which men should take advantage of women, and Íaxíshiílichesh himself steps in to explain that Absároka men routinely lord it over their women because Old Coyote did it before them.

One of the basic tasks of science and of mythology is describing how things are and setting them in context. "Setting them in context" is often called "explaining *why*" – and, as everybody knows, it is a never-ending process. One *why* always leads to another, and science and mythology march on. But explaining the shape of the universe is one thing; justifying habitually shabby behavior is something else. Myths that set out to explain something overtly – *etiological* myths, as they're called – often slide into justification, especially if what they explain is sociological. The mythteller, like the geneticist and the philosopher, should never have an agenda.

None of the other stories that Yellow-Brow told to Lowie makes that sudden lurch into defensive etiology. So what went wrong in this case? Did Yellow-Brow – then an old man with no teeth and a much-admired storyteller – have a permanent grudge against women? Did he simply feel like throwing his narrative weight around on that particular day? Or did he deliberately scuttle the myth to bait his old friend Robert Lowie, a man of intense propriety and reserve,[4] who in 1931, at the age of 48, was at long last contemplating marriage? Luella Cole, the Berkeley psychologist whom Lowie did in fact marry in 1933, was also in Montana in 1931, watching Lowie and Yellow-Brow work. Yellow-Brow would have watched her watching. The joke he played did damage to the myth, but it is evident that Yellow-Brow and Lowie both thought it was a good one.

III

By coming to North America with his parents in 1893, Robert Lowie was spared direct involvement in two world wars – but as an Austrian of Jewish descent, he spent a lot of time thinking about what he had escaped. It might be good for us to think about it too.

In the autumn of 1918, while Lowie was in New York, the German army was on maneuvers in the Ardennes. Among the many units on that front was a meteorological team. One member of this team was a young man, 29 years old, whose civilian occupation was teaching philosophy. He was then very active in the Catholic Church but had been called, like many other academics, into military service. His military job was making periodic checks on windspeed and barometric pressure, then reporting these to senior officers, who used the data to schedule attacks with poison gas. This soldier's name was Martin Heidegger. Twenty-five years later, in the midst of another war, he continued to insist that it was noble to be German and godly to die for the fatherland.

Heidegger liked myths, he liked poetic stories, just as Plato and Yellow-Brow did, but he seems to have lacked Plato's suspicions. I don't believe that Heidegger ever suggests that poets be banished from anywhere. And I wonder if that has something to do with the fact that he missed the crucial difference between the social myths, or pseudomyths, of the National Socialist movement and genuine myths – those to be found, for example, in Sophokles' plays.

The centerpiece of Heidegger's *Introduction to Metaphysics* is a chorus from Sophokles' *Antigone*. That play has lasted a long time – but so has the social myth of Teutonic supremacy, so perhaps longevity is no test of social value or of truth. The play, in any case, and especially the chorus Heidegger chose, seems to me to shine some light on the distinction between social myths and real myths, or the false myths and the true. Poetry, actually, is the test. The myth of racial superiority doesn't shine like a flowering apple tree or a star. It isn't poetic. That's evidence – possibly not proof in itself, but certainly evidence – that it isn't true.

A few decades ago, when the War in Vietnam was at its height, *Antigone* seemed a very powerful and current piece of theatre to me and some of my friends. Much more recently, I've learned, it's been important to a group of native women in Saskatchewan – and for equally good reasons. Antigone, remember, is thinking about connections and relations: about the tough coexistence of resemblances and differences. The people she's surrounded by are obsessed with homogenization and division. They want absolute distinctions between enemies and allies. Their world has shrunk from one to two. The two are known as "them" and "us."

In Sophokles' play, just as in Germany in 1918 and again in 1943, and among the Crow in Yellow-Brow's youth, all the able-bodied men are in military service, and the women are therefore busy. No one is left to sing in the chorus except the elders. Again and again, the old people of Thebes come out on stage and do a geriatric dance. And while they dance, they sing, and while they sing, they think. At the core of the play, sung by these elders, is the song that reappears, like a lost dream, at the center of Heidegger's book. In Greek, it sounds like this:

πολλὰ τὰ Δεινὰ κοὐΔεν ἀνθρώπου
δεινότερον πέλει·
τοῦτο καὶ πολιοῦ πέραν
πόντου χειμερίῳ νότῳ
χωρεῖ, περιβρυχίοισιν
περῶν ὑπ᾽ οἴδμασιν, θεῶν

τε τὰν ὑπερτάταν, Γᾶν
ἄφθιτον, ἀκαμάταν ἀποτρύεται,
ἰλλομένων ἀρότρων ἔτος εἰς ἔτος,
ἱππείῳ γένει πολεύων.

κουφονόων τε φῦλον ὀρνίθων
    ἀμφιβαλὼν ἄγει
καὶ θηρῶν ἀγρίων ἔθνη
πόντου τ' εἰναλίαν φύσιν
σπείραισι δικτυοκλώστοις,
περιφραδὴς ἀνήρ· κρατεῖ
δὲ μηχαναῖς ἀγραύλου
θηρὸς ὀρεσσιβάτα, λασιαύχενά θ'
ἵππον ὀχμάζεται ἀμφὶ λόφον ζυγῷ
οὔρειόν τ' ἀκμῆτα ταῦρον.

καὶ φθέγμα καὶ ἀνεμόεν
    φρόνημα καὶ ἀστυνόμους
ὀργὰς ἐδιδάξατο καὶ δυσαύλων
πάγων ὑπαίθρεια καὶ
δύσομβρα φεύγειν βέλη
παντοπόρος· ἄπορος ἐπ' οὐδὲν ἔρχεται
τὸ μέλλον· Ἅιδα μόνον
φεῦξιν οὐκ ἐπάξεται·
νόσων δ' ἀμηχάνων φυγὰς
    ξυμπέφρασται.

σοφόν τι τὸ μηχανόεν
    τέχνας ὑπὲρ ἐλπίδ' ἔχων
τοτὲ μὲν κακόν, ἄλλοτ' ἐπ' ἐσθλὸν ἕρπει.
νόμους παρείρων χθονὸς
θεῶν τ' ἔνορκον δίκαν
ὑψίπολις· ἄπολις ὅτῳ τὸ μὴ καλὸν

ξύνεστι τόλμας χάριν.
μήτ᾽ ἐμοὶ παρέστιος
γένοιτο μήτ᾽ ἴσον φρονῶν
ὃς τάδ᾽ ἔρδοι.

Heidegger translated the song into German. This is one
attempt to put it into English:

> Strangeness is frequent enough, but nothing
> is ever as strange as a man is.
> For instance,
> out there,
> riding the grey-maned water,
> heavy weather on the southwest quarter,
> jarred by the sea's thunder,
> tacking through the bruise-blue waves.
> Or he paws at the eldest of goddesses,
> earth, as though she were made
> out of gifts and forgiveness,
> driving the plough in its circle year after year
> with what used to be horses.
>
> Birds' minds climb the air, yet he snares them,
> and creatures of the field.
> These
> and the flocks
> of the deep sea. He unfurls
> his folded nets for their funeral shrouds.
> Man the tactician.
> So, as you see, by his sly
> inventions he masters
> his betters: the deep-throated
> goats of the mountain,

and horses. His yokes ride the necks
of the tireless bulls who once haunted these hills.

And the sounds in his own throat
gather the breezes that rise in his mind.
He has learned how to sit on committees
and learned to build houses and barns
against blizzards and gales.
He manages all and yet manages
nothing. Nothing is closed
to the reach of his will,
and yet he has found no road out of hell.
His fate, we all know, is precisely
what he has never outwitted.

Wise, yes – or ingenious.
More knowledge than hope in his hand,
and evil comes out of it sometimes,
and sometimes he creeps toward nobility.
Warped on the earth's loom
and dyed in the thought of the gods,
a man should add beauty and strength to his city.
But he is no citizen whatsoever
if he is tied to the ugly by fear or by pride
or by greed or by love of disorder – or order.

May no one who does not still wonder
what he is and what he does
suddenly arrive at my fireside.

I hold the very simpleminded view that everything is related to everything else – and that every one is related to everyone else, and that every species is related to every other. The

only way out of this tissue of interrelations, it seems to me, is to stop paying attention, and to substitute something else – hallucination, greed, pride, or hatred, for example – for sensuous connection to the facts. I think it is not the world's task to entertain us, but ours to take an interest in the world.

I also subscribe to the view – not original with me – that the world is constructed in such a way as to be as interesting as possible. This is a deep tautology. Our minds, our brains, our hearts are grown out of the world, just as buttercups and mushrooms are. The world is us, and we are little replicas and pieces of the world. How could the world be anything other than as interesting as possible to us?

Yet all it takes to break that link is to try to control the world, or take it for granted, or ask it not to change or not to complain while we continue to carve it up. All it takes – and this is not, evidently, very difficult to do – is to sever the identity of poetry and thinking.

NOTES

1 Simone Weil, *Cahiers*, vol. 3 (Paris: Plon, 1974): 67.

2 Weil, *Attente de Dieu* (Paris: Fayard, 1966): 65.

3 This and the following quotations are retranscribed from Robert H. Lowie, *Crow Texts*, edited by Luella Cole Lowie (Berkeley: U of California Press, 1960): 204–28. The orthography used here is the standard modern spelling system for Crow, except that initial *mb-* is used consistently where the standard spelling uses either *m-* or *b-*, and initial *nd-* is used where the standard spelling calls for either *n-* or *d-*.

4 How much reserve can be seen from Lowie's autobiography, *Robert H. Lowie, Ethnologist: A Personal Record* (Berkeley: U of California Press, 1959).

THE TREE OF MEANING AND

THE WORK OF ECOLOGICAL

LINGUISTICS

I

When the European invasion of the Americas began, there were about sixty languages being spoken in the territory now known as Canada, another sixteen, more or less, in Alaska, and at least 220 in what are now the forty-eight contiguous states of the USA. Some of these straddle the borders, of course. I count a total of about 280 in North America north of the Rio Grande. There were another two hundred or more from the Rio Grande to the Isthmus of Panama. About five hundred, you could say, in North America as a whole. More than that – perhaps in the vicinity of seven hundred – were spoken in South America. That's a total of twelve hundred or so in the Americas, out of six thousand or more in the world as a whole.

Other things being equal – which of course they never are – it is probably true that language density increases as biomass increases. In practice, languages go where speakers go, and speakers go, when they can, where the living is good. They also go where migration routes allow them to go, and in difficult times, they go where refugees are suffered to exist. So there are some interesting pockets of aboriginal language density on the map of North America. California was a magnet for immigrants in precolonial times, the same as it is now, and in

Conference on Environmental Ethics, Yukon College, Whitehorse
19 July 2001

the year 1500 it had more human languages per unit of land than anywhere else north of Oaxaca. This pattern held right up the coast, to the southern tip of Alaska. The West Coast of North America, not the East Coast, was the most densely peopled region before the Europeans arrived. As an old migration corridor, the West Coast acquired more languages per unit of population as well as more humans per unit of land. And the languages that lived on the West Coast were more varied – they represented a much wider taxonomic range – than on the East Coast or elsewhere on the continent.

It's wrong, of course, to speak about these things in the past tense, but present tense is not entirely right either. Of about three hundred languages formerly spoken in all the native nations gobbled up by the USA and Canada, about 170 still survive. That is a little over half. But most of those surviving languages have fewer than five per cent of the number of speakers they used to have. Most of those languages are eroding, simplifying, losing the rich vocabularies and grammars they had acquired over centuries of relatively peaceful maturation, and the odds are very good that most of these languages will vanish in your lifetime.

A lot of effort is going into language revival and language maintenance nowadays – very important effort, which needs all the support and all the encouragement it can get. But languages, like all living things, have to live within environments, to which they must adapt. A language that only survives in the classroom, like a plant that only survives in a flowerpot, or an animal that only survives in the laboratory or the zoo, is a different thing – and in some respects a lesser thing – than one that survives in the wild.

For a language, life "in the wild" means life as a functioning part of a cultural ecosystem, where chatter, laughter, conversations, stories, songs, and dreams are as continuous as breathing. It means the luxury of *being taken for granted*, in the same way that a tree is taken for granted by the birds that perch in its branches, by the earth, water, light, and air it grows in, and by the beetles, lichens, and mosses growing upon it.

Life in the wild, for a language as for any living entity – animal, plant, fungus, protozoan, or bacterium – means a dependable and nourishing interconnection with the rest of life on the planet. It means a place in the food chain. It means a sustaining, sustainable habitat. That perennial connection to biological and physical reality is what feeds and shapes and calibrates a language. In conditions of natural equilibrium, languages have ranges, no more permanently fixed than the ranges of plants and animals, but also no less vital, no less real. The native range of a language is the domain it keeps up to date with: a territory it inevitably shares but one it can't and doesn't take for granted. It is the portion of the world which that language ceaselessly catalogues and explores. A language can only do this, of course, with the help of its speakers.

Its speakers are in a sense the lungs of the language. Without them it will neither speak nor breathe. But without that other nourishing attachment – not to its speakers but to the world that surrounds them – the ability to speak would be of little value. A language severed from the world might go on talking, but the memory of its referents would fade, and its standards of truth and beauty would wither. After a time we would find it had nothing of substance to say.

A language, you may say, cannot have living speakers and yet have no connection to the world, because its speakers also have to eat and breathe. But they can eat and breathe indoors, and if they do that all the time, their language shrinks. The indoor world becomes the only world it knows.

Because the number of speakers has, in most cases, shrunk, and because the world of those speakers has, in most cases, stiffened and contracted, the languages native to North America are endangered now in nonpolitical as well as political ways and have much less security than before the colonization. Teaching them in the schools doesn't change that. Raising the GNP doesn't change it either. On the contrary, raising the GNP appears to endanger languages severely.

You all know something about the accelerated destruction of plant and animal species that began with the European colonization. You know that some species – Steller's sea cow and the passenger pigeon for instance – have been exterminated, while many others, including the buffalo, the whooping crane, and the Port Orford cedar, have come very close. You also know that the process – habitat destruction and species annihilation – is still galloping along in North America and elsewhere in the world.

The strange thing is this: there are more humans alive than ever before – more, it seems, than the planet can comfortably tolerate – and yet human languages and cultures rank right up near the top of that list of threatened beings. Over a space of four centuries, from 1500 to 1900, while the immigrant population was steadily rising, the total indigenous population of North America fell by more than ninety per cent. Given that much death, and the forced dislocation, missionization, and cultural transformation that went with it, it's astounding that over half of the languages spoken in North America five centuries ago are still spoken today.

When you wipe out a community, a culture, and leave five or ten or twenty speakers of the language, you can claim that the language survives, that it isn't extinct. But what happens is every bit as terrible as when you clearcut a forest and leave a strip of trees along the edge, to hide the clearcut from the highway. In both cases, something will eventually grow back – but what was there before is gone forever.

A language is an organism. A weightless, discontinuous organism that lives in the minds and bodies of those who speak it – or from the language's point of view, in the bodies and minds of those *through whom it is able to speak*. Languages change over time and eventually they perish, like other living things – but in a state of environmental health, when languages die, other languages – neighbors and children of those that are dying – are growing up to replace them. When you kill a language off and replace it with an import, you kill part of the truth. A language is a means of seeing and understanding the world, a means of talking with the world. Never mind talking *about* the world; that's for dilettantes. A language is a means of talking *with* the world. When you kill a language off – even a language with only one speaker – you make the entire planet less intelligent, less articulate, less capable, and so decidedly less beautiful than it was.

What is it that people say when they're conversing with the world? They sing songs and tell stories. They make poems, in other words: lyric poems and narrative poems. And wherever there is language, that is what happens. Wherever in nature there are humans, there are human languages, and wherever in nature there are languages, there are stories. If we dress that statement up so it sounds like it belongs in the university, it will say, *Every natural human language has a literature*. But in its own unprintable way, every *nonhuman* language has a literature too. If something speaks well, literature is what it has to say. (If you prefer a more self-centered definition, we can also put it this way: any well-told story, and maybe even any earnest statement, turns out to have literary properties when you pay it close attention.)

In Europe, China, and other regions of the earth where industrial technology has become a fetish, many people seem to believe that literature is a rare and special achievement, only created by "advanced civilizations." Some historians claim that great literatures are only created by great empires. It is true that the resources of empire can do a lot to increase literary *quantity* or literary *storage capacity*, but literary *quality* is independent of that.

Literature, in fact, is as natural to language as language is to human beings – and for human beings, language is as natural as walking. Language, in fact, is as natural as eating, which all living creatures do. Humans have a proven ability to out-talk and out-eat everything else on the planet, at least in the short term, and some people seem immensely proud of that. Why, I'm not quite sure.

Scripture – that is, writing – is a technology, but a seemingly simple technology, like fire. Unlike fire, however, writing is not – and in the long run can't be – a cultural universal. This may be why mythographers (myth *writers*, as distinguished from myth *tellers*) usually say that writing wasn't stolen from the gods but was freely given to humans instead.

Any society that wants this technology can obtain it, but only those prepared to pay the price, in social self-absorption and bureaucratic overhead, can keep it. And like other potent technologies, writing radically alters every society into which it is introduced. It involves, after all, a kind of ritual mutilation of the intellect, a sort of cerebral circumcision. To this day there are missionary agencies, both secular and religious, going about the world attempting to spread literacy, claiming that this technology will empower and enfranchise and enrich all those to whom it is given. What these missionary agencies are doing in actual fact is exterminating the earth's last oral cultures. Those who seek to improve human welfare by exterminating ancient oral cultures are in need of greater wisdom – just like those who seek to improve human welfare by clearcutting the earth's last virgin forests.

11

People often notice that language helps them think – and then they sometimes ask, *Are there other ways to think besides in language?* Doubtless a good question; but that, I think, is not the way to ask it. What the question means is, *Are there languages to think in other than the ones in which we talk?* And the answer is, *Of course!* There are the languages of mathematics, the languages of music, languages of color, shape, and gesture. Language is *what something becomes when you think in it.* Life as we know it thinks, it seems, in nucleic acids. The forest thinks in trees and their associated life forms: asters, grasses, mosses, fungi, and the creatures who move through them, from annelids and arthropods to thrushes, jays, and deer. Humans often, but not always, think in words and sentences.

Ideas, according to Marx, do not exist apart from language. Many others say the same. They are asserting that the only way to think is in the speech of human beings. The entire natural world stands as proof that this is false. Yet in a broader sense – a sense that is equally alien both to Marxist and to capitalist values – I suspect the claim is true: where there are ideas, there is language. Mythtellers, however, are prone to remember (and writers to forget) that the languages of words are not the only kind of human language, and that the languages spoken by humans are only a small subset of language as a whole. Some deeply human stories tell us this is so.

In the hands of an expert mythteller, stories are a form of wisdom. In the hands of anyone else, they may be nothing more than narrative clichés. Here as elsewhere, everything depends on the tradition – yet everything depends on the individual as well. If you treat the stories with respect, you have to learn to hear them in their language – their tradition – but also in the voices of the real individuals who are telling them.

The anthropologist Franz Boas, who spent half a century taking dictation in Native American languages and studying the results – and who inspired a whole tribe of able people to do likewise – often tried to separate the tale from the teller. For much of his career, it seemed to him unscientific to do otherwise. Though Boas never said so, he apparently believed that stories underwent an evolutionary change, akin to speciation, as they passed from language to language and culture to culture. If that were so, then to study the comparative anatomy of stories, we would have to disregard individual performances as such, and individual artistry. We'd have to find the holotypes instead: the canonical "Haida version," "Tlingit version," "Tagish version," and so on for each story. Some of Boas's students – Alfred Kroeber and Robert Lowie in particular – swallowed this unspoken idea whole. And it is wonderful to see, through their footnotes, personal letters, and other remarks, how they all – Boas and Lowie especially – chafed at the constraints of this self-imposed, untenable assumption.

As long as they sat in the classroom or the library, reading synopses and translations, they could believe in the ethnic speciation of stories. What taught them otherwise? Love of their work, and love of reality. Repeated trips to the field, hearing storytellers speak in their own languages. There they heard and saw and felt the incredible variation – anatomical, physiological, and behavioral – with which stories can unfold, depending on who's telling and who's listening. Ethnicity, language, and culture have no more effect on the speciation of stories than on the speciation of people.

It does, however, seem to me that a course in literary history ought to begin with linguistic geography: a close look at the map and the calendar, to see what languages are spoken in what places, and whose words have been transcribed and when and where and under what conditions. If we taught

North American literatures that way, we would be well into the course before we came to the moment in history when Spanish, English, French, and the other colonial languages were imported to this continent and the big colonial literatures started to build. Most people teaching literature in the USA and Canada teach only the top layer and forget to even mention the foundations.

There is in fact no boundary, so far as I'm concerned, between linguistics and literary history. Linguistics is a branch of natural history – the branch that focuses, let us say, on the statements made by speaking creatures, and on the stories that they tell – in the same way that conchology focuses on the shells made by shell-making creatures, and osteology on the bones made by creatures that possess internal skeletons. This approach frightens many linguists away. Many of them don't know what "literature" is, but they know it sounds awfully subjective and unscientific, so they'd like to think it has nothing to do with their field. And to some scholars of literature, "linguistics" sounds morbidly objective, technical and dry.

I prefer to think about literature and language as a continuum that includes everything from birdsong to linear algebra and symbolic logic. Most of that continuum, or all of it, is occupied with stories.

So linguistics, as I understand it, deals with the stories creatures tell. But what about the stories creatures *are*? Can we do a linguistics of that? I don't see why not. What kind of linguistics would it be? It would be biology. If that's the case, it appears not only that linguistics is a branch of natural history, but that natural history is a branch of linguistics.

Now maybe we're getting somewhere. That is, maybe we're getting to where we are, which is deep in a net of stories and interconnections from which, even in death, there is no escape. Each of us tells stories, and each of us *is* a story. Not just each of us humans, but each of us creatures – spruce trees and toads and timber wolves and dog salmon. We all tell stories to ourselves and to each other – within the tribe, within the species, and way beyond its bounds. Roses do this when they flower, finches when they sing, and humans when they speak, walk, sing, dance, swim, play a flute, build a fire, or pull a trigger.

A lot of the messages humans send are audible messages, transmitted by the fancy apparatus of the mouth, received by the even fancier apparatus of the ear. Those are the sorts of messages most linguists choose to study. But a number of Native American languages – including American Sign Language (ASL), the Langue de signes de Québec (LSQ), and their Latin American relatives – are altogether silent. These exceptions prove a very important rule. The words *language* and *linguistics* are made, of course, from *lingua*, which is the Latin name for the tongue. But language isn't limited to the tongue. People speak with their hands, arms, shoulders, heads, faces as well as their voices. Speakers of LSQ and ASL speak with these silent organs exclusively. This tells us that the terms *language, linguistics, syllable, phoneme, phonetics* and so on – all those words fixated on sounds and on the tongue – are really metaphors. So is the dichotomy *oral* versus *written*, which invites us all to choose up sides and have a tournament or a war between the People of the Mouth and the People of the Hand. Talking and writing are different, it's true, but those are only two of many ways to speak, and they can enter into many sorts of partnerships and collusions – which, by the way, is what is happening here and now.

Language isn't confined to the system of mouth and ear any more than emotions are restricted to the heart or dancing to the feet. There isn't any one organ or one anatomical process to which language is confined. Nor any human language to which certain forms of stories are confined.

III

Humans, in any case, send messages. Analytical linguists parse these messages into components – phonemes, morphemes, suffixes, prefixes, infixes, roots, particles, words, phrases, clauses, sentences. A lot of linguists stop there, just at the point where, for me, the study of language gets most interesting.

A story is to the sentence as a tree is to the twig. And a literature is to the story as the forest is to the tree. Language – that metaphor – is the wood the tree is made of, an engineer might say, but a biologist would notice something else. The wood the tree is made of is created by the tree. Stories make the language they are made of. They make it and keep it alive. You can kill the tree and take the wood, kill the story and take the language, kill the earth and take the ore, kill the river and take the water – but if you really want to understand the wood, the water, the minerals, and the rocks, you have to visit them at home, in the living trees, the rivers, the earth. And if you really want to understand the language, you have to encounter it in the stories by which it was made.

What's more, if you really want to understand the tree, you have to encounter it in the forest. If you want to understand the river, you have to explore the watershed. If you want to understand the story, you have to go beyond it, into the ecosystem of stories.

If you'll forgive me, I'll make a little detour here into the dreary realm of terminology. I have not lived for the thousand years it would take to become conversant with all five hundred Native North American languages, but as far as I've been able to make out, most of these languages distinguish two major kinds of stories: those that occur in mythtime and those that occur in human time or historical time. In Cree, for example, the former are called *âtayôhkan* or *âtayôhkêwin* and the latter

âcimôwin. In Haida, the former are *qqaygaang* and the latter
gyaahlghalang. In Kwakwala, the former are called *nuyem* and
the latter *q'a'yoł*. In Osage, the former are *hígo*, the latter *úthage*.
In Winnebago, they are *waiką* and *worak*. These are not the only
names for literary genres in any of these languages, but this
basic distinction between two kinds of time, and two kinds
of story, seems to be important. Like the distinction between
oral and written, it's a distinction we should be careful not
to get trapped in. The Cree mythteller Kâ-kîsikâw-pîhtokêw
loved to play around with this pair of terms in Cree, calling
the same stories *âtayôhkêwin* at one moment and *âcimôwin* the
next, teasing his student, the linguist Leonard Bloomfield, and
anyone else who tried to pin these notions down.

The etymology of these terms naturally differs from one
language family to another, but consider the two Cree words
for example. The word *âcimôwin*, meaning a story set in human
time or historical time, comes from the verb *âcimo-*, which
means to tell, to explain, to report. The word *âtayôhkan*, meaning a myth, a sacred story, a story set in mythtime, is related
to – in fact, on the surface, it is identical to – one of the
words for spirit being or guardian spirit. Is such a story merely
"something told"? Its name appears to mean it has a little more
reality than that.

It's easy to get into trouble translating these terms into English. One reason is that English is a very acquisitive language
that keeps putting words in the bank. We have a surplus of
terms: *myth, story, tale, legend, reminiscence, memoir, history, tradition, chronicle, epic, fiction, narrative, novel, travelogue*, and so on,
not to mention compound terms such as *fairy tale, true story, science fiction* and the rest. In the real life of language, these terms
overlap; in fact, they sprawl all over each other like teenagers
lounging around on the couch. A pedant could make them all
sit up straight and proper and measure off the space assigned

to each, but the moment the pedant left the room, that order would dissolve. And while we have that surplus of words for different kinds of stories, there are some other equally basic terms we lack.

We have the word *myth*, in any case, and we can use it for any kind of story, any kind of narrative, happening in myth-time. A *mythology*, then, is an ecosystem of myths, a forest of language where those kinds of stories are dominant. What do we call an ecosystem made of the other kind of stories, the ones that are sited in human time? This kind of language forest embraces both history and fiction. The English word *history* had that larger sense once upon a time, but we would have to do some work to get it back. And what about the larger ecosystem, including mythology, history, and fiction? I've been using the word *literature* for that kind of ecosystem, even though I know the term *literature* has been tainted by academic use. I need a name for the big watershed of stories, human and nonhuman, and that's the most suitable term I have found.

This detour into terminology is all in aid of making a simple point. A story – whether it's myth or fiction or history – typically has a beginning, a middle, and an end. We may not start at the beginning and may never get to the end, but we expect them to exist, like head and foot. This is a sign that stories, like sentences, are individual organisms more than they are communities. An ecosystem is different. A forest has an *edge*, it has a *boundary*, and it may, vaguely speaking, have a *middle*, but it has no beginning and no end, because it isn't a linear structure. It simply starts wherever you enter it and ends wherever you come out. The same is true of a mythology. History may or may not be linear, like a river, as many people claim. Mythology, like the forest, clearly is not.

IV

Trees grow in and on the earth. Where do stories grow? They grow in and on storytelling creatures. Stories are epiphytes: organisms that grow on other organisms, in much the same way staghorn ferns and tree-dwelling lichens – Alectoria, Bryoria, Letharia and so on – grow on trees.

I have a hunch that from a lichen's point of view, the basic function of a tree is to provide a habitat for lichens. I have a hunch that from a story's point of view, the function of storytelling creatures – humans for example – is to provide a habitat for stories. I think the stories might be right. That's what you and I are really *for*: to make it possible for certain kinds of stories to exist.

We don't know very much, strange to say, about the biology of stories. Aristotle studied their anatomy, but not much more was done, in a scientific way, until the twentieth century. The comparative work of Boas and Lowie and Stith Thompson added a little. Then Vladimir Propp and Claude Lévi-Strauss and the linguist Dell Hymes began to study the anatomy and physiology of stories more intensely. One of the first things Propp and Hymes discovered is that, whatever the language they're told in, stories tend to have branching, fractal structures, very much like trees.

Those trees, the trees of meaning we call stories, grow in your brain and the rest of your body. And there seems to be a symbiotic relation between those trees of meaning and ourselves. What the stories get out of it is that they get to exist. What we get out of it is guidance. Stories are one of the fundamental ways in which we understand the world. They are probably our best maps and models of the world – and we may yet come to learn that the reason for this is that stories are some of the basic constituents of the world.

Most of you, I suspect, are familiar with a twentieth-century proverb, *the map is not the territory*. We owe this statement to a linguist by the name of Alfred Korzybski. (Semantics, Korzybski's field, is of course a subdivision of linguistics, though Korzybski did his best to make it sound like something else.)

Thirty years ago, in a lecture in honor of Korzybski, Gregory Bateson proposed an idea that startled and frightened his audience. The idea was simple enough. It was that *the units of biological evolution and the units of mind are one and the same*. This thesis owes something to Darwin, of course, and something to Lamarck – an often vilified biologist for whom Bateson had a refreshing degree of respect. And it owes something to Parmenides, the Presocratic poet who said, among other things, τὸ γὰρ αὐτὸ νοεῖν ἔστιν τε καὶ εἶναι. This is a short, sweet, simple Greek sentence which no equally sweet and short and simple English sentence matches. It takes more than one English map, in other words, to portray this little parcel of Greek territory. Here are two approximate translations: (1) *To be and to think are the same*; (2) *To be and to have meaning are the same*. The implication of the Greek verb νοεῖν [noeîn] is that thought and meaning form a unit which ought not to be dissolved.

The English words *noesis, knowledge,* and *narration* all stem from the same root. Thought and meaning are connected not just to each other but to storytelling too. What Parmenides is saying extends to what he's doing. *To be and to tell a story are the same*. Or: *To be is to be a story*. Or: *I am, therefore I think* – and not the other and more arrogant way around.

Put the Greek philosopher-poet Parmenides and the English biologist Charles Darwin in the same room for a moment and you have the makings of Bateson's thesis, positing the unity of biological evolution and mind. Put Parmenides and the Haida philosopher-poet Skaay together for a moment in the same canoe and you have the implicit beginnings of what I like to call ecological linguistics.

I have a hunch that fields of learning worth their salt grow up from their own subject matter. I don't imagine they can be generated by lightning bolts of theory hurled from above. But lightning storms are welcome now and then, if only for the glory of the show, and Bateson's thesis looks to me like an illuminating flash, giving an instantaneous glimpse of what ecological linguistics ought to be.

Bateson was 65 years old when he delivered his Korzybski Lecture, and this was the time of his own awakening. I'd happily quote you the whole lecture, but here two paragraphs will do:

If you put God outside and set him vis-à-vis his creation, and if you have the idea that you are created in his image, you will logically and naturally see yourself as outside and against the things around you. And as you arrogate all mind to yourself, you will see the world around you as mindless and therefore not entitled to moral or ethical consideration. The environment will seem to be yours to exploit. Your survival unit will be you and your folks or conspecifics against the environment of other social units, other races and the brutes and vegetables.

If this is your estimate of your relations to nature AND YOU HAVE AN ADVANCED TECHNOLOGY, *your likelihood of survival will be that of a snowball in hell. You will die either of the toxic byproducts of your own hate, or, simply, of overpopulation and overgrazing.*[1]

An idea, as Bateson says, is *a difference that makes a difference.*[2] A *meaningful* difference in other words. A thought worth thinking is a meaning. A tree of meaning is a story. A forest of such stories is a mind. So is a tree with birds in its branches. So is a human with ideas (plural) perching in its brain.

V

We owe many things to David Abram, not the least of which is the rallying cry, *The rejuvenation of oral culture is an ecological imperative*.

Why is oral culture a key to our continued coexistence with the world?

Because oral culture means much more and less than simply talking. Rekindling oral culture means rejoining the community of speaking beings – sandhill cranes, whitebark pines, coyotes, wood frogs, bees and thunder.

Oral culture also means much more than telling stories. It means learning how to hear them, how to nourish them, and how to let them live. It means learning to let stories swim down into yourself, grow large in there, and rise back up again. It does not – repeat, does *not* – mean memorizing the lines so you can act the script you've written or recite the book you've read. Oral culture – and any culture at all – involves, as nature does, a lot of repetition. But rote memorization and oral culture are two very different things.

If you embody an oral culture, you are a working part of a place, a part of the soil in which stories live their lives. There will in that event be stories you know by heart – but when the stories come out of your mouth, as when the trees come out of the ground, no two performances will ever be the same. Each incarnation of a story is itself. What rests in the mythteller's heart are the seeds of the tree of meaning. All you can tape or transcribe is a kind of photograph or fossil of the leaves: the frozen forms of spoken words.

To put it in other terms, the text is just the map; the story is the territory. The story however is also a map – a map of the land, a map of the mind, a map of the heart, a map of the language in which the story is told. Every map is also a territory, and every territory a map – *but not its own*. To be and to mean and to think and to tell are the same, yet all of them rest on that tissue of interconnection. The story that you tell and are is you *but not your own*.

You find the words by walking through the vision, which may be in the heart that is there inside your body, or it may be in the heart that is out there in the land. You learn the trail if you walk it many times, but every time you walk it, you reinvent the steps. There may, of course, be steep and narrow stretches where you memorize the moves – those places in the story often crystallize as songs – but they are subject, even then, to variation and erosion and other forms of change. And they connect you to yourself and to the world.

In an oral culture, stories are given voice. They are also given the silence in which to breathe. Very rarely in oral cultures do you meet people *who talk all the time*. In literate societies, I meet them rather often. Here, what's more, I am in danger of becoming one myself. I therefore beg to be excused.

NOTES

1 Gregory Bateson, *Steps to an Ecology of Mind* (San Francisco: Chandler, 1972): 468.

2 *Steps to an Ecology of Mind*, pp 271–2; see also p 459.

THE HUMANITY OF SPEAKING:

THE PLACE OF THE INDIVIDUAL

IN THE MAKING OF ORAL

CULTURE

I

It is possible to speak in complete isolation. Roses bloom whether or not there is anyone present to admire them. Loons and hermit thrushes sing to themselves and to the air and to the trees if there are no loons and thrushes there to hear them. Human language can do the same. It is not, however, possible to *learn* to speak in isolation – not for humans, not for birds. Language, hard as it is, is formed on the soft anvil of community. It is something that links us to each other as well as to the world beyond ourselves, the larger music which we echo when we talk.

Language is also, of course, something that sets us apart from each other. Language defines and protects, more than anything else, our cultural watersheds, dividing us up into speakers of French, speakers of English, speakers of Greek or Creek or Cree. But humans are mammals, not trees. Humans can move, if they choose, from one linguistic watershed to the next. And they frequently do.

Every people has a language; every language has a literature. Most of those that have existed have never made the

Laurier Lecture, Wilfrid Laurier University, Waterloo, Ontario
8 November 2001

leap from the oral to the written. But if you follow any of the great and famous written literatures back in the direction of its roots, you will come to such a moment, when oral works were caught in the snare of the page. The *Odyssey*, the *Iliad*, the Song of Deborah and the story of Adam and Eve in the Garden of Eden, the *Rāmāyana*, the *Beowulf*, the *Poema del Cid*, the *Nibelungenlied*, are all oral works that were captured in writing.

Cultural historians often use these terms, *oral* and *written*, as if they were opposites or alternatives. They are not. *All literature is oral*. Writers are simply that unusual or deviant class of storytellers and singers who take their own dictation.

It is true that writing changes literature. It changes it, first of all, by leaving things out. A transcript of an oral poem never captures the fullness of a living performance tradition. And this is where writers become more deviant still. As they take their own dictation, they begin to try to use the resources of writing to patch up the holes and mend the tears they cannot help but make in the fabric of literature as they slip from the oral tradition.

The presence of an audience changes literature too, and oral composition also leaves things out. It leaves out what is whispered or unspoken. Writing opens the door to those who speak *sotto voce* or in solitude. It can make the process of speaking in solitude more fruitful, more socially acceptable, even more lucrative for some, but it doesn't create the phenomenon.

The Okanagan storyteller Peter Seymour is an informative example. He was born near Colville, Washington, in 1896 and died in 1979. In 1968, he dictated several stories in the Okanagan language to the linguist Anthony Mattina. One of these stories, called *The Golden Woman*, was published in 1985. It's essentially a European tale, full of flying horses, keys and locks, money and writing, all handsomely refracted through Salishan oral tradition, and full of good jokes about white men.

Kʷlìwt yəʔ nk'ʷcwíxtn
t'əxʷ axàʔ táwn, sílxʷaʔ tàwn.
Uɬ aɬìʔ nax̌əmɬ lut t'ə cmystìn iʔ skʷistúlaʔxʷs,
swìt captík̓ʷɬ.

Uɬ axàʔ kɬymíxʷməlx ixìʔ ‖ táwn,
sìlxʷaʔ ylmíxʷəms, smysqílxʷ.
Uɬ kɬəɬsqʷsíʔ, kmúsəms,
yəyˤàt tuʔtwít.

Ixìʔ uɬ n̓px̌'mùs iʔ scm'aʔm'áyaʔ,
way' t'əxʷ sqípc, way' taʔmúlaʔxʷ.
Uɬ ixìʔ txʷùymsəlx axàʔ
iʔ sxaʔx̌ʔìtx iʔ tkaʔkaʔɬìs yəʔ ‖ʔíwsəlx....¹

PEOPLE *were living in that place,*
another town, a big town.
And yet I don't know what the place is called,
only the story.

And there's a chief in that town,
a big chief, someone everybody knows.
And he has four sons,
all still just boys.

And then there's no more school,
yes, spring, yes, the place is free of snow.
And there they went,
the oldest three, to see their father....

Okanagan, like other Salish languages, bristles with clus-
tered and glottalized consonants. To English speakers it can
look and even sound, on first acquaintance, like someone

chewing broken glass. But if you look or listen closely to those few lines of Seymour's story, you'll begin to see how intricate the narrative structure is. It's built of quatrains, couplets and subcouplets, syntactically rhymed and nested into ever-larger two- and four-part structures.

Seymour told this tale over several days in an abandoned farmhouse. Only he and Mattina were present, and if Mattina had not used a tape recorder, no one would ever know what Seymour said. He always spoke so quietly, according to Mattina, that he could not hold an audience *even of native speakers*. He loved telling stories but got little practice. "The Golden Woman" is a long and complex tale, and Seymour got lost in it as he went, so the telling we have is in shards, like a broken vase, yet much of its shape and finish are clear. With a louder voice and a bigger ego, Seymour could have learned to tell it well. There may be many Peter Seymours in the world, but the only ones we learn of are those who live where oral culture, writing, and portable voice recorders happen to coexist.

II

From the oldest extant documents and inscriptions we learn that the first uses of writing weren't literary at all. The earliest writers were clerks and accountants doing administrative tasks: counting sheep and goats, and keeping track of stores of wine and grain and oil. But wherever writing persisted – in Mesopotamia, Egypt, China, India, Greece – someone noticed sooner or later that writing could be used to record the words of storytellers and singers. Writing had to discover literature, and it discovered it where it lives, in the speaking voice.

In North America, this process of transcription began in Mexico in the 1540s – two decades, that is, before Shakespeare was born – and again in Guatemala in the 1550s, where it yielded the earliest extant Native American classical text, the *Popol Vuh*. Bernardino de Sahagún, a graduate of the University of Salamanca, was ordained as a Franciscan in 1524, and in 1529 he was sent to what the Spaniards called New Spain. There he spent most of his time running residential schools for Aztec children. Unlike his colleagues, Bernardino realized that his students could teach him as much as he could them, or maybe more. He learned their language, Nahuatl, at the same time he was teaching them Spanish and Latin. He taught them how to write all three. And he sent them out to interview their elders and write their findings down.

The process was not without its risks. In 1570, some of Sahagún's manuscripts were seized by ecclesiastical authorities. After that, he started hiding copies of his work – a wise precaution. By 1577, rumors about him had reached the palace in Madrid, which issued an order saying

que luego que recibais esta nuestra cédula, con mucho cuidado y diligencia procureis haber estos libros, sin que dellos quede original ni traslado alguno, los envieis á bueno recaudo en la primera ocasión á nuestro Consejo de las Indias, para que en él se vean; y estareis advertido de no consentir que por ninguna manera persona alguna escriba cosas que toquen a supresticiones y manera de vivir que estos indios tenian, en ninguna lengua, porque así conviene al servicio de Dios Nuestro Señor y nuestro.[2]

that as soon as you receive this instruction of ours, you are to obtain, with great care and diligence, these books, leaving neither a single original nor copy; send them under proper guard at the first opportunity to our Council of the Indies to be examined; and be advised not to permit anyone, under any conditions, to write, in any language, things reflecting either the superstitions or way of life of these Indians, for this will suit the wishes of the Lord our God and of ourselves.

It would not have been wise, under these conditions, for Sahagún to give his sources names, even if he knew them. But it looks as if he rarely worked himself with Aztec elders. He was learning the tradition indirectly, through his students. This was good, no doubt, for the students. They were encouraged to listen to their elders, and to think that indigenous and colonial traditions could coexist – a lesson that not everyone in Mexico has mastered even yet. But because he was working second-hand, Sahagún did not produce a literary record. He collected a lot of information, and he did collect it in the Nahuatl language. But he did not preserve – nor even, it seems, attempt to preserve – a real tradition-bearer's voice.

Literature has nothing necessarily to do with letters or writing. It has to do with *content* and with *voice*. In literature, these two are fused. When you hear a great mythteller or read a great writer, you don't just get some information; you receive a kind of transfusion. You come *voice to voice* with the voice you hear, as though you were *face to face* with the speaker. The voice becomes part of your mind and stays with you forever. That is what it means to listen to literature, whether you listen with your ears to words an oral poet speaks or with your eyes to words a writer has put on the page.

There were missionaries in Canada and the northern USA at an early date, and some of them at least were learning Iroquoian languages. Some made lists of words. I have not discovered any who transcribed texts dictated by native speakers, but their manuscripts too, if they ever existed, may have been made to disappear. These missionaries did, at any rate, introduce the alphabet to Iroquoian communities. Over the next two centuries, native speakers of Mohawk, Onondaga, and Cayuga used the Latin alphabet to create their own indigenous scribal culture. A linguist named Horatio Hale, who lived most of his life in Clinton, Ontario, worked with Mohawk and Onondaga speakers to copy and translate some of these texts, which he published in Boston in 1883.[3] Those are the first printed editions of Native Canadian texts – and since the manuscripts Hale was working from were already a century old, these are probably the oldest texts we have from north of the Rio Grande. (Prayers, hymns, and scriptures translated into Native North American languages had appeared before this date, but these were the first published texts that were really of Native North American origin.)

One of Hale's contemporaries, a missionary by the name of Stephen Return Riggs, spent most of his life working with speakers of Lakhota – a Siouan language spoken in North and South Dakota and in parts of southern Saskatchewan. Riggs taught many of his converts to read and write their language and compiled a short anthology of texts written by three of them: Michael Renville, David Grey Cloud, and Walking Elk. This collection wasn't published until 1893, well after Riggs's death, but it again is the first book of its kind: a collection of texts written for publication by Native American writers in a Native American language.[4]

In the meantime another missionary linguist, Émile Petitot, had been working in the north. From 1862 to 1883, he recorded stories told in Chipewyan, Dogrib, Gwichin, Slavey, Inuktitut and Cree. In 1888, in Alençon, he published the result: *Traditions indiennes du Canada nord-ouest: textes originaux et traduction littérale*[5]: a 450-page anthology of stories in a panoply of Native Canadian languages, with parallel French translation. That was the first anthology of Native Canadian oral literature ever published. Many more texts, and better texts, have been recorded since, but no one has yet sifted them and assembled them into such a useful form. Petitot's remains even now the most substantial anthology of its kind.

From a literary standpoint, there are problems with each

of these books, as there are with Sahagún's. The Mohawk and Onondaga texts published by Hale, though known as "books," are brief (a total of 15 pages); at base they are ossified ritual texts, offering limited room for literary artistry; and Hale's grasp of the material leaves something to be desired. The Lakhota texts commissioned by Reverend Riggs show that their authors found writing a peculiar and unfriendly thing to do. They were living, after all, in a functioning oral culture and might have left us better work if Riggs had asked them to dictate stories which he would transcribe. Father Petitot relied on children as much as on adults, and he evidently condensed his transcriptions, leaving out the formulaic openings and closings and the structural repetitions that are crucial to Native American oral narrative. How do we know? The oral tradition is still alive in Chipewyan, Dogrib, Slavey, and Inuktitut. You can still hear what Petitot omitted. And there are other texts, transcribed by other linguists after Petitot's return to France, to prove the continuity of the tradition.

It was not altogether auspicious, but that was the beginning of the overlap of indigenous oral culture and the imported culture of writing in northern North America.

III

The next phase opens with Franz Boas, his colleagues and his students. These scholars and the mythtellers they worked with have left us a large legacy. I will focus on one example: John Swanton's work with the Haida poets Skaay and Ghandl.

Swanton met the Haida mythteller Skaay on 8 October 1900, in the mission village of Skidegate, built where the old Haida village of Hlghagilda had stood. Swanton had just started learning Haida. He could say very little directly, but he explained, through an interpreter, that he wanted to transcribe stories in Haida. And he said that he especially wanted to transcribe the story of the Raven. Skaay agreed to tell him stories, they settled the rate of payment, and then Skaay outlined in advance what he would tell. He would tell a story he called *Xhuuya Qaagaangas*, "Raven Traveling," but he would tell another cycle of five stories first. They started the following day, Tuesday, October 9. And this is how the story began:

Ll giidagang wansuuga.
Ll jaadagang wansuuga.
Skyaamskun ghinwaay llaghan ttl gitghan
        jihlgwagaangang wansuuga.
Ll xhaatgha llagha kkuugagang wansuuga.

Ll daaghalang stins: 5
nang dlquunas
gyaan ising nang hittaghaniina.

Waaygyaanhaw ll xhaatghaga llanagaay gu ga
        xyaahldaal ttl xhaayang wansuuga,
tluugha tlaahlgugha.
Waaygyaan xyaahldaalang wansuuga.   10
Waaygyaan gaytlgistlaayang wansuugang.

Gyaanhaw at nang kyanangsghaayang wansuuga
ll xhaatgha ghulsqaawugha aa,
«Gustanggha tluwaay haw iijang?» ...

THERE *was one of good family, they say.*
She was a woman, they say.
They wove the down of blue falcons
        into her dancing blanket, they say.
Her father loved her, they say.

She had two brothers: 5
one who was grown
and one who was younger than she.

And then they came to dance at her father's town, they say,
in ten canoes,
and then they danced, they say,   10
and then they sat waiting, they tell me.

And someone – her father's head servant, they say –
went out and asked them,
"Why are these canoes here?"[6]

The whole poem – the tightly woven cycle of five stories – lasts about eight hours. Swanton transcribed every word, and longhand phonetic transcription is slow and arduous work. So dictating the poem took roughly two weeks. In printed form, it's two hundred pages, yet it's just as economical as haiku: no wasted words, no decorative adjectives, no picturesque details. Whenever Skaay says something that sounds obvious – something like Ll *xhaatgha llagha kkuugagang wansuuga*, "Her father loved her, they say" – he does it for a reason. That line is one of the fulcra on which the whole work turns: a little verbal arrow quietly aimed at the heart of the story.

We can study these features of Skaay's work – his tone, his sense of structure, and his style – because Skaay was free to work in the mode he knew and loved – the oral mode – and because Swanton wrote down every word, not a digest or paraphrase. Though he still knew very little of the language, Swanton sensed, as he listened to Skaay, that he was hearing the real thing. Months later, working through the text word by word with his bilingual Haida colleague Henry Moody, he learned that he'd been right: Skaay's artistry was real.

1 The Haida village of Hlghagilda, 26 July 1878. Photo by George Dawson. National Archives of Canada PA 37755.

IV

The Haida had no writing, nor did the Aztecs, with whom Sahagún had worked three centuries before. The Aztecs did, however, have a rich tradition of visual art – painting and carving – in which the stories could be seen. So did the Haida. The Haida, like the Aztecs, created a visual world that helped to keep their oral literature healthy. Then the missionaries came, and they deliberately destroyed it.

When the geologist George Dawson arrived in the Haida village of Hlghagilda on Friday morning, 26 July 1878, this (figure 1) is what he saw – except that he saw it in the fullness of three dimensions, changing light, and vivid color. He could photograph it only in static, two-dimensional black & white.

The poles were as dense in the front of the village as trees in the forest: every house adorned with its own steeple and most with an assortment of memorial poles as well. This is the world in which Skaay was born and raised. When Swanton arrived, in 1900, all of that was gone. Skaay if he closed his eyes could see it because he had lived in it; Swanton could not.

Swanton went looking for what he couldn't see – and this (figure 2) is the form in which he found it. This is a portion of Swanton's typescript: his transcription of a story told in the Haida language. The story was dictated by a man named Sghaagya in December 1900, in the mission village of Skidegate, but it is set in the precolonial Haida world.

The typescript, like the photograph, filters and compresses features of reality. We have to learn to read it – and I don't just mean we have to learn the language. Learning to read transcriptions of oral literature is something like learning to read historical photographs. The depth and the color, the sounds and the smells, the coughing and spitting, and a lot of the rest of the nitty-gritty is missing. Through informed imagination, much of that can be restored. And it's like learning to read music. The point is not just to grasp the grammar and the syntax but to envision, and maybe re-create, a genuine performance.

The typescript looks at first to be plain prose, which is a form designed to minimize the outward individuality of any human voice. Almost no one speaks in genuine prose, but the form is often used – by journalists, linguists, and court reporters alike – for transcriptions. The typographic form we associate with prose makes speakers look like writers.

Swanton went looking for what he couldn't see, and his typewritten texts are the result. I went looking, in the typescript, for what I couldn't hear: the oral art, the form and meaning hidden in the flattened landscape of the page.

On this particular page, Sghaagya is talking about a dispute between two lineages belonging to the two Haida moieties, the

2 Part of page 700 of Swanton's Skidegate Haida typescript, Ms. ACLS Coll. N1.5 (Freeman 1543). American Philosophical Society Library, Philadelphia.

Eagle side and the Raven side. An old man of the Kyaanusili lineage (Raven side) attempts to settle the quarrel. He pays a visit to the enemy, urging peace by performing a dance and a poem.[7] Sghaagya was a boy when this occurred – it must have been about 1850 – but he quoted the poem to Swanton, and there it is, embedded in his story (lines 4–10 in figure 2), as if it too were only so much prose.

The poem is not in prose; it is in verse. But the story in which it occurs is not prose either. It has the structure of oral narrative, which is neither verse nor prose. Its form can be felt and understood in performance – but Swanton did not hear a performance; he heard dictation, at a pace artificially slowed by systematic repetition. The form survived dictation because it was real – like the form of a sound philosophical argument or a well-constructed play, or the form of a plant or

THE KYAANUSILI PEACE POEM

littlxhagit hl qiyadagan,
Naay Injawa llaana yaguhlsi gha
    gagaalang kkyuwaay at hltangghu kkyuwaay
        kitgitxhan ttlxhagan.
Gagaalang kkyuwaay gut hl qaylgan.
Hltangghu kkyuwaay gut hl qaattlxhaga.

«Gasing llaana ghiida haw aa iijin?»   5

«Kilstlaay hlqin, Gaala dang ghunggha llanaagha iiji.
Dang ghunggha llanaagha yaguhlsi gha
    gagaalang kkyuwaay kit·ttlxhagan gut
        daa qaydan.
Dang ghungghalang danggi ngaygulgan.
Hltangghu kkyuwaay guthaw daa qaattlxhaga.»

Aa dii ghunggha llaana gwa iija – aa hayingii?   10

animal. And because it is real, it can still be extracted from the typescript and mapped typographically, not only in transcription but even in translation. Part of that form belongs to the species, Homo sapiens; part belongs to this particular human culture and its language, Haida; and part – a substantial part, I think, in this case – belongs to the individual speaker or singer. If we restore the form to the voice, we get more of all three.

We also get something else in this case: we get what is almost certainly the earliest surviving piece of Haida literature, tiny but whole, preserved for half a century in the amber of Sghaagya's memory, and preserved for a century more in Swanton's typescript like a fossil in the shale. Only one impor-

THE KYAANUSILI PEACE POEM

Princes, I am one of those who are married to your sisters.
At Trophy House in the middle of the town,
    the path of vengeance and the path of feathers
        start and end together.
On the path of vengeance I departed.
By the path of feathers I arrive.

"What town have I come to?"   5

"Prince, my son, this is your father Gaala's town.
From the middle of your father's town,
    where the path of vengeance starts,
        you departed.
Your fathers were concerned about you.
Now by the path of feathers you arrive."

Is this my father's town — or someone else's?   10

tant thing is missing: the author's name. Sghaagya must have
known who composed this poem, but he did not tell Swanton,
and Swanton evidently did not ask.

    V

Figure 3 (overleaf) is a model of a Haida house. Few people
have ever been lucky enough to see such a house in real life,
but almost everyone who has taken a university course in the
history of art, anywhere in the English-speaking world during
the past half century, has seen this photo. It appears in Ernst
Gombrich's textbook The Story of Art, a book that was first pub-

3 Daxhiigang. Model of Qqaayganga Naas (Myth House), Kkyuusta. 1901.
Redcedar. The frontal pole is 92 cm high. American Museum of Natural History,
New York, 16/8771, neg 36150. (The cornerpost on the right is displaced in this
photograph.)

lished in 1950 and is now [2001] in its 16th edition. It is an
excellent book in many ways, and I have learned a great deal
from it myself. Its author died just a few days ago,[8] at the age
of 92, and it is with great respect for his work and his memory
that I want to suggest, at this late date, a slight revision to his
much-loved book. Chapter 1 is entitled "Strange Beginnings:
Prehistoric and Primitive Peoples; Ancient America." In this

chapter, Gombrich discusses paintings from Lascaux and works from several African, Australasian, and Native American cultures. That is where we find this illustration.

John Swanton commissioned that model in 1901 from the Haida carver Daxhiigang, known in English as Charlie Edenshaw. To Gombrich, however, this is an artwork *outside history*. He therefore fails to give the artist a name. In the first fifteen editions of his book, he also failed to give the work a date. The illustration, Gombrich says,

> is a model of a chieftain's house of the Haida tribe of the north-west with three so-called totem poles in front of it. We may see only a jumble of ugly masks, but to the native this pole illustrates an old legend of his tribe. The legend itself may strike us as nearly as odd and incoherent as its representation, but we ought no longer to feel surprised that native ideas differ from ours.[9]

Next we have a summary of what Gombrich calls "the legend":

> Once there was a young man in the town of Gwais Kun who used to laze about on his bed the whole day till his mother-in-law remarked on it; he felt ashamed, went away and decided to slay a monster which lived in a lake and fed on humans and whales. With the help of a fairy bird he made a trap of a tree trunk and dangled two children over it as bait. The monster was caught, the young man dressed in its skin and caught fishes, which he regularly left on his critical mother-in-law's doorstep. She was so flattered at these unexpected offerings that she thought of herself as a powerful witch. When the young man undeceived her at last, she felt so ashamed that she died.[10]

Gombrich goes on to elucidate the housepole of this model house in terms of this rather painfully summarized story. In doing so, he gets a bit mixed up, changing a whale into a fish, and changing a creature called *Sins Xhiitadaay*, "Holding Up the Daylight," into a "fairy bird" – but Gombrich inherited some of these errors from Boas and some from Swanton himself. It is sad to see them in a textbook (especially one in its sixteenth revision), but they are easy errors to fix. What concerns me is something else. The underlying problem surfaces at the beginning of chapter 2, where Gombrich turns his attention to Egypt, Mesopotamia, and Crete. These, for him, are parts of a world and a tradition he can think of as his own, while the indigenous cultures of Africa, Australasia, and the Americas are not. Chapter 2 begins as follows:

Some form of art exists everywhere on the globe, but the story of art as a continuous effort does not begin in the caves of southern France or among the North American Indians. There is no direct tradition which links these strange beginnings with our own days, but there is a direct tradition, handed down from master to pupil, and from pupil to admirer or copyist, which links the art of our own days, any house or any poster, with the art of the Nile Valley of some five thousand years ago. For we shall see that the Greek masters went to school with the Egyptians, and we are all the pupils of the Greeks.[11]

If you divide the world into *them* and *us*, and history into *ours* and *theirs*, or if you think of history as something only you and your affiliates can possess, then no matter what you know, no matter how noble your intentions, you have taken one step toward the destruction of the world.

Suppose Gombrich had looked at this model house with the same profound affection and curiosity that he brings to works by Renaissance Italian architects and sculptors such as Brunelleschi and Donatello. What might he have seen? He could easily have learned the artist's name, to start with. He could have learned his English name, Charles Edenshaw, or with a little more effort his Haida name, Daxhiigang. Then he could have learned that a large body of work, including full-size poles, masks, drawings, and other items, by this artist are preserved. We have everything we need, in this case, for a study of individual style. Gombrich could have learned something about the artist's life. He also could have visited the landscape where Daxhiigang lived and worked. He could have read, in Franz Boas's English translation, the 34 pages of stories that Daxhiigang told to Boas near the mouth of the Skeena River in 1894. One of those texts is a two-page version of the story which Gombrich reduced to a paragraph. Next, he could have set that rendition of the story side by side with others to see how they fit. And then he could have looked for other works by Daxhiigang that are based on the same theme.

When the Haida poet Ghandl told "the same" story to Swanton, in the Haida language, at Skidegate in November 1900, he linked it to several other themes, creating a work that is unlike any other ever recorded on the Northwest Coast. This is normal and typical behavior for a good mythteller. Mythtellers are, as a rule, creative artists; they don't just go around repeating one another. Ghandl's story takes about half an hour in spoken form and fills about a dozen pages in print. I'll read you the last section, where the poem matches up with the figures on this housepole. But now I've put myself in a jam. To get us quickly to that section of the story, I have to resort to a summary, just like Gombrich. Summaries are very rarely literature, but sometimes they are useful.

The story begins with a man who hunts sea lions. He is abandoned by his colleagues on a reef. His wife's youngest brother tries to save him but cannot. Once the hunter is all alone, a diving bird invites him into the sea, where he learns some things from killer whales and sea lions. Then he returns to his home in secret, gets his tools from his wife, builds a trap and catches a seawolf – the so-called "monster" mentioned by Gombrich. After that, he creates two pods of living killer whales by carving them in wood. He tells these orcas to destroy the hunters who left him on the reef, saving only his wife's youngest brother – the one who tried to save his life. Now we come to the final movement of Ghandl's poem.

> Gyaan llanagaay gu lla iisugwaang qawdi 241
> ttl qqaastlas ttaahlgha
> lla qaaaxhuls.
>
> Gyaan waasghaay qqal ghii lla qattsaayasi.
> Gyaan llanagaay gyaawgi sttlang at sghun lla
>   xhaaghatgaayasi
> ttaghun taadlju lla xhadlgihls.
>
> Gyaan ll jighunaan·gha lla ttalgi kinggangas.
> Singghaayxhan ll qqaahlugangas
> ll kkyaawgha naagaay qqaatgu lla lla istaasi.... 249

> AND THEN, *after he'd been in the village awhile,* 241
> *at a time when the others were sleeping,*
> *he went out.*
>
> *And then he dressed in the seawolf skin.*
> *And then, at the edge of the village, he reached out*
>   *to the water with one paw,*
> *and he had half of a spring salmon.*
>
> *And the mother of his wife, who always nagged him,*
> *always got up early in the morning.*
> *He laid the salmon down at the door of her house.*

Early in the morning, she came out.   250
She found the chunk of salmon
and was happy.

That night again, he dressed in the seawolf skin.
He went into the water up to the elbow.
He came back with half a halibut.

He set it down beside the door of his wife's mother's house.
She found it in the morning.
The people of the village had been hungry up till then, they say.

Again that night, he dressed in the skin of the seawolf.
He put his foreleg all the way into the water,   260
and he got a whole spring salmon.
He set it, again, at the woman's door,
and she found it in the morning.

He dressed again the next night in the seawolf skin,
and then he let the water come over his back.
He brought in the jaw of a black whale
and left it at his mother-in-law's door.
She was very pleased to find it there.

His wife's mother started to perform
    as a shaman then, they say.
They fasted side by side with her for four nights.   270
He was with them too, they say.
It was his voice that started speaking through her —
through the mother of his wife.

The next night again, he got inside the seawolf.
He swam seaward.

He killed a black whale.
Fangs stuck out of the nostrils of the seawolf.
Those are what he killed it with, they say.

He put it up between his ears
and carried it to shore.   280
He put it down in front of the house.
She had predicted
that a whale would appear.

And again, as they were sleeping,
he went out inside the seawolf.
He got two black whales.

He brought them back to shore.
He carried one between his ears
and the other draped across the base of his tail.
He swam ashore with them   290
and set them down again in front of the house.

When night came again,
he swam way out to sea inside the seawolf.
He got ten black whales.

He carried several bundled up between his ears.
He carried others in a bunch at the base of his tail.
He had them piled on his body,
and he put one in his mouth.
He started swimming toward the shore.

He was still out at sea when daylight came, they say,   300
and when he came up on the beach,

the mother of his wife was there to meet him
  in the headdress of a shaman.

He stepped outside the seawolf skin.
"Why," he asked her, "are there spearpoints in your eyes?
Does the spirit being speaking through you
get some help from me?"
She died of shame from what he said, they say.

The seawolf skin swam out to sea alone.
Then the hunter took the string of whales
and said that no one was to touch them.   310

The sale of those whales made him rich, they say.
And then he held ten feasts in honor, so they say,
of the youngest brother of his wife.
He made a prince of him.

This is where it ends.[12]

Does the story still strike you as "odd and incoherent," as Gombrich says, or have we got close enough to the humanity of the teller for the story to start to make sense? And what about the humanity of the carver?

In the spring of 1901, while Swanton was in the Haida country, he commissioned ten small carvings from Daxhiigang. Seven of these were model memorial poles – freestanding poles that were placed out in front of Haida houses to commemorate dead members of the aristocracy. One was a model mortuary post: a type of memorial pole designed to hold the deceased's remains. The remaining two were model housepoles – and in these two cases, Daxhiigang reinterpreted the commission to include the entire house. Both were models of houses built and owned by his uncle Gwaayang Gwanhlin. Daxhiigang lavished special care on the model we've been looking at. He made not only the house and housepole but the interior house screen too (figure 4) and a model canoe that went with the house.

4 Daxhiigang. House screen from the model of Qqaayganga Naas (Myth House). Redcedar and paint. American Museum of Natural History, New York, 16/8771, neg 2A18684.

Divider screens like this are called *laal* in Haida. In the old days they were often set behind the central fire to shield the private quarters of the headman's immediate family from the area used by everybody else. The figure on this screen looks like a giant frog, and in Haida and Tlingit cosmology, the frog is a figure involved in the acquisition of wealth. But according to Daxhiigang, this frog-like being is G̲unaaqadeit. That is the Tlingit name of a mythcreature known in Haida as Tangghwan Llaana, "Sea Dweller." He is the master of wealth, presiding over the world beneath the sea, and one of his forms or emblems is that of a giant saltwater frog.

In the spring of 1904, the Tlingit mythteller K̲aadashaan, headman of Wrangell, Alaska, clarified for Swanton why a house with the image of G̲unaaqadeit on the screen behind the fire would have the shamanizing mother-in-law and the seawolf on the frontal pole.[13] According to K̲aadashaan, after dying in the service of his mother-in-law, the son-in-law, dressed in his seawolf skin, *was transformed into* G̲unaaqadeit.

His wife then joined him in the sea, where she gave birth to all the headwater women – those quintessential creatures known in Haida as *qaasgha jiina*. They are the spirit beings who draw the spawning salmon up the streams and so enable us to eat. Gwaayang Gwanhlin (an avid collector of Tlingit titles and dances) was well acquainted with Ḵaadashaan's elders and would have known the story. So should we, if we are going to put a model of that house in our museum and its picture in our books.

Gwaayang Gwanhlin, who built the house and lived in it, was the artist's maternal uncle, his teacher, and his predecessor as headman of the Stastas lineage of the Eagle side in the Haida social order. In other words, Daxhiigang was the nephew and the heir of the owner of this house.

So this is not just a model of a house. It is a model of the house the artist's uncle built for himself at Kkyuusta, which is modeled in turn on the house of Tangghwan Llaana, source of all food and riches, at the center of the mythworld, on the bottom of the sea. It is a model of the house that Daxhiigang would have inherited and lived in if things had been different: if smallpox and the church and the British Empire had not wreaked havoc on the Haida world.

VI

I would like to repeat that I have great respect for both the late Professor Gombrich and his book. But I have no faith at all in the principle he uses to cut history down to manageable size. I don't agree that there is *no continuity* between "us" and "them" – between the inhabitants of the modern university, where Gombrich's book is used as a text, and the artists in oral cultures of Africa, the Americas, and Australasia, or in prehistoric Europe. Continuity of culture is never guaranteed, but where that continuity is lost, artists *re-create* it. That is one of the services art performs. Bill Reid's work, as an example, reaches back to Benvenuto Cellini, to Titian, to Pietro Bernini, whose sculpture of a sunken boat sits in the Piazza di Spagna in Rome, and to Pythokritos of Rhodes, who carved the Beached Ship of Lindos and in all probability the Victory of Samothrace, now in the Louvre. It also reaches back to Daxhiigang, Gwaayang Gwanhlin and their forebears, who created the great carvings of Haida Gwaii, dozens of which are now to be seen in major museums around the world.

Meaning is not a thing; it is a relationship. It is, in other words, a difference – between or among things perceived, or between the perceived and the perceiver, or between the perceiver and his family, his community, his species, or his world. Some people say these are two or three quite different kinds of meaning: the objective, the subjective and maybe something else. But meaning is a relationship, in every case: a difference rather than a rupture or disjunction. To deny that a relationship exists is to deny that meaning is present. A break, of course, can be meaningful – but then the meaning lies in the *relation* between the break and the thing broken.

A week ago yesterday [1 November 2001], in New York City, the latest Nobel laureate in literature, Vidiadhar Surajprasad Naipaul, gave a lecture recounting a voyage he had made through Pakistan, Afghanistan, Iran, Indonesia, and other non-Arab Muslim countries: those nations which have over the past twelve centuries been converted to Islam. He spoke about the fact that in cultures of conversion such as these, history begins with the arrival of the faith. Everything before the moment of conversion loses its relation to the present. In other words, it ceases to have meaning.

Canada and the USA, on this score, bear some resemblance to Afghanistan. They are patchwork quilts of languages and cultures, yet at the same time they are cultures of conversion. This explains why Canada, in its quiet, deferential, Canadian way, can be every bit as philistine as Pakistan, Afghanistan, Iran and the rest of Naipaul's list. With us, moreover, the conversion is very recent. That is why the Canadian philosopher George Grant was able, in 1967, to describe North America as "the only society on earth that has no indigenous traditions from before the age of progress." What that statement says is that traditions native to Canada do not exist, or that if they exist they are meaningless. Or in Gombrich's more polite terms, that there is no continuity between Native Canadian traditions and the life of the present day. The act of parliament, passed in April 1884, which prohibited Native Canadians from practicing the potlatch or owning the regalia it required was of course intended to ensure that no such continuity would ever be created or discovered. So was the order issued by the Spanish Crown in 1577, requiring the seizure of Sahagún's manuscripts. So was the Taliban ruling council's order, issued earlier this year [2001], to destroy all evidence that the people of Afghanistan were once in large part Buddhist.

I knew George Grant and loved him. I choose to believe that he would graciously retract his statement now if he were here to do so. Since he is not, I think that as a courtesy to him and to ourselves, we should retract it for him. Native Canadian and Native American traditions do exist and do have meaning. Finding and asserting the continuity between these traditions and the strange new world in which we live is crucial to our survival. It is also crucial to our self-respect. It is a task in which Native Canadians have to participate – and they do. But it is not a task confined by racial identity. It is not, in other words, a task that we can sit back and let aboriginal people do for the rest of us. That too is part of what I mean by the humanity of speaking.

NOTES

1 From pp 75–6 of *The Golden Woman: The Colville Narrative of Peter J. Sey-mour*, edited by Anthony Mattina (Tucson: U of Arizona Press, 1985). In this orthography, based closely on Mattina's, the acute accent indicates primary stress, grave accent secondary stress, and the underdot marks a syllabic consonant.

2 *Códice Franciscano*, quoted by Arthur Anderson in his introduction to Bernardino de Sahagún, *General History of the Things of New Spain: The Florentine Codex* (Nahuatl text, edited & translated by A.J.O. Anderson & C.E. Dibble, 13 vols in 14 parts, Santa Fe: School of American Research, 1970–82): vol. 1: 37.

3 Horatio Hale, *The Iroquois Book of Rites* (Philadelphia: D.G. Brinton, 1883). The best recent edition is that published by U of Toronto Press in 1963, with a useful introduction by William Fenton.

4 Stephen Return Riggs, *Dakota Grammar, Texts, and Ethnography*, edited by James Owen Dorsey (Washington, DC: Dept of the Interior, 1893).

5 Émile Petitot, *Traditions indiennes du Canada nord-ouest: textes originaux et traduction littérale* (Alençon: Renaut de Broise, 1888) [= *Actes de la Société philologique* 16/17: 167–614]. There are two editions of this book. One is made from sheets printed for the *Actes*, paginated 167–614 and dated on the title page 1888. The other, paginated i–vi + 1–446, includes a new preface dated 2 juillet 1888 but is misdated on the title page 1887. These editions are otherwise identical to one another, but both differ radically from Petitot's earlier book with a similar title: *Traditions indiennes du Canada nord-ouest* (Paris: Maisonneuve & LeClerc, 1886). That work is in French only, with no aboriginal texts, and the French versions are dressed-up and toned-down literary paraphrases rather than translations.

6 Skaay, *Being in Being* (2001): 39.

7 See John Reed Swanton, *Haida Texts and Myths: Skidegate Dialect* (BAE Bulletin 29. Washington, DC: Bureau of American Ethnology, 1905): 384–9; Bringhurst, *A Story as Sharp as a Knife* (1999/2000): 165–8.

8 Gombrich died on 3 November 2001. This lecture was delivered five days later.

9 Gombrich, *The Story of Art*, 16th ed. (London: Phaidon, 1995): 49. Compare p 29 of the first edition (1950).

10 Gombrich 1995: 49; cf. Gombrich 1950: 33 and Swanton, *Contributions to the Ethnology of the Haida* (Jesup North Pacific Expedition 5.1, New York: American Museum of Natural History, 1905): 126.

11 Gombrich 1995: 55; cf. Gombrich 1950: 33.

12 Ghandl, *Nine Visits to the Mythworld* (2000): 106–10.

13 See Swanton, *Contributions to the Ethnology of the Haida*, p 127, and *Tlingit Myths and Texts* (BAE Bulletin 39, Washington, DC: Bureau of American Ethnology, 1909): 165–9.

PROSODIES OF MEANING:

LITERARY FORM IN NATIVE

NORTH AMERICA

I

I would like to begin, if you'll forgive me, with a long quotation whose relation to the subject of this talk may not at first seem clear.

Die Vorstellungsart: daß ein lebendiges Wesen zu gewissen Zwecken nach außen hervorgebracht, und seine Gestalt durch eine absichtliche Urkraft dazu determiniert werde, hat uns in der philosophischen Betrachtung der natürlichen Dinge schon mehrere Jahrhunderte aufgehalten, und hält uns noch auf, obgleich einzelne Männer diese Vorstellungsart eifrig bestritten und die Hindernisse welche sie in den Weg lege gezeicht haben.

Es kann diese Vorstellungsart für sich fromm, für gewisse Gemüter angenehm, für gewisse Vorstellungsarten unentbehrlich sein, und ich finde es weder rätlich noch möglich sie im ganzen zu bestreiten. Es ist wenn man sich so ausdrücken darf eine triviale Vorstellungsart, die eben deswegen wie alle triviale Dinge trivial ist, weil sie der menschlichen Natur im ganzen bequem und zureichend ist.

The idea that a living being is created for external aims, and its form thus chosen for it by deliberate force, has interfered with philosophical

Belcourt Lecture, University of Manitoba, Winnipeg
1 March 2002

contemplation of the natural world for several centuries already and is trammeling us still, though several individuals have challenged it with vigor and have shown what a hindrance it creates.

This idea may be well-intentioned in itself, appealing to certain temperaments and indispensable to certain points of view. I find it neither desirable nor possible to reject it altogether. But it is, if one may say so, a trivial idea, and like all trivial things, it is trivial because on the whole human nature finds it flattering and rests content with that.

This passage is found in one of Goethe's writings on natural history, *Versuch einer allgemeinen Vergleichungslehre*, written around 1792.[1]

II

Form is a large subject; meaning is another, and Native North America is home to several hundred languages and literatures where form and meaning thrive. I hope nevertheless to say a few things here about relations of meaning and form in Native American oral narrative, and especially about the larger context in which they might be seen. By "context" I mean that I will often stray a long way from the subject – because sometimes, if you hike a little farther, you get a better view.

Early in my life, I turned from the study of physics to the study of language and literature. I was never a real physicist and am not now a real linguist; I am merely a student of language, and a sort of linguistic mechanic. The proof of this is that I am much less intrigued by language as such than by the things that language can say. Even more than that, I am intrigued by what it can almost *but not quite* say and what it almost *but not quite* allows us to hear.

Language is, by definition, a self-transcending medium, and fascinating therefore in itself. But I am fascinated more when language seems to transcend not just language but also those who speak and understand it. These are the moments when language permits or propels us to the verge of saying, and of hearing, more than we thought we knew or were able to say, more perhaps than we thought possible either to utter or to understand. This happens sometimes when a person is driven to scream, reaching beyond the boundaries of language. It also happens sometimes when someone sings a song or tells a story, passing through the heart of language to a place that is, as Melville says, "not down in any map; true places never are."[2]

There are those who think of literary form as a way of tying language down and keeping it in order. I'm more interested in form as a kind of catapult: an articulating skeleton that allows meaning to leap or dance or glide amazing distances, taking us along. Musical form is part (not all, but part) of what it takes for sound to enter the realm of music. If the form constrains the sound, it does so to enable it to hover like a dragonfly, leap like a deer or pounce like a cat. The constraints, if they succeed, become a source of freedom and power. Literary form is part of what it takes for language to enter the realm of *literature* or *poetry* – I'll use those two quite different terms as synonyms for now. If the form is a constraint, it's the kind of constraint that allows a song or a story to go where others can't. Wings are a constraint that makes it possible to fly.

I don't say this will happen every time a form appears. I say that that's what form, in art as in biology, is *for*.

III

The "problem," from the colonial perspective, is that Native American narrative poetry is not composed in rhyming couplets or rolling dactylic hexameters, nor is it sung to a stringed instrument like heroic song in the Balkans, nor is it full of

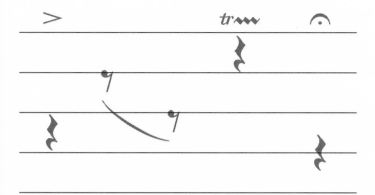

1 One-bar Impromptu: a prosody of silence

elaborate evocations of the glory of princes and warriors, the beauty of women and landscape, or the complexities of the self. In other words, it lacks some basic features that people trained on European literature associate with poetry. In the 1950s, after a lifetime studying Native American languages and cultures, Alfred Kroeber made a list of things he *did not find* in aboriginal America. On the list he put *philosophy* and *poetry*.[3] It is odd to encounter Kroeber, with all his experience and all his undoubted humanity, sitting in his leafy house in Berkeley, wearing starched collar and spats, but there he is. He missed some things that sat there right in front of him – things he'd been actively engaged with, in fact, for half a century – *because they took an unfamiliar form.*

The cure for this "problem" is excruciatingly simple. Abandon the colonial perspective and the problem goes away. There is no one now in Skidegate or Aishihik, Ermineskin or Long Dog Lake, Waskaganish or Odanak, fretting over the lack of iambic pentameter in Haida or Southern Tutchone or Cree or Penobscot.

But suppose, at long last, we want a productive dialogue

between Native American and European cultures. Suppose we want to read and hear the literature, the poetry, the stories, of these worlds side by side. Then we need a sense not just of how they differ but of what they have in common.

You could say, in that case, we need a theory. Theory in the humanities is often a sort of therapy: something we turn to when we find ourselves at odds with where we are or somehow out of touch with immediate reality. It is a medicine whose function is to calm us down enough to let reality make sense again. Theory in this sense is a substitute for time – a splint and bandage for the fractured limbs of history. Where time is short, theory abounds.

In astrophysics – my old calling – theory is not that: it is the one form of mythtelling that still retains its dignity and prestige in the academy. But this is something I never could have learned by continuing in physics. To learn what modern physics is, I had to study Native American literature. The kind of theory we call *myth* – the dominant genre in classical Native American poetry – is a way of honoring time and the world, and not a device with which to synthesize or replace them.

My theory, if you want to call it that, is a simple observation: literature occurs wherever human communities occur. Stories, like the human beings who tell them, are part of the natural flora and fauna, endemic to the world. All stories, of course, have form, just as tamarack and black spruce, jack pine and juniper have form. The only formless flora and fauna are those that have been eaten or cooked and stored, becoming fuel for other forms. The observable fact is that philosophy and poetry, like language, are human universals. It seems to me, in fact, that poetry *provokes* human language to exist, and that poetry is what language – even philosophical language – generally aspires to rejoin. Poetry, that is, is a characteristic of reality, echoing in every human tongue.

Linguistics as it has imagined itself over the past century has started with the phoneme, worked its way up to the sentence, and then stopped there, as if it thought that literature were none of its affair. It's odd that this is so, when many great linguists – Franz Boas, Edward Sapir, Melville Jacobs, Roman Jakobson, Kenneth Hale, for example – have known better. Some of these linguists – Sapir, Jacobs, and Jakobson at least – have made their intuition of the seamlessness of language and literature absolutely clear.

Dell Hymes, who is a member of this lineage, has argued for nearly half a century that linguistics should *not* stop with the sentence but should look far beyond, at the form and structure of stories, because stories, just like sentences, are found wherever human language is found. I wonder what would happen if we *started with the story* and worked our way both up and down from there: to mythology on one side; on the other to the sentence, phrase, word, morpheme, phoneme, tagmeme, and other sublogical particles catalogued by the great particle linguist Leonard Bloomfield. I wonder, in other words, how things would change if we looked afresh at the *natural history* of language as well as its microbiology.

The naturalist starts with the tree, the shrub, the avalanche lily or the moss, then works his way up to the forest and down to the leaf, the stem, the petal and sepal, stamen and pistil, or the spore case and the spores. Or she starts with the mouse, the grouse, the wolf, the moose, the deer and works her way up to the pack, the flock, the herd, the larger patterns of territorial interaction and routes of migration, and down to the leg, the foot, the wing, the beak, the hoofprint and details of the skull.

Early European students of Native American languages did two things, as a rule. They collected lists of words – not sentences, just words – based in almost every case on Indo-European lists, leaving precious little room for any Native

American thinking. Some of them also tried to learn enough vocabulary and grammar to translate songs and stories they'd brought with them – Bible stories and hymns – *into* the languages they were learning. That is a far cry from the method of the naturalist. Naturalists are sometimes invasively curious, but in general they confront the world *organism to organism*. This method at its best involves considerable humility and respect as well as aggressive curiosity.

The blind collection of standardized wordlists continued into the twentieth century, but before the end of the nineteenth, another phase was clearly under way. It started with Silas Rand, Émile Petitot, Horatio Hale, Albert Samuel Gatschet and several others. Its most eminent exemplars are Edward Sapir and the man we call the father of American linguistics: Franz Boas.

An early symptom of the change was the passion for collecting artifacts and stories. The artifacts were often misunderstood, but they were usually real, while the stories were more often – especially in the early days – collected *in translation*. Millions of these artifacts sooner or later made their way into museums of natural history. That is not a place where nationalists, creationists, or other kinds of romantics generally like to see their art, but it might be where all art does belong once it ceases to be used. Putting an artifact in a museum is a lot like putting a mythteller's words in a book. Much is left behind, but what is kept becomes available for study. The artifact itself (and through the artifact, the artist) is free at last to teach whatever it or he or she can teach. The same is true for any literary text – any story, song, or history – transcribed in the original. It is then free to teach what it can teach. That is not the case for a story captured only in translation. When the original is lost, the story cannot teach what it once knew or what its author understood; all it can teach is what its hearer thought he heard.

If you study the form and structure of Native American artifacts – moccasins or parflèches, totem poles or baskets, let us say – the museum is often an excellent place to work. The displays may be too artful and intrusive, but once you get something removed from the case, you can usually see what it is. It's widely understood – though it wasn't always – that the custodians shouldn't tinker with the works. If you study the form and structure of Native American stories, you soon learn that interpreters, translators, editors, and explainers are very dangerous people. What you need is a clean transcription, a museum-quality text. For the early period – up to roughly 1880 – those are very scarce.

The postmodernist view is (1) that the place to look for meanings is in relations involving human beings and (2) that these relations may be altogether different for different human beings. That opinion is now very widely held – in amusement parks and universities, in the city and on the reserve. I take a different view myself. It seems to me that things have meaning before they are ever seen or touched by human beings, and that humans can *participate*, as trees can, in the meaning-making process. I think that humans can put meanings into things in such a way that they will stay where they are put, and other humans can come by, even centuries later, and draw those meanings out. Some meanings – if that is the right name for them – are highly individual; some are peculiar to certain communities and cultures; but there is a rich fund of meanings that is shared by the whole species, and a fund of meanings richer yet that is the common property not of the species but of the planet. Those are among the meanings we draw on, and the meanings *language* draws on, whenever we tell stories, say hello, carve masks and totem poles, or read and write literary texts. This is why some people read, and why some read so obsessively that they end up writing books and giving lectures about literary form.

I hold, in other words, that the pyramid of meanings is pointed at the human end, wide at the ecological end. There are others who hold the opposite.

IV

The first Europeans to collect Native North American oral literature were, as I've mentioned, generally content to collect translations. In fact, they *preferred* translations, because then they could control the moral tone. Henry Rowe Schoolcraft (1793–1864) and Silas Tertius Rand (1810–1889) represent the feeble best of that tradition. Rand was a missionary working with speakers of Micmac in Nova Scotia and Prince Edward Island; Schoolcraft, during his most productive years, was a government Indian agent in northern Michigan, heavily dependent on the skills of his Ojibwa-speaking wife, Jane Johnston. Both Schoolcraft and Rand were more concerned with changing native people than with recognizing who they really were, and both felt a similar moral duty not just to gather but to change the native stories they were told. The tales they collected resemble the engravings in contemporary travel books. Their method, like that of the engravers, allows for and encourages *correction* of anything that seems insufficiently picturesque or insufficiently refined to suit the gentle temperament of European readers.

Rand became fluent in Micmac and did take several texts in the original, but some of what he heard appears to have disturbed him. He retreated to the safety of translation. It used to be said that all his Micmac manuscripts had perished in the Wellesley College fire of 1914, but Peter Sanger has recently located a couple of these texts, and they are handsomely transcribed. (I find it hard to imagine Henry Schoolcraft doing anything so useful.)

The earliest Rand text we have – and it must be one of the first he ever took – is a complete story dictated by Susan Barss near Charlottetown in 1847. I'm far too ignorant of Micmac to render any informed judgement of Barss's skill with her native language, but after working slowly through the text, I can say that it is a gem in literal translation: more interesting and informative by far in my opinion than Rand's soft English adaptation, posthumously published in 1894. One of the reasons I prefer a faithful version, or an interlinear gloss, is of course that it allows me to come face to face at last with the story's form.

The forms of *sentences* and *words* are often beyond the reach of translation. Syntactic sequence – subject-object-verb, object-subject-verb, and so on – can be mimicked (Milton does it often), but a sequence that is natural in one language and unnatural in another is a hurdle the translator has to walk around. A greater hurdle yet is verb morphology. The Haida poet Ghandl, in one of his stories set in the Tsimshian country, uses the verb *skitghayghadaangghagwagaangang*. This means "flipping something roundish back and forth repeatedly with sticks" – playing something like lacrosse or field hockey, in other words. Except for the verb, the words in the sentence are simple enough, but their morphology too is beyond the reach of English. So is their sequence, which is subject-object-verb with postposition articles and particles where English would insist on prepositions. There is also a supplementary verb that wags the sentence like a tail that wags the dog:

Llanagaay ghaxhagaay
    huunaanda at
skitghayghadaangghagwagaangang
    wansuugang.

"Village-the children-the
    burl with
stick-round-across-flip-each-other-toward-repeatedly
    there-saying."

Or in something more like English,

The children of the village
    whacked a pine-burl puck
back and forth with sticks relentlessly,
    they tell me.

Above the sentence level, speakers are sometimes more adaptable, and form becomes increasingly translatable. Translating word for word, though people often claim to do it, is frequently impossible. Translating phrase for phrase is difficult enough. Translating sentence for sentence and episode for episode is more sustainable by far. But *all of these* are aspects of the form and structure of the story. At each level of language, form *includes* the forms of all the levels below it. This is as true in a Haida story as it is in a Periclean drama or Elizabethan sonnet.

v

To the best of my knowledge, that story which Susan Barss dictated to Silas Rand in Micmac in 1847 is the earliest surviving piece of indigenous oral literature from anywhere in Canada. Not long ago, I thought the earliest pieces we had were a short and wonderful Haida poem from roughly 1850 and some stories written down in rather abbreviated form by Petitot at Great Slave Lake in the 1860s. More discoveries might be made at any time – we might for instance find Petitot's missing manuscripts and fieldnotes, and we might find more of Rand's – but there is no reason whatever to think museum-quality transcriptions from before 1880 will ever be plentiful.

Boas started out only one rung above Schoolcraft, collecting artifacts and words in the original, but stories in translation. The big initial difference is that Boas knew the methods of natural history. His first field of serious study was botany; his PhD was in physics; geography was his first professional calling. Nineteenth-century physics was in essence still a naturalist's field, very different from physics as practiced a century later, and Boas's doctoral dissertation, *Beiträge zur Erkenntnis der Farbe des Wassers*, submitted at Kiel in 1881, is as much concerned with sensory psychology as it is with physical science.

Two events, it seems to me, jolted Boas out of his wordlist-and-translated-plot-summary phase. One was the publication, in 1888, of a volume of texts collected by Petitot. This book, *Traditions indiennes du Canada nord-ouest: textes originaux et traduction littérale*, has its defects, to be sure. The stories are truncated. Structural repetitions and variations, and formulaic openings and closings, have been cut. Yet Petitot wrote a lot of genuine Northern Athapaskan narrative, and a few bits of genuine Inuktitut and Cree. Boas's *Indianische Sagen* – essentially complete by 1889 though not published in book form until 1895 – is a longer work, and richer in some respects, but of all those tales – nearly 250 of them – Boas had transcribed no more than ten in the original (and for several of these, the transcriptions are incomplete).

The other crucial event, as I understand it, was Boas's meeting, in July 1890, with a quadrilingual oral poet named Q'eltí, who lived on Willapa Bay, near the mouth of the Columbia. Q'eltí was the first real Native American literary artist Boas met – or at any rate the first one that he recognized – and Q'eltí became the focus of Boas's work for most of the next decade.[4] The scholar spent three summers – 1890, 1891, and 1894 – taking dictation from the poet in three languages – Chehalis, Chinook, and Kathlamet – using a fourth, Chinook Jargon, to interpret and negotiate. Out of this came two bilingual books: *Chinook Texts* and *Kathlamet Texts*. The one substantial Chehalis text that resulted from this collaboration – only recently rediscovered, though it lay there in plain sight – is now being edited for publication and translated into English more than a century after its author's death. That is a reminder of how original texts retain their value.

In Q'eltí's work, form can be studied in full, because form is *present* in full. Q'eltí had a repertoire of themes which he was capable of weaving into story after story, the way a fluent speaker weaves morphemes into words, and words and phrases into sentence after sentence. He insisted on telling his stories in full, despite the slow pace of manual transcription, and Boas took them down in full. In fact, Boas insisted on taking some of them down in full *more than once*, in different years, so the versions could be compared. There you have a reason why, in my terms, Q'eltí is a major oral poet and Boas a major scholar of oral literature. Boas made no close analyses of the structures of these stories and developed no theories to account for or elucidate their form, but he got the goods. He paid Q'eltí immense respect by taking down the stories just the way their author told them, going over them morpheme by morpheme and phoneme by phoneme, correcting the transcription and making an English gloss – and then by publishing the results, so the rest of us, generations later, can come to them afresh and measure ourselves against them.

In 1917, in the opening pages of issue number one of the *International Journal of American Linguistics*, Boas announced a humanistic program, recognizing literature and linguistics as parts of a single field. He did not invent this point of view. It is present already in the work of his predecessors Jeremiah Curtin and Albert Gatschet, and his students John Swanton, Paul Radin and Edward Sapir, more perhaps than it is in the work of Boas himself; but in inaugurating IJAL, he openly embraced it. He admitted first of all that individual artistry is important in Native American oral literatures – or as he elected to put it, "Collectors of texts are fully aware that in the art of narrative there are artists and bunglers in every primitive tribe, as well as among ourselves."[5] For Boas, "there is practically no poetry that is not at the same time song." This is, in my terms, a very narrow view, but for him it marked a practical division between linguistics and musicology. "The literary aspects of this subject," he decreed, "fall entirely within the scope of a linguistic journal." I think we have to thank Q'eltí, more than anyone else, for teaching him that lesson.

VI

Petitot started taking texts in 1863. Boas began to do the same in 1886 and really converted to this approach in 1890. Between these dates many others contributed their share. The Cherokee writers Gatigwanasti, Inoli, and Ahyų'ini compiled manuscripts of ritual texts which they sold to the ethnographer James Mooney. An old warrior and tribal policeman named Miwákhą Yuhá (George Sword) and a precocious young student named Othéxi (George Bushotter) wrote significant texts in Lakhota. Dayodakane (Seth Newhouse) wrote a book in Mohawk. Skanawatii redictated even older written texts in Onondaga to Horatio Hale. Albert Gatschet, a genuine humanist, joined the Bureau of American Ethnology when it was formed in 1877 and within the year had transcribed texts in Klamath, Maliseet, Molala, Tonkawa, Tualatin, and Tunica. Nor did he stop there. In 1883, James Dorsey took dictation from Habazhudse in Osage and Jeremiah Curtin began to take dictation in Seneca from John Armstrong and Solomon O'Beal. In 1884, Washington Matthews started work with Hataałinééz in Navajo, and in 1888 John Napoleon Brinton Hewitt – another scholar of major importance – began to take dictation from his Tuscarora elders. In all of these texts, because we have them in the original, questions of form can be explored. But in the works of Q'eltí we have literary art, in which form doesn't just exist; it dances.

While he was working with Q'eltí in the 1890s, and for three full decades after, Boas trained younger scholars to do what he had started doing: transcribing texts, making linguistic photographs rather than bowdlerized pastels of works dictated by Native American mythtellers. That half century – 1890, let us say, to 1939 – was the great age of text transcription in North America. Linguists were taking dictation from Native American oral poets whose worlds, in many cases, had been demolished by colonization but who had grown up in touch with a precolonial tradition. Repeatedly the magic worked: an oral poet with a voice and a scholar with an ear found a chance to work together. Yet the scholars said little, as a rule, about the form and structure of the works they were transcribing, and the poets said still less.

Text transcription remains important work and sometimes still produces quite spectacular results. But the Second World War changed Native North America as much as it changed black and white America. With the end of the war, another phase begins.

Dell Hymes, who was born in 1927, came of age as the war was ending. In the 1950s, he began a close study of Kathlamet, using among other things the book of Kathlamet texts that Q'eltí had dictated to Boas more than fifty years before. Over time, he began to notice patterns in these texts. He began to map them out. He began to see that, while there were no acoustically rhyming quatrains, alexandrines, or elegiac couplets, there were equally clear patterns of a different kind: syntactic rhymes and recurrent shapes of incident and event.

Hymes expanded his study to other languages over the years and found that things kept happening in clusters – threes and fives in some languages, twos and fours in others. He called these patterns *measured* verse as distinct from *metered* verse. What he meant by that, he said, was that the patterns arose *among* lines, not *within* lines. "Line" may suggest something visible and written, but here a line is something audible and tactile – cerebrally tactile – rather than visual. A *line* in unmetered oral narrative is generally a *clause*: a unit of meaning and syntax, even though named for its visual form.

The term *measured verse*, like the word *line*, seems to me imperfect, but that is a terminological quibble. What matters is that Hymes discovered the narrative structures in Q'eltí's poems, and then discovered similar structures in the oral poems of many other Native American mythtellers. The study of these structures has come to be called *ethnopoetics* – again perhaps an unfortunate term, but one we are also probably stuck with.[6]

Hymes's discovery looked like the great breakthrough in Native American language and literature studies: the answer to Alfred Kroeber and many others who had thought the stories "formless." But the breakthrough didn't stop there. Hymes himself, his wife Virginia, William Labov and others began to understand that *everyone* tells stories in this way. Inner-city children, English nannies, traveling salesmen, Africans and Fijians, Glaswegians and Sahaptins, Poles and Indonesians talk in patterns – very different from the patterns in which we're taught to write – and they do this most reliably when invited to tell a story.

Does this mean everybody is an oral poet? Yes, it does. It does *not* mean we are all *great* oral poets. It suggests, as I said before, that stories are part of the natural flora and fauna – and like birds' nests, spiders' webs, scallop shells, and snake skins, they have form. In fact, they *are* form. It also goes a long way toward proving Hymes's contention that the sentence is not the upper limit of language.

As of the year 2000, more than forty other scholars, inspired by Hymes's example, had contributed to this investigation, and narrative texts in more than sixty Native American languages had been successfully subjected to this kind of formal analysis. This has taught us a great deal about Native American oral literature. When the results are more widely digested, we will see that it has also taught us a great deal about poetry and literature as a whole.

Now and then I meet a linguist who thinks that poetics is to linguistics as astrology is to astronomy. Hymes's work suggests to me that if linguists and literary critics both raised their gaze a little, they would see that their fields are actually one and the same, though they habitually dwell on different portions of the spectrum. No one knew this better than Edward Sapir.

It might be useful at this point to try to distinguish two related concepts: structure and pattern. Patterns are produced by structures, and pattern is often what we see when we are looking at a structure – a maple in winter, a fir tree in summer, basketwork, the weave of a piece of cloth, construction scaffolding, the framework of a building before it gets its skin.

Other patterns are not structural in this sense. The patterns of vinestocks in a vineyard, trees in an orchard, checkers on a checkerboard, and wind on water are examples. The pattern there is overlaid: produced by habits, rules, appetites, or forces extrinsic, not intrinsic, to the thing.

It isn't hard to separate a pattern from its structure. We can copy a basketwork pattern in clay, etch the image of a palm frond into glass or emboss the texture of a hand mold into smooth, machine-made paper, but the pattern which revealed an inner truth about the basket or the palm leaves or the hand-made paper doesn't bring the structure with it. Such a pattern tells us little or nothing of the structure of the clay or glass or dandyrolled paper to which it's been transferred. It's also easy to make a pattern that has little or no structural foundation – and all too easy to derive the imaginary structure implied by such a pattern. Exercises of that kind – frequent enough in the study of both literature and language – have given the movement known as structural-*ism* a bad name.

In metered verse – Arabic and Chinese as well as Greek and English verse – the reigning pattern is acoustic, and the prosody is audible to most human beings, including those who do not know the language. Students of meter tend to keep their focus tight, and the largest prosodic unit they recognize is generally quite small: the line in stichic verse, the stanza in stanzaic verse. These units are usually somewhere between five and fifty syllables. In performance terms, that is somewhere between two and twenty seconds, though the poem might last for hours. While we could look for larger units, it is not clear why we should. The reason is that metrical patterns *usually* appear to be extrinsic or imposed, like the order in an orchard. Most of the time they are surface figurations, refracting, not reflecting, the semantic and noetic structure underneath.

In Greek strophic verse – the choral odes of Pindar and the

playwrights – the metrical fabric is enlarged. The prosodic units here are often larger – up to a couple of hundred syllables – and the number of repetitions is always few. But whether the verse is in strophes, stanzas, or lines, sound and sense are largely separate. This does not mean poets can't or don't bring them together. Poets do that all the time, and people notice when it happens. Sound and sense are fundamentally distinct, both in language and in verse, and that is why we notice and enjoy it when they momentarily fuse.

There is a tendency as well, in Indo-European poetry, for the sense to separate from itself, or from the lexicon. Then we get a layer of figured language simultaneous with but semi-independent of the layer of plain sense. This more than anything else gives poetry in Europe – in Plato's time and ours – its bright but not untarnished reputation, as language one can love but not quite trust.

The patterns in Q'eltí's poems are patterns of meaning, patterns of thought, that manifest themselves as patterned incidents or events. You will certainly hear sounds when these patterns are performed; you will hear the poet speak. But you will hear very little of the pattern in the sound itself; you have to hear it in the sense, which means you have to learn the language. The patterns are semantic and noetic.

Unlike the surface patterns known as meter or verse, the noetic patterns encountered in oral narrative tend to repeat at varying scales. You may have, for example, a story in five acts or movements, in which each act consists of three or five scenes, and each scene of three or five subscenes, and each of these subscenes will unfold in statements patterned in threes or fives. The structures are *fractal* and *cladistic*, meaning that they branch and branch again in consistent, predictable ways. That's another clue that they are natural, not artificial patterns: meaning nobody had to invent or consciously copy them. They are part of what one learns when one acquires a language fully and by natural, not artificial means.

Where do these structures come from? I don't know how to answer such a question except to say that the most basic narrative forms, like Platonic solids and crystal lattices, come from the possible working its way through the actual. The narrative seeds of very complex stories can be found in the simplest of sentences. "He died" is a story in itself, told in two essential elements, a subject and a predicate. "She left him" is a story told in three. "She killed him and ran" is a story told in four simple elements. "She left him and took the children" is a story told in five – and like many pentamerous statements found in oral narratives, it is built as three plus two. Single-element statements are quite possible, though rare; and if we wished to, we could certainly frame statements with more elements – nine, say, or thirteen. Two, three, four and five are the common numbers because, as a rule, they are enough.

Is it significant that the number four keeps cropping up in Algonquian languages and the number five in Haida and Chinookan? It depends what you mean by significant. I don't suppose these numbers mean anything more – or anything less – than the structural numbers of plants. Binary structures predominate in the grasses, ternary structures in the lily and iris families. Plants in the mustard and evening primrose families are structured in fours; those in the rose, pea, phlox and harebell families are in fives. What look like six-part structures in the irises and lilies turn out to be ternary structures in pairs. Simple integers, again, seem quite enough to do a very complex job, but the numerical structures are easy to see in some plant families, more difficult in others, and so it has proven with oral narrative.

"Prosody rhymes with cosmology," says my colleague Dennis Lee.[7] I would only like to add that it rhymes with crystallography, botany, and zoology on the way. Is that a surprise? Language is no more unnatural than the hair on your head or the limbs on the trees. Like laurel leaves and hair, it can be combed, teased and braided in artful or just artificial ways, but combed or not, language has a sophisticated morphology that it shares with the rest of the world – and so do the stories we use it to tell.

VII

Broadly speaking, the external patterns of metrical verse are associated with song, and with *speech under the influence of song*, while more internal, branching, and fractal structures are associated with story, and with *speech under the influence of story* – speech propelled by some kind of narrative impulse. If it is not tautological to say so, these different modes of speech, which are global in distribution and have been with us a long time, appear to be the hallmarks of two elemental conceptual modes: *lyric* and *mythic*. I wonder if there are other, equally elemental, ways to think out loud.

Plainly not everything metered is lyric; not everything fractally structured is mythic. Literature, like physics, is more complex and various than that. Sung narrative – oral epic and ballad – which thrived in neolithic cultures from ancient Greece and India to Africa and Japan, and may have been present in ancient Mexico and Peru – appears to draw upon both modes. So does lyric drama. So does lyric prose. And who's to say that spoken oral narrative cannot be just as lyrical as any lyric prose? But the analytic structures that thrive in *expository* prose seem determined to be *neither* lyric nor mythic. (Perhaps, then, analytic structures represent another basic mode. If so, it is a mode that has so far only been identified in literate societies. And since the last of the world's truly oral cultures have been annihilated during my lifetime, hypotheses concerning them are now very difficult to test.)

When I speak of phonological patterns as external or surface patterns, I do not mean "superficial" in any evaluative sense. Verse *can* be superficial, like anything else, but there is nothing inherently superficial in singing while you think.

I think the difference is more like that between lake and river water. The turbulence you see in flowing water may look chaotic at first. Watch it closely and you'll see it's highly ordered, and the order it possesses (or the order it's possessed by) arises from inside and underneath, like the structures that occur in oral narrative. Lake water, however, answers the wind with structures that belong, in a sense, to neither wind nor water. This metaphor rests on the cheerful assumption that language is like water, that what-is is like the rock beneath the water, and that the heartbeat, music, speech, and maybe the entire social architecture of those who speak the language is like wind across the water. When the river is flat it responds to the wind in much the way a lake does (this is how epic resembles lyric), but when the fall of the river is steep, the breeze has very little discernible effect.

Many examples of highly accomplished oral narrative are preserved in Native American languages, while an enormous body of lyric and narrative verse, and of literary prose, has been preserved from Asia and Europe. This gives the impression that cladistic, fractal literary structures are typical of Native American cultures while prose and verse (*metered* verse, in Hymes's terms) are typical of Asia and of Europe. This seems to be the fruit of historical accident. There is no good evidence yet, so far as I'm aware, that it represents any linguistic difference. (Still less is it connected in any way with the superficial genetic distinctions known as "race.") Lyric structures, lyric prosodies, are found worldwide – in Native America just as in

Europe.[8] Story structures – prosodies of meaning – are global phenomena too. But under given cultural conditions, some kinds of structures and not others become primary bearers of serious thought and armatures of major works of literature.

The oral literatures of paleolithic and mesolithic Europe are lost. If we had good examples of oral narrative from the same cultures that left us the great paintings of Chauvet, Lascaux, and Altamira, we might be able to draw a few meaningful comparisons between European and Native American literary art. As it is, there is no extant European literature *in the genre of spoken oral narrative* that measures up to the greatest extant examples of Native American mythtelling.

We have important works of literature *written* in Native American languages dating back to the 1550s, but all of these are isolated works. A genuine reading public is only now beginning to develop, and only in a few indigenous languages – Inuktitut and Nahuatl, for instance. It would be nice to know how the indigenous literatures of the Americas might have changed if Mesoamerican hieroglyphs had developed into syllabic or alphabetic scripts and spread throughout the hemisphere without European intervention. If that had happened, we could compare the written literatures of the Americas with those of Asia and Europe. But so far as I know, we can't go back and rerun the experiment.

We might have a little more basis for comparison where neolithic literature is concerned. The neolithic city states of the Mississippi Valley perished before Europeans and their writing systems came to North America, and the neolithic empires in Mexico and Peru were destroyed before much could be learned, but we have some very impressive salvaged texts. These can be read against early European works – the Homeric hymns and the poems of Hesiod, for example. What we don't seem to have is any reliable information on how Precolumbian oral literature and music fit together. That link was crucial to the oral literatures of early agricultural societies in Europe, Asia and Africa. It was probably crucial to Aztec, Mayan, Otomí, and Incan oral literatures as well.

VIII

If the patterns and structures of oral narrative are so wide-spread, why didn't anyone see them long ago? I'm sure that people did – but most of those who saw them evidently felt no need to write a book or give a lecture on the subject.

Jerome, the patron saint of translators, who was born in Slovenia about 340 CE and died in Bethlehem about the year 420, made what might be called an ethnopoetic translation of the Bible. In doing so, he broke the so-called "prose" texts of the prophets into lines. The preface he attached to his transla-tion of Isaiah tells us something about what he had in mind:

Nemo cum prophetas versibus viderit esse descriptos metro eos aesti-met apud Hebraeos ligari, et aliquid simile habere de Psalmis, vel operibus Salomonis; sed quod in Demosthene et Tullio solet fieri, ut PER COLA SCRIBANTUR ET COMMATA, qui utique prosa, et non versibus conscripserunt: nos quoque utilitati legentium providentes, interpretationem novam, novo scribendi genere distinximus.[9]

No one, seeing turned lines in the books of the prophets, should con-clude that these texts are metrically structured in the Hebrew, or are in some way comparable to the Psalms or the works of Solomon. In fact – as is the custom with Demosthenes and Cicero – they are COMPOSED BY RHYTHMIC CLAUSE AND PHRASE, and so as prose, and not arranged on the page as verses. I, however, being certain *it would benefit my readers, have divided up the text to make a new translation newly ordered on the page.*

The key phrase here is *per cola … et commata*. To a gardener this would mean *by limbs and branches*; to a charioteer it would mean *by laps and stretches*; to a grammarian it would mean *by clauses and phrases* or, more pedantically, *by main clauses and subclauses*. There are other quite legitimate interpretations, befitting other contexts, but it seems to me the sense of limbs and joints or limbs and branches underlies them all.

Jerome chose to punctuate the text in a highly visible (and accordingly visceral) way, not by inserting the small, economical *positurae* and *virgulae* of the medieval scribe but by breaking it up into units of sense – the limbs and branches of meaning – and treating each such unit as a line. This takes more vellum and is therefore not a change that could be casually introduced. Some of Jerome's later prefaces (to Ezekiel, for instance) prove he'd met resistance, but the prophetic and poetic books of the Vulgate are printed with his linebreaks to this day. His successor Cassiodorus – concerned, like Jerome, with learning to read inherited texts and teaching others to do the same – claims that good punctuation is as helpful to readers as the most lucid of commentaries.[10]

There is a sense in which Hymes and his followers are doing just what Jerome and Cassiodorus were doing: punctuating texts to bring their meaning to the fore. But in working with fractally structured texts, one has to punctuate on a number of levels at once. It's not enough to lop and stack the branches; you have to map the tree. This is feasible in part because the texts Hymes and the rest of us work with have usually come direct from the speakers. They've been transcribed, but they usually haven't passed, like the Hebrew scriptures, through a team of scribal editors trying to meld a group of authors and traditions into one.[11]

Jerome did not invent the simple notion of treating a clause as a visible line. Sumerian scribes used such a form for the *Epic of Gilgamesh* and other texts several thousand years before Jerome was born – and long before the Hebrew prophets made the poems Jerome was turning into Latin.[12] The scribes of Alexandria owed some of their conventions and inventions to the scribes of Egypt and Sumeria; Jerome inherited in turn from the scribes of Alexandria and Rome. Centuries later in New Jersey, Walt Whitman saw editions of the Vulgate and based his sense of lineation partly on Jerome's. Ezra Pound and William Carlos Williams learned some things from Whitman. Dell Hymes and his college roommate, Gary Snyder, learned from Pound and Williams in their turn. The notation of the linebreak and the line, as a visible image of thought and speech, is apparently as old as script itself: much older than the spaces between words. But the spatial disposition of a written text may tell us much or tell us nothing about what goes on inside. Hymes's lineation, like Jerome's, is analytic.

Some centuries after Jerome, Hebrew scholars also started to *articulate* the Torah in this sense: to punctuate the written text with Masoretic accents.[13] A sixteenth-century Jewish layman, Azariah dei Rossi of Mantua and Ferrara, reflected on this process in an essay on the form of Hebrew sacred poetry. It is a short work, forming part of the last chapter of his long (actually overlong) book known as ספר מאור עינים, *Sefer maʾor ʿênayim*, "The Book of the Light of the Eyes," published in Mantua in 1573.[14] The poetry found in the Hebrew scriptures, Azariah says, is cast in a kind of verse that has nothing to do with counting syllables; it has to do instead with מספר הענינים [*mispar haʿinyanim*], the prosody of *concepts* or of *meanings*. This, so far as I know, is the first published mention of *noetic prosody* – a term I once mistakenly believed I had originated myself, while searching for alternatives to Hymes's "measured verse."

Outsiders, if I may say so, have been of some importance in the history of learning – partly because outsiders are free to think for themselves and partly because thinking, if it gets to be a habit, makes outsiders of insiders. The Native American oral poets who are often regarded by distant outsiders as semi-official spokesmen for the cultural groups into which they were born are themselves very frequently outsiders – visionaries, dreamers, and social or physical misfits. The two greatest Haida poets on record, Skaay and Ghandl, are powerful examples. And though scholarship depends on a sense of community, scholars are not by any means exempt from the centrifugal force of learning. Q'ix̌itasu' (George Hunt), Francis La Flesche, William Beynon, Archie Phinney, and other Native North American linguists and anthropologists all experienced the centrifugal as well as centripetal effects of education and found themselves marginalized in two (sometimes three) cultures at once. That is something they might have discussed with Azariah dei Rossi.

As a Jew in Renaissance Europe, Azariah was always both outsider and insider, but his devotion to Jewish tradition pushed him out much farther yet. His learned book was condemned as heterodox by Jewish leaders in Italy. After two years as an outcast within his own community, he attempted to appease the conservative rabbis by issuing, at considerable expense, a censored third edition.

Within the Jewish tradition, Azariah was well and thoroughly ignored until Joanna Weinberg began, not long ago, to call attention to his work. But on the margins of that tradition, his description of Hebrew traditional verse has had considerable impact.

Robert Lowth, an eighteenth-century English scholar of biblical Hebrew, read Azariah's essay on prosody in a Latin translation made in the 1650s by Johann Buxtorf Jr. That is why, in the preface to his own translation of Isaiah, Lowth speaks of versification based on "the rhythmus of things" and "the rhythmus of propositions." In Buxtorf's Latin version, עניין [ʿinyan], which means *meaning* or *concept* or *matter-at-issue*, is translated *res*, "thing." The plural of עניין [ʿinyan] is עניינים [ʿinyanim]. Azariah's key phrase, מספר העניינים [mispar haʿinyanim], is Lowth's "rhythmus of things or propositions."

Linguists and poets alike can take some pleasure, by the way, in the etymology of מספר, *mispar*, the Hebrew word for prosody. Its root is the Hebrew verb which corresponds to Greek λέγειν (*légein*, as in λόγος): *to say* or *tell* or *count*. That verb in Hebrew is ספר, *sapir*.

Early Hebrew verse is scanned, as Azariah says, by counting עניינים [ʿinyanim] – meanings or concepts – instead of syllables or stresses. In practice, these ʿinyanim are mostly nouns and verbs: the *semantically* stressed or heavy parts of a statement. This makes it fairly easy to mimic the formal character of early Hebrew verse in Latin or English translation, whereas mimicking the character of early Greek or Latin verse, or of classical Arabic verse (which like classical Greek is quantitative), is notoriously difficult in English. Semantic meter operates at a layer of language that is closer to conceptual and cognitive foundations. Quantitative and qualitative meters operate nearer the phonological surface.

There is little doubt that early Hebrew poets were conscious of these matters, but they have left us no treatise on the subject. In the early Christian era, Jewish and Christian scholars alike saw that something was happening, and several tried to describe it – but in terms better suited to Greek than to Hebrew. Philo, Josephus, Origen, and Jerome all suggested at one time or another that parts of the Old Testament had a form that corresponded to the Greek dactylic hexameter.[15] Azariah read all these authorities and saw past their mistake.

Hymes's analyses also depend on counting semantic loci, though they usually begin not by counting nouns and verbs but by counting verbs alone. Each main verb is the nucleus of a clause, or a clause in itself; each clause or subclause, as a rule, is treated as a line; and lines, when they're identified this way, are found to constitute a structure and its pattern, not only in Native American oral literature but wherever oral narratives are told.

This makes it sound extremely simple; it is not. There are just as many subtleties involved in scanning Native American narrative as there are in scanning John Donne's verse or the choral odes of Aiskhylos' plays. But there is a simple idea here, which is that as prosody comes to the surface of language, it leaves the realm of meaning and structure behind and enters the realm of phonology. In studying the form of Native American oral narratives, we follow it back down. I think this means that the definition of *prosody*, both in the poet's sense and the linguist's sense, needs to be enlarged.

There is also a complication. It is that meanings can be lifted out of structures and ordered into surface patterns too. *Semantic weight* can become a simple prosodic feature just like syllable length or stress, which only operate within a small domain. When Azariah coined the phrase *prosody of concepts*, he was not describing Hebrew oral narrative; he was analyzing the versification of early Hebrew prophecy and lyric. He was confronting simple patterns, in which semantically weighted words occur in little clusters – twos or threes – which are grouped in turn in twos or threes or fours. He described these clusters, quite correctly, as prosodic feet, and the groups they form as verses (prosodic lines). Yet the elemental units in these feet are semantic, not acoustic.

That is a different kind of noetic prosody than Hymes discovered in the narratives of Qʼeltí, and it is different from what Hymes and his colleagues have been finding in oral narratives worldwide. The prosody that Azariah found in early Hebrew is (to borrow Hymes's terms again) a relationship *within* lines, not *among* lines. It is a pattern, not a structure: metrical, imposed, and so non-fractal.

IX

Another of Hymes's farflung predecessors – one better known to linguists than Azariah or even Jerome – is the Russian Vladimir Propp. In Leningrad in 1928, Propp published the intriguing little book he called Морфология сказки [Morfologiya skazki], *The Morphology of the Tale*. After its first translation into English, in 1958, it attracted wide interest. Claude Lévi-Strauss read it as an early landmark of structural analysis. Wayne O'Neil, one of my teachers at MIT, read it as proof that transformational grammar could as well apply to stories as to sentences.[16] I like to think of it myself as yet another instance of the natural historian's approach to literary form.

Propp learned the word *morphology* from Goethe, who in 1817 published what I think is the first work ever written on plant and animal morphology. Three long and prominent quotations from Goethe's study of morphology appear as epigraphs in all Russian editions of Propp's book (and are missing, for some reason, from every edition of the English translation).

In 1926, while Propp was still busy writing his book, another careful reader of Goethe, the historian Johan Huizinga, delivered a public lecture at the University of Leiden. The lecture was called *De Taak der cultuurgeschiedenis*, "The Task of Cultural History." One of the basic principles enunciated there is this:

De cultuurgeschiedenis vindt haar voornaamste taak in het *morphologisch* begrijpen en beschrijven der berschavingen in haar bijzonder en daadwekelijk verloop.[17]

The chief task of cultural history is the morphological understanding and description of the actual, specific course of civilizations.

Here, it seems, we have a man willing to approach not merely literature but the whole of human culture as a naturalist might: willing to assume that human history unfolds like natural history, through forms that can be grasped whole if studied in detail – but which are lived out in any case, like every plant and animal morphology, whether anybody studies them or not. (Huizinga's later application to human history of certain crucial medical concepts – infection, contagion, and the like – rests securely on this base.)

Morphology means the study of form and structure. Μορφή [*morphē*] is shape or form; it is also the virtue or goodness of form; in other words, shapeliness, beauty. Σοὶ δ' ἔπι μὲν μορφή ἐπέων, Alkinoös says to Odysseus: "A handsomeness [μορφή] of speech is on you." Then he explains what he means: μῦθον δ' ὡς ὅτ' ἀοιδὸς ἐπισταμένως κατέλεξας: "You tell a story with a minstrel's skill." (That predicate is worth a closer look: μῦθον κατέλεξας: "You *tell your way across* a myth, a story.") Μορφή is also tied to the verb μορφάζω [*morpházō*], which means to make a sign, to gesture, to gesticulate, to mime. It means to reach for morphemes through bodily hieroglyphics, eschewing the organic high technology of speech. Implicit in this web of etymologies is an assumption or an article of faith: a patterned set of morphemes that the words are miming while they speak. It is that *shape, beauty*, and *meaning* are one and the same or inseparably linked. This identity or marriage is μορφή.

236

Linguists generally marry the term *morphology* to the form and structure of *words*, and I wonder if this is incongruous. In biology, the same term usually implies, first of all, a study of the form and structure of *whole organisms*. It extends from there, of course, to mapping out the structure (and savoring the *shapeliness*, remember) of their parts. Are plants and animals more like words or more like stories? Before you answer that, Huizinga has something else to tell us: "The organism of history," he says, "if there is one, lies outside human psychology."[18] I don't know whether Huizinga would agree, but my hunch is that the organism of literature lies for the most part outside human psychology too. History and literature tell us a great deal about the human mind – not because *they* are inside *it* but rather because *it* is inside *them*.

The leaps I mentioned earlier – those moments in which language transcends its speakers as well as itself – are, I think, the moments in which the mind can see itself in the form, and so can be, momentarily at least, inside history or literature and outside both at the same time. In certain kinds of stories, as in certain kinds of circuses, such leaps are part of the routine. In others, they are unexpected and sometimes unwelcome, like an acrobat in a drawing room or a poet at the annual general meeting.

The title of Propp's book, Морфология сказки, "the morphology of the story (or the tale)," has routinely been translated into English as "the morphology of the *folktale*." The Russian title is broader than that, but Propp himself is careful to explain that its actual focus is narrower. It is a morphological study of one particular species of tale, the волшебная сказка [*volshebnaya skazka*], the Russian wondertale. Волшебство [*volshebstvo*] is the Russian word for *magic*. What Propp purported to have made is a morphology of how indigenous Russian storytellers portray the relation between magic and human affairs. A morphology, in other words, of one particular kind of extended metaphor.

Skeptics look at Native American oral poetry and ask, "If this is literature, where are the figures of speech, the fine Homeric similes, the metaphors, the tropes?" Metaphor, as Paul Ricœur reminds us, is an informative kind of *deviant predication*. (The informative kind of deviant *nomination* is called *metonymy*.) But in Native American narrative, the metaphors, the deviant predications, are usually stated so directly, with so little rhetorical fanfare, that readers trained on European literature don't notice them as literary figures. They are perfectly embedded in the narrative. They are what I like to call *declarative* metaphors. Take them out and there is not only no poetry left; there is no narrative either. So I don't suppose these metaphors *are* literary *figures*. I suppose they are structural components, each one syntactically related to the rest of the components of the poem where they appear.

Look where the morn in russet mantle clad / peeps o'er the brow of yon high eastern hill is a different sort of metaphor, clad in the russet mantle of elaborated diction. What it means – at least in one sense of that word – is "Look, the sun is rising." Now *that* is a real metaphor: the sun is *rising!* Go to the Department of Astronomy and Physics, where the mythtellers congregate these days, and they will tell you that the sun is doing nothing of the sort. You are imputing rising to the sun, committing deviant predication: speaking in metaphor. So let's try again to strip the metaphor away. Let's reduce those two pentameters to one monosyllable: *Sun!* Now we have a pure, true, 24-carat metaphor. We haven't spoken any predicate out loud, and yet a predicate is there. *Sun!* – and Bloomfield will confirm this – is a sentence. What the sentence *Sun!* means is *The sun is up; the sun can now be seen; the sun's presence is demonstrating itself in* its *wonderful, irrefutable way. The universe is glowing; we are basking in its light. Look where the morn in russet mantle clad....* And that's a metaphor as powerful as any we will get.

How can it be a metaphor when it's a monosyllabic acknowledgement of matter-of-fact reality? By *being exactly that.* When you come down to elemental things – earth, air, fire, water, wind, sun, moon, a flake of lichen on the rock, a scrap of birdsong, Orion in the clear, winter sky – you find that metaphor – or poetry, to call it by its other name – is a fundamental property of things. You find that *things are deviant predicates of themselves.*

A myth is (among other things) a story that allows you or propels you to see that this is so: one that acts out, demonstrates, explores, and in its own way even "proves" the truth of a deviant predication – and suggests, perhaps, the deviance of predication itself. It is a story reaching out beyond the safe and ordered world into the metaphoric, metamorphic strangeness that inheres in simple acts and things. It's a story that lets reality shine.

I don't suppose a myth can do that without form, but I am sure that form alone is never enough to turn the trick. At any rate, no one has yet shown that the morphology of Native American myths is necessarily much different from that of oral histories or autobiographical tales. To the contrary, mythification seems to be a universal process, in oral and written literatures alike. That is to say, as stories are told, they seem to gravitate toward forms familiar in the myths. This does not guarantee they will acquire mythic resonance. You can lead a story to form, but I don't believe you can, by formal means, make it burst into flower or rise up and dance.

So a story has a form, in something like the way that a sonata or a sentence has a form. It could, like a sentence or sonata, be *well-formed* and still say nothing of evident value, or it could be poorly formed and still say quite a lot.[19] I know which one I'd choose. But now and then, as connoisseurs of stories, sonatas, or sentences, we might just ask for everything at once: stories or sonatas that are not only beautifully formed and say wonderful things, but those in which the form and content egg each other on. That is what happens in the best classical Haida and Navajo texts I have studied, and in the stories that Q'eltí dictated to Boas in Kathlamet and Shoalwater Chinook.

x

The British linguist Michael Halliday has been interested primarily in European languages, but he is one of the few linguists who have focused, in the past half century, on larger units, not on microparticles. He likes to call these larger units "texts," as if they were normally written. For Halliday, however,

> A text is … a unit of language in use [and] not a grammatical unit…. A text is not something that is like a sentence, only bigger; it is something that differs from a sentence in kind…. A text is best regarded as a SEMANTIC unit: a unit not of form but of meaning…. A text does not CONSIST of sentences; it is REALIZED BY, or encoded in, sentences.[20]

This is an invitation to pursue the sociology of language, not to study language or literature itself. English teachers and linguists may adore grammatical units, but for the actual users of language – storytellers, poets, and ordinary speakers – and for linguists and English teachers too, when they are trying to get a point across – all units of language are units of language in use.

I concede that some texts – in the modern world, many texts – differ in kind from a sentence. Many things that pass for texts nowadays are accumulations, like piles of lumber. A sentence is something *grown* or something *built* or something *found*, like a tree or a nest or a house. The texts that interest me most – those I call works of literature – are indeed, in this sense, like a sentence, only bigger. They resemble trees and forests. This also brings us back to a sociological frontier. Some people think of forests as simply accumulations of trees; others know the forest is a fabric and a structure in itself, a form that other forms create. A story is a story by virtue of the fact that it has form as well as meaning – and in the literary world, we like to claim that form and meaning spring from a single root, like space and time in physics.

Can anything have form and not have meaning? The suggestion seems absurd – but urban life is full of such absurdities. Do they prove the case? I guess they do – in the same way that ghost stories and haunted houses prove the existence of ghosts.

Can anything have meaning and be formless? I don't expect to prove, one by one, that every text that has a meaning has a form, but Propp, Hymes and others have begun this endless task, with quite spectacular results.

Texts are units of form, as sentences are – and sentences, like texts, have long been understood as units of meaning. More than forty years ago, in an Alberta country school, I heard a teacher say, "a sentence is a combination of words expressing a complete thought." I don't know where or when or how she might have learned this definition – and I was not then concerned enough to ask – but I remember the delight with which, at least a decade later, I stumbled onto the real source. I hope she knew that she held one end of a thread stretching back from that Alberta country school to the country schools of early Greece.

Dionysios the Thracian was a school teacher in Rhodes in the second century BCE. His short grammatical handbook,

Τέχνη γραμματική [*Tékhnē grammatikḗ*], which is still widely
read by students of Greek, includes the following passage: λέξις
ἐστὶ μέρος ἐλάχιστον τοῦ κατὰ σύνταξιν λόγου. λόγος δέ ἐστι
... λέξεως σύνθεσις διάνοιαν αὐτοτελῆ δηλοῦσα. "A word is the
smallest rearrangeable part of a sentence, and a sentence is ... a
gathering of words disclosing a self-sufficient thought."

The word used here for *word* is λέξις [*léxis*], the word for
arrangement of parts is σύνταξις [*sýntaxis*], and the word for *sentence* is λόγος [*lógos*]. This is good classical usage. Throughout
De Interpretatione, λόγος is the word that Aristotle likewise uses
to mean *sentence*. His own definition is this: λόγος δέ ἐστι φωνὴ
σημαντική, ἧς τῶν μερῶν τι σημαντικόν ἐστι κεχωρισμένον,
ὡς φάσις ἀλλ' οὐχ ὡς κατάφασις: "A sentence is a meaningful
utterance [*phōnḕ sēmantikḗ*], the parts of which are separately
meaningful, as signs though not as propositions."[21]

That final phrase is worth a closer look. *As signs though not
as propositions* is a tolerable rendering of the sense, but it misses
something vivid in the Greek: ὡς φάσις ἀλλ' οὐχ ὡς κατάφασις: "as *phásis* but not as *katáphasis*." This is to say, a solitary
word can *send a signal* but cannot, like a sentence, *send it back*;
it can't *converse*. A word proffers a meaning, but unless it is a
sentence in itself, it cannot give that meaning any confirma-
tion or response.

That, incidentally, is the sort of thing I think T.S. Eliot had
in mind when he pegged Aristotle as "a great writer."[22] Even
among dedicated classicists, this was not a popular view when
Eliot voiced it in 1920. It is equally unpopular today, but it
seems to me entirely correct – and I think that one could say
the same thing, for pretty much the same reasons, of Edward
Sapir. Neither was anything close to a great poet, but their
relationship to poetry was crucial to their writing and their
thinking. Both understood that reading and writing poetry is
a normal and healthy thing for busy humans to do.

Definitions are practical things, either imperfect or tauto-logical, but those two definitions of the sentence – Dionysios the Thracian's and Aristotle's – share a significant virtue: they accept the interdependence of form and meaning. Both in their way agree that a sentence is *something like a story only smaller*. It is a unit of language in use. It exists because it has something to tell, and that something is itself. The form has meaning and the meaning has form; that's how and why it works.

What about that other famous statement on the *lógos*, the opening lines of the gospel of John? Ἐν ἀρχῇ ἦν ὁ λόγος, καὶ ὁ λόγος ἦν πρὸς τὸν θεόν, καὶ θεὸς ἦν ὁ λόγος…. An Aristotelian or Dionysian reading of this passage would suggest a new translation: *In the beginning was the sentence, and the subject of the sentence was the god, and the sentence was a god*…. In Greek as in English, to get the word, you have to hear the story, and the sentence is the bridge between the two.

Sapir's view of the sentence, formulated as much from Na-tive American as from European models, is thoroughly Aristo-telian too – and at the same time thoroughly Sapirian:

The sentence is the logical counterpart of the complete thought only if it be felt as made up of the radical and grammatical elements that lurk in the recesses of its words. It is the psychological counterpart of experience, of art, when it is felt, as indeed it normally is, as the finished play of word on word.[23]

This is more an *appreciation* of the sentence than it is a defin-ition (and all the better for that), but it reaches out, again, to larger as well as smaller units of language and suggests a root conception of the sentence as the molecule of narrative and logic.

Sapir's remarks on the sentence appear in his most widely known work, the book called *Language*, published in 1921. Twelve years later, Leonard Bloomfield published another book, twice as long, twice as methodical, not half as poetic, with precisely the same title. I have heard Sapir and Bloomfield described as the Plato and Aristotle of American linguistics – and perhaps there is something to the claim. Bloomfield, at any rate, loves to subdivide and parse, and does it well; Sapir takes much more obvious delight in making connections and spotting resemblances.

Bloomfield's discussion of sentence *types* is a model of its kind. The definition that comes with it, though, is narrow. For Bloomfield, the sentence is defined not by the satisfying way in which it integrates its parts, but by its lack of integration into anything beyond: a sentence is "an independent [linguistic] form, not included in any larger (complex) linguistic form."[24]

I would not like to stir up posthumous disagreements between Bloomfield and Sapir, nor disputes between their followers. They are two great humanist scholars in a field where not everyone remembers humanist values. But in defining the sentence as a wall which linguistics cannot leap, Bloomfield (inadvertently perhaps) defined linguistics as a science that cannot see past the sentence.

Not so very long ago, large numbers of biologists insisted that their proper field of study stopped with the individual organism. It was eventually remembered that organisms really do belong (and *must* belong) to their environment, that they function as environments in turn, and that changing their surroundings can be just as catastrophic as tampering directly with their body fluids and tissues. If, as I like to think, the proper parent science of linguistics is biology, then it might be good to do some ecological linguistics. This ought to mean not only looking beyond the sentence to the forest of the text where the sentence lives and breathes; it should also mean examining the structures of plants, texts, animals, and sentences side by side.

XI

Gesang ist Dasein, Rilke says.[25] "Singing is being." In Stephen Mitchell's fine translation, "Song is reality." That is why meaning, and meaningful statements, have prosody. It also, I think, explains why prosody takes many different forms.

In early Jain and Buddhist writings, the precious fiction of human identity is dismissed as an illusion masking a bundle of three quite separate parts. The parts are known in Sanskrit as *kāyavakcitta*: body, speech, and mind. (Later Buddhist thinkers sometimes added a fourth, *hrdhaya*, the heart, but the favorite number is three, and the bundle they form is called *triyoga*, the triple link. In Chinese it is 三家 *sānjiā*, the triple relation or triple house.) My hunch – speaking merely as a practitioner, not a theorist, of literature and language – is that the study of prosody ought to embrace the physiology and comparative anatomy of body, speech, and mind – or (in the interests of inclusiveness) of body, speech, and mind and heart.

This is neither to assert nor to deny that there is a *mental organ* of language – a problem I am not equipped to solve. But we could surely get closer to that question by refining the analogy. Is language artificial yet essential, like a parka in the cold? Intrinsic yet prosthetic, like an antler or a coxcomb? Integral yet finally expendable, like an eye, a leg, a hand? Quintessential and internal, like the lungs? Or is a language a distinct and symbiotic entity? If so, is its relation to its speakers parasitic, like a tapeworm's to its host? Commensal, like the link between the turtle-shell algae and the turtle? Superficially mutualistic, like the relation of horse and rider? Or profoundly mutualistic, like the marriage that occurs when an alga and a fungus coadapt to form a lichen?

A comparative anatomy of language would ask not only what forms language takes but how these forms arise from the underlying *appetite* or *aptitude* that language represents. Loco-motion, for example, is an aptitude manifested differently in snakes, fishes, gastropods, ungulates, and birds. Even within the class Mammalia, the aptitude for movement takes quite different forms in whales, bats, ruminants and humans. And even within the species Homo *sapiens*, language demonstrates amazing and insistent adaptability – finding its way through eyes, hands, arms, and upper body, for example, if the route through tongue and ear is blocked.

I find it easier, myself, to think of individual human languages as organ*isms* than of *language* in the abstract as an *organ*. But if languages are organisms, how do they propagate? Through their speakers, evidently – though not by the well-loved method that their speakers use to propagate themselves. From the perspective of us humans, language is exogenetic: part of culture rather than nature. But would that distinction hold from the perspective of languages themselves? My hypothesis is this: stories are the reproductive organs of languages. Where stories cease to be told, languages die, or have to be sustained by means that are patently artificial. If this is so, then the forms that stories take are as crucial in their way as the forms of flowers and fruits.

In a state of nature, where languages and literatures are oral, stories are almost always built of three- or four- or five-part structures. In botanists' terms, they are trimerous like irises and lilies, tetramerous like the fireweeds and crucifers, or pentamerous like the roses and mallows and pinks.

It is easy to sound like a simpleton while contemplating the prosodies of meaning that emerge out of the structures of oral narrative. You find yourself repeating simple integers over and over: two, three, four, five. This is a realm in which ten is a very large number – but linguists should find nothing strange in that. Linguists work in a world where phonemes are perceived to a large extent as contrastive pairs, where four or five levels of stress are all that a fluent speaker perceives, and where grammatical structures are very rarely more than six tiers deep. Yet good linguists, like good poets, good musicians, and good botanists, know that counting to five, or even to two, can get very complex. (The Buddhist in me wants to remind myself and you that counting to one is harder yet.)

But what are we counting? What are we counting when we scan a stanza of verse or a page of music, or map the structure of a story or a starfish or a pine? We are always counting two things at once, doing double-entry accounting. When you scan a passage composed in iambic pentameter, for instance, you count whatever comes. *Let me not to the marriage of true minds | admit impediments. Love is not love | which alters when it alteration finds....* You count that against the empty grid: *ta* DUM, *ta* DUM, *ta* DUM, *ta* DUM, *ta* DUM. Only the former is meaningful and interesting, but it is interesting in part *because* of the imperfect way it fits that empty shell. The same is true when counting beats in music, when counting leaves and veins or toes and teeth or other salient parts of a creature's anatomy, and when counting the loci of meanings in Native American oral narrative. You have in front of you a landscape – of xylem and phloem, tissue and bone, or sound and sense; and you have in your mind a simplified pattern. Neither one is the form itself. One is its ghost or its echo, the other its body. In the former it is obvious and perfect but not present. In the latter it is sensuous, irregular, and real. One is a memory, the other a fact. If you perceive the two together, you get a sense of depth, a sense of context and perspective, essential to experiencing literature as literature. Still you never touch the form itself. And never need to.

XII

The terms in common use for discussing the forms of Native American narrative – such terms as *line, scene, episode, prosody,* and *verse* – suggest that linguistic and literary reference points are everything we need to understand what we are doing. I don't believe that's so. It seems to me the numerical patterns, the prosodic structures, found in these narratives resemble time signatures in music and cladistic structures in biology far more than they resemble the metrical patterns typical of Indo-European verse. One way to express this is to say that we are mapping *the way the stories grow,* not *the surface they present.*

It used to be claimed that living creatures were expressions of the will of God – a beautiful idea; but it followed from this that species had no ecological interrelations and no phylogeny, no developmental history, that wasn't foreordained. It is still widely claimed that *literary* creatures – lyric and narrative statements, stories and songs – are expressions of the will of human beings, and that their forms are therefore mere expressions of human habit or human whim, allied with the habits and whims of the language being spoken. As Goethe understood, that point of view demeans the study of morphology, by denying its nontrivial results.

Why should this be true – or why should it be obvious – in the case of Native American narrative literature when it has long gone unnoticed among scholars deeply versed in European literatures?

The dominant genre of classical Native American oral literature is, as I mentioned earlier, myth. (This is true despite the fact that myth, like poetry, is more than just a literary genre.) Mythtelling stands at the opposite pole from that kind of literature or literary language which (as Roland Barthes says) *celebrates itself* and which is therefore likely to be lost (as Robert

Frost says) in translation. Myth celebrates the world and not itself. That, I think, is why it is attracted to literary forms (or why it *generates* literary forms) that echo in their way so many structures present elsewhere in the world; and that, I think, is why it is translatable.

This is not to say, with Lévi-Strauss, that "the mythical value of the myth is preserved even through the worst translation." The mythical value of the myth is, on the contrary, easy to lose, and mistranslation is always a danger. One of the easiest ways to mistranslate the telling of a myth is to obliterate or alter its literary form. And much is lost – the *value of value* is lost – if the myth is cut adrift from the literary value of its telling.

This kind of mistranslation can occur even within the domain of a single language.

One of the unsolved puzzles of Native Canadian literary history concerns a body of texts I mentioned earlier, transcribed in the 1860s and 1870s, in Dogrib, Chipewyan, Slavey, and Gwichin, by Father Émile Petitot. The question is, why do so many of these texts seem crippled in form? One explanation that has been suggested is the age of the narrators. Many of Petitot's stories came from adolescents, whose company he seems to have preferred. But others came from elders. And we know from the work of William Labov, Virginia Hymes and others, that children's stories, just like children's sentences, though they may lack certain kinds of sophistication, can be perfectly well formed.

Another possible explanation – more promising in my view – is that Petitot was transcribing *himself* instead of taking direct dictation from his sources. His purpose, after all, was to learn the languages so he could preach in them. Other missionary linguists, and some professional explorers, have done the same. Father Adrien-Gabriel Morice, who worked in northern British Columbia long enough that he claimed to speak his adopted language, Carrier, more fluently than he did his native French, described his own method as follows:

> I have a reliable Indian narrate to me as clearly as possible the whole of one myth (when this is not too long) in his native language. I then repeat as verbatim as I can what I have heard, subject to corrections when such may be necessary, and then I write down the whole in Indian. My last step is generally to read out my version in the hope of provoking further notices of inaccuracies.[26]

Knud Rasmussen, whose hugely enthusiastic yet oddly stunted versions of Inuktitut stories also raise unanswered questions about form and literary style, makes a similar boast and confession:

> Det er første Gang, der er nedskrevet Sagn hos disse Polareskimoer, og mit Princip under Arbejdet har været aldrig at gengive nogen Fortælling før jeg selv havde lært den og fortalt den. Derved tilegnede jeg mig hele Fremstillingsformen; og jeg har bestræbt mig for saa vidt muligt at give ordrette Oversættelser.[27]

> This is the first time the legends of the Polar Eskimo have been recorded, and it has been my working principle never to reproduce any tale before I have learned it and narrated it myself. Thereby, I picked up the whole mode of presentation; and I have tried to give as exact a translation as possible.

Learning to tell a story well in any language, especially a language learned in later life, is a considerable achievement. The best that many of us do is learn to recite: that is, to imitate, not to participate in, a narrative tradition. But that is the place to start. The scholar's first duty, like the poet's, is to learn to listen, not to learn to talk.

Many people, when they acquire a second language, learn a lot of words and a bit of grammar but neglect to learn the conventions of sentence formation. Then they make hybrid sentences, fitting one language's lexicon into the syntax of another. Such sentences are often fully intelligible (especially to other bilinguals) though not what a native speaker would call well formed. At the next level of competence, people learn to form their sentences according to the customs of the language they are speaking but continue to form *narratives* (literary or otherwise) according to conventions brought from elsewhere – or according to a salad of conventions, some from here and some from there. That may have happened in Rasmussen's case.

When languages atrophy – sometimes centuries before they are clinically dead – what happens is that they are learned *incompletely*, even by those who learn them first. So the last things learned in the best conditions – or the things most rarely learned in full – are the first things lost. Those are the big trees and forests of language: the structures and textures of whole mythologies and metaphorical systems, then of complex stories, metaphors and arguments. That is to say, the shapes of things much larger than the sentence.

Languages need multiple speakers not because they are used to communicate. That is not it at all. Languages need multiple speakers because that is the minimum space in which they will fit. No individual ever learns a language completely.

Rasmussen – let us return to him for a moment – did have advantages which Morice and Petitot lacked. Though raised among Danish speakers in Denmark, he was born in Greenland to a mother who spoke Kalaallisut, the Greenland form of Inuktitut. He was therefore exposed from infancy to a form – albeit a missionized form – of Inuktitut language and culture. Returning to Greenland as an adult, he also knew that he was going there to learn and not to teach. Moreover, the expedition that he joined was called the Danske literære Grønlands-Ekspedition. Literature was the avowed subject of inquiry. Even so, there was no plan to study literary *form*. "Literære" in this case meant the collection of plots and motifs.

Some people say that the shaping of stories is all about personal style, and that style is the expression of one's personal identity. On that view, literary form is a personal prerogative, something that belongs to the province of the self.

In traditional Jain and Buddhist anatomy, as I mentioned a moment ago, the self is a delusion, a misinterpretation of kāyavakcitta, the temporary overlap or interpenetration of body, speech, and mind. Perhaps that is the microcosmic version of another famous triad: *race, language, and culture*, the anthropologists' *triyoga*: three quite separate entities which tend to fall together in the moment and are all too easily, suicidally, disastrously confused.

In comparative anatomy as well, the self is nowhere to be found – but something else is found instead: an endless tissue of relations, linking individual to species, species to genus, species to species, and so on.

When you listen to a well-told story, much of what you hear does come – it has to – from the individual teller. Some of it comes from the teller's language and culture. And some of it comes – a lot of it comes – from what the storyteller shares with the rest of the species (and used to share with other species, now extinct, which were members of our genus). What is speaking, in other words, is not just a person and a culture but humanity. If that doesn't happen, literature doesn't happen.

But if it *does* happen, other things speak too.

The ecology speaks, for one thing: the community of which that speaker, that culture, this species, this genus all form small concentric parts.

The ecology speaks in stories in at least two ways: through lexical reference and through form. It speaks through lexical reference because the world as a whole, addressed through some of its parts, is the subject of every durable story. It speaks through form because the world has form, and the things of the world have form, and the forms that the things of the world have are all contributory parts of the form of the world, and the things of the world include languages, their speakers, the thoughts they think and the stories they tell.

Another thing that's speaking is, of course, the story itself. And another is the language. And it might just be that languages and stories are worthy to be listened to for what they have to say, independently of those who speak and tell them. Permit me to remind you, though, of my old and deep suspicion: what they *almost* say is more important yet.

NOTES

1 Johann Wolfgang von Goethe, *Zur Naturwissenschaft überhaupt, besonders zur Morphologie* (Stuttgart/Tübingen: Cotta, 1817).

2 *Moby Dick*, ch. 12.

3 Alfred L. Kroeber, *A Roster of Civilizations and Cultures* (Viking Fund publication 33, New York: Wenner Gren Foundation, 1962): 81–6.

4 In letters written from the field between the fall of 1886 and the summer of 1890, Boas expressed admiration, affection, and respect for many of the mythtellers he worked with. Some were generous with their stories and skilled with their delivery, others not. Since the actual texts Boas transcribed in those years are so slender, it is impossible to compare those mythtellers fairly against Q'eltí. We can only say that either Q'eltí was an artist of a different order or Boas had by then become alert to literary qualities and values that eluded him before.

5 Franz Boas, "Introductory," *International Journal of American Linguistics* 1 (Chicago, 1917): 7.

6 The word *ethnopoetics* was coined, I believe, by Jerome Rothenberg in 1968 or 1969, but not with Hymes's work in mind. It served in the 1970s as the subtitle of a journal (*Alcheringa: Ethnopoetics*) edited by Rothenberg and Dennis Tedlock. The work this journal published – including some by Hymes – reshaped the meaning of the term but then was saddled with it. Hymes has often called the work he does just "verse analysis."

7 Dennis Lee, *Body Music* (Toronto: Anansi, 1998): 199. For a better text of the same essay, see *Thinking and Singing: Poetry and the Practice of Philosophy*, edited by Tim Lilburn (Toronto: Cormorant, 2002): 19–58.

8 There is no comprehensive study of Native American lyric prosody. Individual studies include, for example, Colleen Fitzgerald's "The Meter of Tohono O'odham Songs," *International Journal of American Linguistics* 64 (1998): 1–36; John Nichols's "'Chant to the Firefly': A Philological Problem in Ojibwe," pp 113–26 in *Linguistic Studies Presented to John L. Finlay*, edited by H.C. Wolfart (Winnipeg: Algonquian & Iroquoian Linguistics Memoir 8, 1991); and Eda Lou Walton's "Navajo Song Patterning," *Journal of American Folklore* 43 (New York, 1930): 105–18.

9 Jerome's prefaces are collected in vol. 9 of *Sancti Eusebii Hieronymi Opera omnia*, edited by Jacques-Paul Migne (Paris: Garnier, 1889) = series Latina, vol. 28 of *Patrologiæ cursus completus* (Paris: Garnier, 1890).

10 *Institutiones* 1.15.12. See also Malcolm B. Parkes, *Pause and Effect: Punctuation in the West* (Berkeley: U of California Press, 1993): 17.

11 Boas himself felt free to blend the works of indigenous authors, so long as they shared a language and culture. He encouraged his students and colleagues to do the same, setting the pattern in *Tsimshian Texts* (Washington, DC: Bureau of American Ethnology, 1902), where pp 7–71 are the fruit of his attempt to construct the Nisgha nation's corporate Raven story from the separate stories told to him at Kincolith in 1894 by Moses Bell and Philip Latimer. Under Boas's influence, John Swanton did the same with the Raven stories told to him in Haida in 1900 and 1901. But unlike early Hebrew scribes, Boas and Swanton took the trouble to show in their notes whose voice is whose. It is possible, therefore, to unblend the works they blended and restore them to something like their original form. Compare for instance Swanton, *Haida Texts and Myths: Skidegate Dialect* (Washington, DC: Bureau of American Ethnology, 1905): 110–38; Swanton, *Haida Texts: Masset Dialect* (Jesup North Pacific Expedition 10.2, New York: American Museum of Natural History, 1908): 293–345; Bringhurst, *A Story as Sharp as a Knife* (1999/2000): 186–8, 208–9 & 221–94; and Skaay, *Being in Being* (2001): 269–344.

12 See Jerrold S. Cooper, "Sumerian and Akkadian," pp 37–56 in *The World's Writing Systems*, edited by Peter T. Daniels & William Bright (New York: Oxford U Press, 1996).

13 "Masoretic" is from מסר, *mâsar*, to hand on, to pass from one to another.

14 Azariah ben Moses dei Rossi, *The Light of the Eyes*, translated by Joanna Weinberg (New Haven: Yale U Press, 2001). The original publication is ספר מאור עינים. Mantua: [Meir ben Efraim, 1573].

15 See Jerome's Preface to Job; chapters 3 & 10 of Philo's Περὶ βίου θεωρητικοῦ; books 2.16 & 4.8 of the *Antiquitates judaicae* of Josephus; Origen's notes on the Psalms; and chapter 11.5 of Eusebius' *De Praeparatione evangelica*.

16 O'Neil was not the first transformational grammarian to take an interest in the realm beyond the sentence, but earlier inquiries by members of the

circle – e.g., Zellig Harris's analyses of discourse in English and Hidatsa, circa 1950 – cast very little light.

17 Huizinga, *Verzamelde werken*, vol. 7 (Haarlem: Tjeenk Willink & Zoon, 1950): 69. The English version is by James S. Holmes & Hans van Marle, from Huizinga's *Men and Ideas* (New York: Meridien, 1959): 51, but the added emphasis is mine.

18 "Het organisme der historie, als men daarvan spreken kan, ligt buiten het menschelijke zieleleven." *Verzamelde werken*, vol 7, p 74 / *Men and Ideas*, p 57.

19 Fred Lerdahl & Ray Jackendoff's *Generative Theory of Tonal Music* (Cambridge, Mass.: MIT Press, 1983) gives a good inkling of some of the things that sonatas and sentences have in common.

20 M.A.K. Halliday & Ruqaiya Hasan, *Cohesion in English* (London: Longman, 1976): 1–2. The rhetorical small caps are in the original.

21 *De Interpretatione* 16b26.

22 T.S. Eliot, "The Possibility of a Poetic Drama," in *The Sacred Wood* (London: Methuen, 1920): 65. The emphasis is his – but forty years later it was evidently different. Then Eliot said what he retained from the study of philosophy was "the style of three philosophers: Bradley's English, Spinoza's Latin and Plato's Greek" (*To Criticize the Critic*, London: Faber, 1965: 20–1).

23 Edward Sapir, *Language: An Introduction to the Study of Speech* (New York: Harcourt, Brace & World, 1921): 33.

24 Leonard Bloomfield, *Language* (New York: Holt, 1933): 170.

25 *Sonette an Orpheus* 1.3.

26 Adrien-Gabriel Morice, "Three Carrier Myths," *Transactions of the Canadian Institute* 5 (Toronto, 1898): 3. Morice appears to have heard a good many indigenous stories, but he preserved very few (so far as we know) in written form.

27 Knud Rasmussen, *Nye Mennesker* (Copenhagen: Gyldendal, 1905): 175. This and a subsequent volume, *Under Nordenvindens Svöbe* (1906), are translated by George Herring as *The People of the Polar North: A Record* (London: Kegan Paul, 1908).

WILD LANGUAGE

Dimension, go beyond dimension,
Calculation, measure nothing,
Only in relation, the cornice balanced
Against the line, the line against
The truth, not as an existence
But as a meaning....

> — RALPH GUSTAFSON,
> "The Philosophy of the Parthenon"

I

Not long ago I moved into a big, shabby wooden house on several acres of forested hillside on an island up the British Columbia coast. The house had never been finished, but it was livable. The land – apart from a small patch just around the house – looked at first to be *perfectly* finished. That is to say, I had the sense it had never been ruined.

People had lived there, of course. People have lived on that island for thousands of years, as they have in every part of North America. Yet it looked to me at first sight as if no one had ever laid hands on the land. Hands are different than feet – a lot more dangerous than feet, it seems to me – and the difference between them is part of the subject I want to explore.

Ralph Gustafson Lecture, Malaspina University College, Nanaimo
6 November 2003

Hands and feet both change the landscape. So do mouths. So do grasses and trees and algae and fungi and tiny bacteria that have no hands or mouths. So do wind and sunlight and rain. But some of this alteration is what we call natural, and some of it – done with hands instead of feet, or with machines that hands have built – is what we label artificial. What does this mean? And where is language in all this? A language is something like a landscape, and something like an animal, and language can be pretty civilized and tame, but can it ever really be wild? I would love to get that clear.

This particular patch of land has been touched by lots of feet and is touched by them every day: the feet of ravens, juncos, nighthawks, varied thrushes, deer mice, voles, red squirrels, land otters, wolves, black-tailed deer, raccoons, the occasional black bear and cougar, and of course some human beings. But most of the humans passing through, so far as I can tell, have either respected it or ignored it. Most of it's never been logged, because it's just too stony, rough, and un-productive to be worth the trouble. It's never been dammed and flooded, because it's steep, and anyway, the streams that run across it are too small to attract the interest of farmers or beavers. For the same reasons, most of it's never been cultivated and planted by any means other than natural progression.

Natural progression can be fierce. Like forests everywhere in the world, this one has known fire. Less than a century ago, there was a major fire on the island, and there are not many trees left on the hillside that survived the conflagration. So this forest, which for me is a living, ever-changing shrine to timelessness, is actually quite young. When I say that it's never been ruined, I don't mean it's never been scourged. I mean that, so far as I know, its basic identity hasn't been fun-damentally lessened – not quite yet – by humankind. In spite of its youth, and in spite of the presence of humans, who do indeed get closer and more numerous every day – and even in spite of the fact that I live there – many people, possibly most, would call it wild land.

It's not as wild as it might be, because roads have been built in the vicinity, which have altered drainage patterns and introduced some noise. It's also been surveyed and deeded and sold in parcels sometimes as small as five acres each. This shift to private ownership changes how some people think of the land. If wildness is in the mind of the human beholder, then the land is already much less wild than it was. In many places, nothing has changed apart from some stakes in the ground, and some flimsy bits of surveyor's tape temporarily tied to a blueberry bush or the limb of a fir. But those are signs the place is doomed. Doomed to further incursion, and doomed to further manipulation: further monkeying around by creatures who have hands.

Maybe we should put this in religious terms. Maybe we should say that the land has been profaned through subdivision. Still, in a sense, the problem is unreal. It doesn't consist of physical change. It consists of a change in perspective. When you carve up the earth into five-acre lots, you change the scale at which some people view it. You encourage them to think of it in smaller and more manageable terms. The wild is by definition *un*managed and unmanageable, and in some sense unconfined by those who would manage it. In spirit and in fact, it is therefore usually *not* privately owned.

In this particular instance, the land may not yet know that it's been profaned. The ravens and squirrels and deer may not yet see much difference. But of course, when people buy land, they start to make plans. And there are, as I said, parts of it that have felt the heavy touch of humans and their machines. The house was built, a septic field laid, a deep well drilled and a shallow one dug, and a garden was planted and fenced, all on roughly half an acre. The part that underwent this treatment wasn't wild when I first saw it, and it isn't wild now, but most of it soon will be. I am giving it back to the world.

Both parts of the land were beautiful in their way when I first saw them. As vegetable gardens go, this garden was beautiful. The wild part, with its mossy bluffs and cliffs and the tall Douglas-firs and juvenile shore pine rising from tiny, often shallow patches of soil; the couple of acres of deeper coastal forest and dense brush; and the acre of spruce and balsam swamp-forest carpeted with sword ferns, were to me the very definition of beauty: the kind of natural-born garden that man-made gardens should be judged by.

The problem lay in the boundary between them. The deer fence made me feel I was in prison when I stood inside the garden. When I approached it from the bluffs or the forest outside, it made me feel I was approaching an armed garrison. I saw it as a wall between indigenous and colonial mentalities, and it seemed to me the house, where I was unpacking my books and belongings – including several hundred books and photocopied manuscripts of Native American texts, and a few dozen grammars and dictionaries of Native American languages – was built on the wrong side.

I addressed this problem in the only way I knew how. I destroyed the garden. I tore out the deer fence. There is still, of course, a boundary between wild and domesticated space, but it no longer coincides with the back fence; it coincides with the front door. One library – mine – is directly contiguous with the other – the world's – and that's the way I like it.

By tearing down the deer fence, I learned a thing or two about the psychology of the man who put it up. He was indeed a master gardener of a kind, but not a man who felt at ease with himself in the wild. He pitched his trash over the fence. It took me months to clean it up. The exquisite natural garden of those bluffs – which must have drawn him there in the first place, because it was he who chose the site and built the house – had apparently receded from his mind. He was more comfortable in prison than he was in the free world, and he had built himself a prison to be proud of. By buying the prison, I set him free, and that's his problem. I also may have saved his life, and that's his problem too. If he'd stayed where he was and continued filling the forest with brush and trash, the forest would eventually have answered in the only way it knows: by setting itself on fire. Destroying his prison exposed the trash heaps; destroying the trash heaps freed the land from prison too.

Now, the question I want to ask myself and you comes down to this: Where is language on this map? Where is it, and where can it possibly be? Is language always a domesticated creature, or is it, or can it be, wild? And if so, in what sense?

To answer that, we'll have to know what *wild* means.

II

We use the word in different ways: the historical baggage of accumulated viewpoints. Some people use it to mean undisciplined, unpredictable, savage, frightening, fierce, raw, crude – connotations that seem to stem from viewing the world as a great and intimidating unknown, or as a resource that humans are entitled and obliged to tame and tap. Some people think that wild rivers are just waiting to be dammed, wild forests waiting to be cut, wild wetlands waiting to be drained, and wild creatures waiting to be tamed or shot and stuffed. In my own dialect of English, *wild* doesn't have those implications. It means undomesticated, unmanaged, uncontrolled by human beings – but it rests on the assumption that there's nothing wrong with that. More loosely, in my dialect of English, it's a term of approbation. "That's wild!" means "that's exciting; that stretches my sense of what-is."

To some people *wild* means formless. This is odd. If you look at a wild plant – a Nootka rose or a clump of salal or a river birch or whitebark pine or anything else – you'll see that it has a magnificent, intricate form: the kind of subtle, adaptable form that the best poets hope to achieve in their poems: the kind of form that makes you think, "This thing's alive!"

Some people think that *wild* means untouched by humans – but if that's the case, there are no wild places on the earth, except deep in the sea or high in the air. Humans have lived for thousands of years all over this planet.

Does *wild* mean having no tools, no clothing, no house? Ground squirrels and marmots and eagles and bears, who make houses, are normally wild. So are ravens and crows, who not only make nests but sometimes use tools. Hermit crabs, who wear clothing, are wild.

The wild surrounds the house, surrounds the tools, surrounds the clothing. We lose it when we try to turn that hierarchy around. The wild disappears from view when we place ourselves in charge. It disappears from view wherever an industry arises. And that includes the tourist industry – because it disappears from view wherever we regard it as a *view*, as something to be cropped and framed, rationed and controlled, looked at like TV and then turned off when it no longer suits our pleasure.

It appears to me that what *wild* actually means is the opposite of undisciplined and crude. It means *extremely sophisticated*. It means capable of living under the most demanding conditions, with minimal tools and housing and clothing. It means self-sufficient in a high degree, and yet part of the fabric, a full working member of the ecology. Could language live up to that standard? Survive at that level? If so, what kind of language would it be? Poetry, maybe? I don't mean polite Neoclassical verse, or florid Romantic verse either, but how about poetry?

III

It is bad manners, where I come from, to talk about one's own work. It is better by far to talk about someone else's. But one of the reasons I am here to give this lecture is to pay my respects to Ralph Gustafson, a man and poet I greatly admired. And it is a condition of the Gustafson lecture "that the lecturer shall be a poet and that the poet shall read poems." I can hear Ralph saying that, in his gracious but non-negotiable sort of way. So let me read you a poem which says (or so I think) some of the same things I have been saying here in prose. The poem is called "And So Do We."

> The ear of language rests
> on the breast of the world,
> unable to know and unable to care
> whether it listens inward or outward.
>
> The world startles it at times.
> And so do we. It is the world's ear
> more than it is yours or mine or ours. Your
>
> speech, of course, is yours. It is another's
> even so. So is your skin. So are your bones.
> So are your fingerprints, your hair.
> The wig of words we wear is no one's
>
> and blows off in half a breeze.
> And so do we. The fact

> *remains. When we are actually*
> *speaking, what we say is not man-made.*

That is the sense in which even human language can and must be wild. The wild is the real, and the real is where we go for form and meaning. Meaning doesn't originate with us. When we are actually speaking, what we say has form and meaning, and those, at root, are not man-made.

There are always some people trying to get closer to the origins of meaning, and always some trying to find out if they can get farther away. I'll read you, if I may, two more short poems that concern two men just trying to be where they are. The first, who speaks here in a voice of his own, is Nányáng Huìzhōng (南陽慧忠), a Buddhist monk living in eighth-century China.

> *Snowflakes, stones and clouds expound it too.*
> *Broken windows, spattered mortar, corpses,*
> *squeaking hinges, slug tracks, stagnant pools*
> *are among its perfected expressions.*
>
> *What is is all false.*
> *What is is all true.*
> *What is is admitting it is,*
> *and what is is recanting.*
>
> *What is is now writing*
> *the word you are reading,*
> *eating the food you are eating,*
> *and keeping your fast.*
>
> *It is giving and taking the breath*
> *you are taking, thinking the thought*

you are thinking, not doing what you
are not doing. Eat it, breathe it, think it too.

The other poem concerns a Japanese monk named Keizan Jōkin (瑩山紹瑾), who lived in the late thirteenth and early fourteenth centuries. Keizan wanted, as good Buddhists do, to free himself from attachments – and he found out, as good Buddhists do, that this did not mean freeing himself from the world, nor from his body, nor from his language, nor from his mind, because those are as real as it gets – and as wild:

> *Give up writing, he wrote.*
> *Give up music and singing, he sang.*
> *Give up poetry, painting, calligraphy,*
> *dancing and miming, he mimed.*
> *Give up thinking, he thought.*

> *But the song kept on singing,*
> *the dance kept on dancing,*
> *thought kept on thinking,*
> *the breezes kept blowing, the sun*
> *continued to shine.*

With very few exceptions, all the world's birds and mammals train their young. Like human beings, they transmit information from generation to generation in two forms: genetic and exogenetic (inside the genome and outside the genome). The genetic route is what we call heredity; the exogenetic path is known as culture. Humans have no monopoly on that.

Both of these avenues depend on language. Genetic information is transmitted through chemical languages, whose morphemes and phonemes are made out of ribonucleic acid. Exogenetic information is transmitted through other kinds of

ROBERT BRINGHURST · *The Tree of Meaning*

language: behavioral languages, some of which are spoken, like the language I am using at this moment, and some of which are silent.

It used to be taught that genetic transmission was strictly linear, never lateral: that it followed the line of parental descent and never crossed from species to species. Now, of course, microbiologists such as Lynn Margulis describe an evolutionary process that involves a great deal of lateral transfer of genetic information. So we ought not to think of ourselves as rising up out of nature or leaving it behind on a lengthening thread. Genetically, we are so deeply enmeshed in the fabric of nature that all separation is an illusion.

We're enmeshed in the natural world in cultural and behavioral terms as well. Behavioral language – including spoken language – also leaks across the boundaries between species. If you spend any time watching other species, and listening to what they have to say, you will learn at least a little of their languages, and something will get through. Birds and nonhuman mammals have taught me a great deal – and told me a great deal – over the years. This, for example, is a poem entitled "Finch."

> I keep a crooked wooden bowl
> half full of birdseed in the garden,
> where the siskins and the finches,
> crossbills, cowbirds, chickadees
> and red-winged blackbirds meet.
>
> Each day among the finches
> there is one – a female house finch,
> Carpodacus mexicanus, I believe –
> who must have tangled with a predator,
> or maybe with a truck.

Not one among the others acts
concerned. No one seems, in fact,
to notice the black cavity that once
was her right eye, the shattered
stump that used to be her upper beak.

And no one gawks or whispers
at the awkward sidewise motion
that enables her to eat. And no one
mocks, crunching a sunflower seed,
her preference for millet.

Where ostracism, charity or pity
might have been, there is reality
instead. I mean that their superlative
indifference is a kind of moral
beauty, as perfect as the day.

If the red-tailed hawk comes by,
or the neighbor's cat, they mention
that to one another and are gone.
They also say hello; they say I am;
they say We are; they say Let's finch

and make more finches. But I never
hear them talk of one another.
They speak of what they are, not who
they do or do not wish to be.
That is a form of moral beauty

too, as perfect as the day. Which is
to say they sing. By nothing
more than being there and being

what they are, they sing.
They sing. And that is that.

IV

What are the essential characteristics of the wild? For one thing, it is coextensive with time: simultaneously ancient and brand new, stable and ever-changing. For another, it is the very essence of wealth: rich and varied and extensive and complex and intertwined with itself beyond our wildest dreams. Third, it's astoundingly beautiful: delicate, fragile, adaptable, strong and immensely intelligent, attentive and responsive. The wild remembers its past and dreams its future and speaks its immediate present. What does it say? It says This, this, this, being here, being here, you, me, us. It will never remember your name, because it has no names for anything, but so long as you live, you are a word in its language. Its vocabulary consists, at any one time, of all the individuals that exist. Its syntax consists of all the ecosystems, watersheds, climates, species and the ecological processes (respiration, photosynthesis, and so on) going on inside them. What a linguist would call its phonology – that is, its material substance – consists of hydrocarbons: proteins, for example, and nucleic acids. It knows how to lie, by imitating itself, but wherever those lies succeed, they double back and add new layers to the truth. (Syrphid flies, which are flies that ward off predators by mimicking the physical features of wasps, are one example.)

The wild isn't something to conquer or subdue; it's something to try to live up to: a standard better than gold. Humans are part of it, and in the long run have no choice but to be so. In the short run, of course, we can try to opt out. We can pretend to be children of god or creatures from outer space, free to leave when our term is up – but what we really are is earthlings. We can also pretend to be so intelligent that we know how to manage the planet more effectively than the planet can manage itself. Those who grow up, as most of us have, in industrialized economies and colonial regimes, are encouraged to think there is no other choice than to take control and manage the planet. But there is another choice. That choice is to *participate* in the biosphere, learning enough about it to recognize and accept that we can never be anything more than junior partners: a few million or billion human cells in a brain the size of the planet. Right now those human cells are acting like a cancer, a tumor in the wise, old brain of planet earth.

As soon as you think your way out of the wild – as soon as depression or arrogance or some other form of exaggerated self-concern leads you to see yourself as distinct from it – the wild looks like a *thing*. You might imagine you can carve it up and sell it. You might even think you can redesign it or manage it and do a better job than the wild itself. But of course you can't. Your only hope, when you are really cut off from the wild, is to rejoin it. The wild is the biosphere: this tiny hollow ball which is the only place in the universe where you or I are free to be what we are.

Nonetheless, people *do* keep thinking their way out of it, or trying to. That makes the wild hard to return to, hard to approach. The Hopi word for wild, *tùmqa*, means exactly that: hard to approach, hard to get hold of. It is used of wild horses, of proud young women, and of certain kinds of food that are served so slippery and hot that picking them up and eating them is a challenge. In Anglo terms, the wild is a hot potato – and one that never cools.

So why do we have the ability to think our way out of the

wild? Why are we capable of the illusion of separation? I don't know why, but I know what the skill is good for. It's good for understanding.

Understanding is something humans do for fun, the same way ravens do aerial somersaults and rolls, and squirrels play chase, and otters and penguins go tobogganing. But the time will come, as any raven can tell you, when you have to straighten up and fly right to keep from crashing. "Straightening up" means, in this case, coming back to a basic fact of bioethics: a principle my friend Don McKay has stated very nimbly and simply in six syllables: *We don't own what we know.*

Years ago, when I lived on Bowen Island, I used to go out from time to time and talk to the frogs and toads who lived around my house. This is part of a transcription of one of those conversations, an excerpt from a poem called *Conversations with a Toad*:

> *Behind you: the owl, whose eyes*
> *have no corners: the owl with her quick*
> *neck, who faces whatever she sees.*
> *The raven, with voices like musselshell, wellwater, wood.*
> *The dippers with voices like water on water.*
> *The ruffed grouse drumming in the Douglas-fir.*
> *And the heron flying in whole notes,*
> *the kingfisher crossing in dotted eighths*
> *and in quarters – both silent; much later,*
> *two voices like washboards:*
> *one bass, coarser than gravel,*
> *one mezzo, crushed gravel and sand.*
>
> *Their beauty bites into the truth.*
> *One way to fail to be is to be merely*
> *pretty. But that beauty: it feeds on you; we*

feed on it. As you feed on this
moth, toad, or may: he may yet be
your dinner: his hazelnut tonsure,
the face like a goat's but clean,
and the mane like brown cornsilk.
Nerves spring from his forehead like fernfronds,
like feathers. He too is transformed.
This is the last life, toad.
Those who eat will be eaten. That
is the one resurrection.

We who kill not to eat but to mark
our domain — to build and breed, in place
of what is, what we choose to create —
have reduced by that much the population of heaven.

...

Woodlice breed in the fallen alder.
Toad, the varied thrush is a beautiful bird.
And the red-shafted flickers, who feed there.
Uses will form for us too in the end.

What is is the truth. What precedes it
is meaning. We will not destroy
being, toad. We will not. But I think
we will overreligiously clean it.

Yet the voices still seep through us too. Even
through us, who have long since forgotten:
to pray does not mean to send messages
to the gods; to pray means to listen.

As students of literature, we are taught to think in terms of finished texts, beautifully honed and polished texts that sit pristinely on the shelves the way artworks hang on the walls of museums. This is fine as far as it goes and as long as it works, but just how far is that? The wild is all about process, not about product. There are plenty of artifacts in the wild – dung pellets, spruce cones and pine cones and maple keys, seashells and sand dollars, pebbles and footprints, owl pellets, bones – but none of these things is the end of the line or the final result. In the wild, there is no final result – except that some day the sun will run down, and then life will go out like a light.

All the native cultures of North America were oral. This means that every year, in every language on the continent, stories were told in the same way flowers bloom and snowflakes fall. The stories were simultaneously ancient and brand new, and never told exactly the same way twice. That is the natural or wild state of literature. The stories were big and rich and complex and sometimes thousands, or tens of thousands, of years old: every bit as sophisticated as anything that occurs in literate cultures. But there were no fixed texts. You couldn't go back and consult the previous version. You could only ask to hear the story again – or if you were able, tell it yourself.

That's the natural state of literature and the natural state of language. No printed dictionaries or grammars on the shelf. The world is the dictionary; the ecosystem – that thin but intricate, rumpled slab of organic memory – is the grammar.

Language and mind are as real to me as rocks and trees. That means they belong to the wild, like rocks and trees and horses and bears and wolves and mice. They can be tamed, but the tamer they are, the less they can teach us.

You don't own what you know, but you must do as you see fit with what we call *your* mind and *your* language. What I am trying to do with mine is to lead them back *into* the wilderness, not back out. My experience so far is that they are leading me as much as I am leading them. I think they know the way. We'll see how far we get.

POSTSCRIPT: WILD TYPOGRAPHY

A couple of years after giving this lecture, I returned to Malaspina for two days at the invitation of Rhonda Bailey, to work with four of her students on turning the lecture into a little book. In defining the visual form of a text called "Wild Language," questions naturally arose. Among them: *What's wild typography?* and *Can there be or is there such a thing as a wild book?*

We could have pelted the page with stoned or drunken letters, letting them sprawl wherever they fell. We could have mixed, at random, a hundred fonts and sizes, and a hundred colors too if the budget had allowed. We could have crumpled up the baseline, carved a rough-edged, one-off textblock into the white space of each page, or deconstructed the text entirely into a random sequence of letters, some of them vanishing into the gutter or flung beyond the paper's edge. We could have roughed the paper up with mud and stones, or dispensed with paper completely and stenciled the text on a pile of leaves. But a grenade going off in a composing room does not bear much resemblance to the symbiotic interchange unfolding night and day in a forest or a wetland, a kelp bed or a coral reef. It resembles more the havoc that occurs when the forest is clearcut or the coral reef is trawled and another piece of the wild – and of reality – is blotted out. Volcanic eruptions, avalanches, hurricanes, landslides, and fire do occur in the natural world, but these are not the essence of the wild. The wild is what methodically starts to rebuild itself in their wake.

Thinking and speaking are as natural to humans as swimming is to fish. Like swimming, they ordinarily leave no trace. But humans, like hairy woodpeckers, don't just love to talk, they also love to leave their mark. A few populations of humans have linked the two and started obsessively making and saving linguistic marks. Only after that has happened does typography exist.

This behavior may be aberrant. It is not evidently, like walking and talking, genetic. (Speech, in humans as in whales, is genetically driven though it is culturally shaped. Literacy, like religion, appears to be socially driven instead.) If writing and printing have no genetic foundation, maybe it's right to call them artificial or *unnatural*, and to say that typography cannot be wild.

Culture, however, is part of human nature: a thick behavioral web in which genetically driven and socially driven activities are inextricably linked. In societies that have enshrined reading and writing, the book is the seed capsule of culture: one of the central parts of a parallel system of reproduction and evolution that mimes in the cultural sphere what genetics achieves in nature. In addition, the book is a favorite way of caching information: stockpiling food for the mind, just as pikas, squirrels, and honey bees (as well as human beings) hoard food for the body. It may still be true that writing is somehow "unnatural" and that typography is never authentically wild – but the wild is at any rate its archetype and source.

Seeds and seed capsules, in nature, are unfailingly elegant. Form not only follows function in these structures; it chases it around, like a mouse with a moth or a cat with a mouse. Immense amounts of information and nutrition are routinely housed in spaces handsome far beyond necessity and compact beyond belief.

Letterforms are inherently abstract, the trace of a hand speaking in silence. They won't get any closer to the essence of the wild by dressing in flowers and leaves, nor in leopard skins and teeth. Still less will they get there by dressing in sleek robotic armor, or in the most egomaniacal costume of all, the explosive-filled vest.

People accustomed to orchards, farms, and gardens very often think of the wild in opposition to the domesticated or tame. The garden, they will say, has greater order than the wild. But it's the other way around. The order of the garden may be easier to see, but it is fragile and superficial. It is artificial and unnatural in a very convincing sense: it cannot take care of itself. The order of the wild is self-sustaining, flexible and deep.

Can typography do that? It hasn't yet. That doesn't mean it shouldn't keep on trying.

Wild typography isn't something I've achieved; it's something I'm always trying to reach. It is typography in which each form is as well made and well placed as the wildflowers blooming in an alpine meadow in the spring, deerprints in a rain-soft stretch of game trail, the feathers in a varied thrush's wing, or the miniature forest of moss and lichen spreading over a stump. It is typography in which the forms still savor of the hands and minds that made them, not of machines that mimic the hands, nor of computers emulating the machines. There is a style of Chinese and Japanese calligraphy known as Wild Grass (kuángcǎo or kyōsō, 狂草) – and the nearest thing we have to wild typography, it seems to me, is the comfortable yet highly disciplined writing of Táng Chinese, Fujiwara Japanese, and Renaissance Italian scribes.

Many would say that Táng Dynasty China, Fujiwara Japan, and Renaissance Italy are high points of human civilization. How can their art be closer to the wild than something from a neolithic village or the colonial frontier?

Forests are wild. Forests are also highly developed civilizations. They are *nonhuman* civilizations – or as my friend David Abram likes to say, *more-than-human* civilizations. Humans can join; they can play a small role. Problem is, humans are sometimes too proud to accept it.

In time and space alike, the forest is incomparably rare, but it is real. It does not need or want our managerial interference. We have the capacity now to destroy it, but not to create it again – and not to create something better with which to replace it.

I think that, at their best, human civilizations actually start to resemble the forest. They start to attain – and to sense and respond to – the forest's supple and self-reinforcing order. And then some of the things they produce – poems, stories, pieces of music, musical instruments, letterforms, buildings – also acquire some of the inexhaustible grace we find in the forest. They're almost wild.

FINDING HOME:

THE LEGACY OF BILL REID

I

Bill Reid lived 78 years, most of them painful, many of them joyful, and all of them productive. I'm going to mention pain repeatedly this evening, though I'm sure that joy is of equal or greater importance.

I'm also going to talk about several pieces of Reid's art, and I'm going to do it without any pictures. I hope that most of you have seen some or all of the works I'm going to mention. If you haven't, I hope you will take the trouble to see them, and to see them in person, whenever you can. If you've seen them already, I hope you will see them again. And again. And again. It is not very difficult to do that in Vancouver. Art is as important to a city as streets and power grids, sewers and cafés. If you replace *works* of art with *images* of art, the city shrivels up and blows away, and suburbs take its place. No one person makes a city or a culture, but the city of Vancouver, insofar as it is more than just a heap of rooms and windows, is largely the creation of Bill Reid.

Besides, as I said, I want to talk largely about pain – not people in pain but pain itself, and joy itself, and art itself – and there are no photographs of that.

Of course, before there was a city here there was a world: a forest ringed by beachfront villages, for which the city may

First Nations House of Learning, University of British Columbia, Vancouver
6 February 2004

ROBERT BRINGHURST · *The Tree of Meaning*

be a very poor replacement. Painful though it may be, it is good to think about that, and Reid is one of the artists who lead us to do so.

Some of the pain Bill Reid encountered in his life was the kind that is sooner or later familiar to all of us: the pain of love and rejection, friendship and loss, misjudgment and mis-understanding – all part of what it costs just to be a human being. There were, in eight decades, many women in his life, three of whom he married, one of whom stayed with him to the end. There was the absentee father he almost never saw. There was the daughter from whom he was all too quickly estranged. There was also the adopted son he never quite got close to and who died a miserable death in 1981 at the age of 25. In 1976, there was the violent death, just a few hundred meters from here, of one of his closest friends, Wilson Duff, and a few years earlier, the drug-related death of a very promising younger Haida artist whose suicidal path Bill had tried in vain to change.

In the Museum of Anthropology, also a few hundred meters from here, is a mask Bill made in Montreal in 1970. Portrait masks are a Haida tradition, and this one looks at first like a perfectly canonical work of late classical Haida art. The carving is very symmetrical and restrained; the formline painting is delicate in weight and gracefully composed, but the painting is powerfully asymmetrical, and it alludes to that ominous new gesture of late classical Haida painting known as the *black field*. The mask is a portrait of a woman. She was originally not, I think, a Haida woman, but her womanhood is stated by purely classical Haida means: the lower lip is extended to hold a labret.

I think I know precisely whom this mask is a portrait of, and I think that scarcely matters. As with many a fine portrait by Botticelli or Piero della Francesca, it is nice to know the

identity of the sitter, but the power of the character portrayed
has superseded that. The identity of the sitter is now important
mostly for the way it illuminates the work of art, and not the
other way around. The human portrayed here has become a
spirit being – *xhaayda* has turned into *sghaana*, to use the Haida
words. That same transformation is the subject of a lot of Haida
literature. Whether the act of making the mask brought the
spirit being into being or the other way around I do not know.
Nor do I know, in the realm of Haida literature, whether the
stories create the spirit beings who inhabit them or the other
way around. What I think is that in art and literature alike,
the relation is basically ecological. That means self-reinforcing
and self-policing. In an ecological system you can never isolate
any component for long as either cause or effect because every
component is both of these at once. Humans, works of art,
and spirit beings, it seems to me, are parts of a single ecology,
one where neither humans nor their artworks have or should
have pride of place.

Joy in Haida is *gudaang llaa*, "goodness of mind." One of the
ways to say "pain" in Haida is *ghuxhagang*, which literally means
"burning from within." Joy, Bill liked to say, is a well-made object, and the mask is superbly made. The fact remains that the
person captured or the spirit being created in that mask knows
a lot about anguish, a lot about pain. Is it his pain projected
onto her, or her pain reflected back at him? And how can there
be such pain in the midst of joy, such joy in the midst of pain?
Those aren't the kinds of questions powerful masks or portraits
answer. Those are the kinds of questions they *ask*.

In 1983, at a panel discussion in what was then called the
BCPM, the British Columbia Provincial Museum, Bill showed
his audience a photo of that mask, and then astonished some
of his listeners by saying,

This is a mask, representing nothing. It's purely decorative. I haven't made very many masks, and I forget exactly why I made this one. I was in Montreal at the time.... I have never done masks or any other equipment for ceremonial use, because I've never been involved in ceremonies. I'm not a dancer, and my relationship to the culture of my people is in fact a very remote one. So this is a mask for the sake of being a mask, for something to hang on the wall. The face painting is merely a formal design. It represents nothing from the tradition. It was an exercise, you could say, in making a mask.[1]

That's one of the cagiest pieces of non-explanation I've ever encountered. At the same time, it's an artist doing just what artists are supposed to do and very often don't: putting the meaning into the work instead of putting it into the catalogue. Putting it into the work and then deliberately suggesting that it isn't even there, because then you'll have to see it for yourself or not see anything at all. It's also an example of Bill's sense of humor in full bloom. I can see him eyeballing the room as he said that, looking to see how many of his listeners were caught in his self-deprecating ruse.

There is a Haida myth, a traditional story, in which a group of hunters sets out, taking their dogs, evidently to kill black bears. First night out they camp, and when they wake up in the morning, they find themselves trapped at the top of a pillar or the bottom of a shaft. They escape by putting their dogs and then each other into the fire. One by one, as they're burned alive, they reappear, at the top of the shaft or the foot of the pillar. When they have all been translated back to ground level, they go on their way. They tell themselves that nothing's changed, but something has.

We have two superb incarnations of this story in the classical Haida language: one dictated in Skidegate in the fall of

1900 by a blind poet known as Ghandl, the other dictated at
Masset in the spring of 1901 by a storyteller and carver known
as Haayas. Both were transcribed by a fine linguist named
John Swanton. As Haayas tells the story, these hunters paddle
back to where they've come from and find that their families
have moved. So they follow them back to their winter village,
known as Ttii.

> Ttii llanagaay qanggayghalan dluu
> ll giinangghuugangghawan.
> Ll kil llghaanga ttla gudangawee ghanuu
> tlagw ll sughaawan.
> Wakkyanan gam llanagaay ghaaqasgadangan.
> Wakkyanan gam giinang·huugangaay ga
>   ll qaynstlghangghaawan.[2]

> *Once they could see the village of Ttii,*
> *they sang paddling songs without stopping.*
> *To let the others hear their voices,*
> *they sang across the water.*
> *In spite of that, the village gave no sign.*
> *In spite of that, they did not falter*
>   *in their singing.*

They come right up in front of the town, and still no one
hears them. One of the group goes ashore. He enters the family
house, banging the doorflap, but no one takes notice.

> Tajigwaa ll tawee jaaghang ahl na llgheegagan ttluu'udaayan.
> Ghaghadeega ll ghuhldaalan.
> « Gasinttlaw tlagw iittl iijing? »
> hin nang na llgheeygas jaaghang ahl guu suudaayan.[3]

> In *the rear of the house sat his friends and his wife,*
> > *with the head of the household.*
> He *sat down among them.*
> His *wife and the headman said to each other,*
> "What's *come over us?*"

Gasinttlaw tlagw iittl iijing? literally means, "Why are we on the other shore?" What it connotes is, "Something funny's going on here. Why do we feel so weird?" When he hears his wife and headman say this, the hunter finally understands: he and his colleagues are spirit beings now: still quite real, and in their own way still perceptible, yet utterly invisible to normal human beings.

That's what has happened to the woman whose face and grief and anger underlie the alder mask. She's disappeared. That's the meaning of the statement, This *is a mask, representing nothing ... a mask for the sake of being a mask.* That's the meaning of I haven't *made very many masks, and* I *forget exactly why* I *made this one.* There is something here that's perfectly transparent – first in the sense that it's perfectly obvious, second in the sense that you can't see it. It's what Rilke meant when he looked at a stone torso of Apollo in the Louvre and called it *durchsichtig*, which means "see-throughable." What's really there is not a piece of broken stone or a piece of painted alder but a presence: invisible, inaudible, unspeakable as well. In the midst of a panel discussion in a museum in Victoria in 1983, the spirit being in this mask is a creature whose power might be felt but who cannot be discussed or even mentioned, because in the language of panel discussions, she has no name.

There is joy in that mask as well as pain, but the pain is what's portrayed. To get the joy, you have to feel the way the object fits the vision and feel the physical object being made. To get the joy, you have to enter, in a sense, into the body of the carver, which is a body trying to come to terms with its pain.

If it were a Greek instead of a Haida mask, you might expect to find its happy twin – and in a sense it has one. Its partner, its inverse mirror image, is a necklace, also made in Montreal at nearly the same time. The two works have never, so far as I know, been exhibited together. They are now in different collections; they are made of entirely different materials; and they rest on two quite different cultural traditions. The necklace, which is known as *The Milky Way*, is a piece of jewelry, built from gold and diamonds using European techniques. Like the mask, it's a powerfully asymmetrical object built on a quite symmetrical plan. The anguish in it is the anguish of the craft, the anguish of day after day, week after week at the workbench using finicky little tools and doing finicky little tasks. What all that anguish leads to is a vessel of pure joy, a constellation of tiny stars floating over a bed of crumpled sunlight. The necklace is a slice of summer sky – night sky and day sky both at once – designed to settle on a woman's collarbones and shine in tandem with her face.

On the same day in 1983, after talking about that mask, Bill said some very interesting things about the necklace. One of them was that it owed its inspiration to "some of the old Skidegate poles [whose] carvers never heard of the law of physics that says that two objects cannot occupy the same space at the same time...."[4] I keep on thinking, though, of something else he might have said, if he had chosen to torment his listeners just a little further. He might have said, for instance,

This is a necklace, representing nothing. It's purely decorative. I haven't made very many necklaces, and I forget exactly why I made this one. I was in Montreal at the time.... I have never done necklaces or any other equipment for ceremonial use, because I've never been involved *in ceremonies. I'm not a nobleman, a magnate or a movie star, and my relationship to the culture of my people is in fact a very remote one. So this is a necklace for the sake of being a necklace, for something to wear on your neck…. It was an exercise, you could say, in making a necklace….*

II

Bill knew other kinds of pain – other kinds of *burning from within* – that most of us are spared. I am not an authority on agony, but I have served in the armies of two countries, under some not altogether pretty conditions, and I can tell you that Bill patiently endured some of the greatest physical torment I have ever seen inflicted on any human being. That was part of the price of his advancing Parkinson's disease, an ailment he suffered more and more acutely, and always uncomplainingly, for roughly thirty years.

There is a certain facial expression, or lack of expression, that comes and goes in people who have Parkinson's disease. It occurs when the victim momentarily loses control of the facial muscles. Then the smiles, the winks, the crinkles, the microscopic liveliness of eyes and lips and cheeks – the things that bring a face alive – just all turn off. The lungs keep breathing, blood keeps flowing, and the eyes keep seeing, but the flesh around them all goes dead. And then, a while later, life returns. That face is known to the victims of Parkinson's and to their relatives and physicians as The Mask.

If you go to the Vancouver Airport, or better yet to the Canadian Embassy's chancery in Washington, D.C., you can see one of the two incarnations of Reid's largest work of sculpture, *The Spirit of Haida Gwaii*. Bill was 70 when that work left his studio, and 71 when the first casting – the Black Canoe, we called it – was unveiled. His Parkinson's was well advanced by then, and he was working largely through the hands of other people, but there is nothing in that sculpture that does not bear his stamp or stem from his decisions. The canoe is full of totemic animals – wolf, eagle, raven, bear, and so on. On the starboard side, tucked in among the larger-than-life cargo, is a roughly life-size human paddler. That figure is the nearest thing you'll find to Reid's self-portrait, and the nearest he ever came to rendering The Mask.

In Rembrandt's self-portraits, the fusion of sitter and painter is always front and center, so when you stand before the painting – which is where the painting wants you – it holds you in its gaze, where you become the painter's sitter and the sitter's painter too. Mantegna's self-portraits are different from that. Mantegna's face is never front and center. He tucks himself into a corner, where he joins you in watching what he's made. Titian's self-portraits, of which there are four at least, cover the range – and it is a wide range – between Mantegna and Rembrandt.

The most obvious of these is the one in the Prado: a side view of Titian in old age, with his brush in his hand. He isn't using the brush; he's holding it close to his body, as if it were an object of no concern to anyone but him. And he isn't looking back out of the front of the painting to see who is looking at him. Nor is he looking at himself. He's facing sideways. Try as you might, you cannot catch his gaze. He's busy looking at everything else. That's how Bill's self-portrait is positioned in the boat. You see him from the side. He's facing toward the bow, not posing for the camera, just getting on with the job.

Another of Titian's self-portraits is embedded in a painting called The Flaying of Marsyas, now in the Archbishop's Summer Palace in Kroměříž, Slovakia. Marsyas – Μαρσύας – was a satyr – a spirit being in other words – who got himself involved in a little musical competition with a more powerful spirit being called Apollo. Marsyas lost, of course, and the price of losing was that Apollo, the gentle god of art and light and poetry and music, skinned him alive. The surviving body of classical Greek literature, like the surviving body of classical Haida literature, is reduced to a small fraction of what it once was, and we have no good Greek version of this story. If we did, I'd quote it to you, because one of the great pleasures in life, so far as I'm concerned, is setting classical Greek and classical Haida poets side by side. They frequently illuminate each other, like that necklace and that mask.

Since we don't have a text, we have to stitch the story together from bits and pieces found here and there in the works of satirists, geographers, and travelers. It's just like piecing together a lost Native American myth – one of those stories that "everybody knows" but which no great storyteller ever dictated to a linguist, in a language of the storyteller's choosing, during the time when a great storyteller could. Stories in that predicament are trapped beneath the surface of literature, condemned to the hazy world we call folklore.

For a painter, that can be a godsend rather than a problem. So it happens that in Italy during the Renaissance, where the most highly developed languages of storytelling were oil paint and fresco, the story of Marsyas and Apollo was painted many times. Titian's version, so far as I know, is the only one containing a self-portrait. Titian has given his own features to one of the judges – the dissenting judge, Midas, who tried in vain to keep this grisly tale from unfolding as it does. In the painting, he sits only inches from where Apollo is working the knife, starting to peel his challenger's skin, and only inches from the dogs who are lapping up the blood.

In *The Spirit of Haida Gwaii*, Bill, like Titian, is caught up in the story he portrays. His own face, or rather his own mask, is worn by the only human paddler to be found in that canoe.

286

The self-portrayal doesn't end there, of course. The other creatures in the boat are part of him as well: the Wolf, who was
his crest, his totem animal; the Raven, who was his alter ego;
the Dogfish Woman whom he loved. Every creature in that
sculpture is part of his identity. Yet he is far from being the
hero or the subject of the sculpture. Like Titian, he is there to
pay the price of what he's seen.

When it came time to talk about *The Spirit of Haida Gwaii*,
Bill was only a little less elusive than he was when he talked
about the mask from Montreal. He identified the paddler wearing the Parkinsonian mask as a "professional survivor" and
gave him the name the Ancient Reluctant Conscript, a phrase
that he remembered from a poem by Carl Sandburg.

> On the soup wagons of Xerxes I was a cleaner of pans....
>
> Red-headed Caesar picked me for a teamster.
> He said, "Go to work, you Tuscan bastard,
> Rome calls for a man who can drive horses."...
>
> Lincoln said, "Get into the game; your nation takes you."
> And I drove a wagon and team and I had my arm shot off
> At Spotsylvania Court House.

The conscript is another of those beings whose relationship
to the culture of his people "is in fact a very remote one" – but
also one of those without whose help no culture is going to
go anywhere.

The only way to have anything *other than* a very remote
relationship to the culture of your people is to give your entire
life to it. When you die, your culture takes you in, and then,
if you've given enough, your place is near the center. Reid
has done that now, and his relationship to the culture of his

people – all his people, all the people fate has brought to the Northwest Coast and all the people of the human species – is now anything but remote. But in 1988 and '89, when the figure of the Conscript first took shape, and in 1991 when it was cast and finished and unveiled, Bill still made no claim to be at the center of anything. Like Mantegna and Titian, he knew that he was part of something vastly larger than himself, which would not be sorted out for many generations.

Reid's head was full of poems – full of the narrative poems of the Haida masters, Skaay and Ghandl and Xhyuu and Kilxhawgins and Kingagwaaw and Haayas, who dictated works to Swanton at Skidegate in 1900 and at Masset in 1901, and full of the poems of Homer, Isaiah and Virgil, Keats and Shelley, Frost and Sandburg, Pound and Eliot, Purdy and Cohen. He read them all in English, not in Haida, not in Greek and Hebrew and Latin, but he read them well, and in his mind they lived together fruitfully and peacefully. Bill's mind, in other words, was a good model for the world: a place where people and their dreams had better and more hopeful things to do than snarl at each other or blow each other up.

Another model or example for the world – one of immense importance to Reid – is the polyphonic music created in the European Renaissance, elaborated during the Baroque, and nurtured through difficult, inhospitable times by the great Neoclassical and Romantic composers. Bill loved that music – Josquin's motets, the Bach fugues, the Haydn and Mozart quartets. That music was one of the things that brought us together. It was like a fire we used to gather around to keep warm. And he loved it with good reason. In polyphonic music, two or three or more melodic lines, independent of each other yet respectful of each other, move in the same space at the same time, sometimes contradicting one another, sometimes dancing with each other, but never giving up their independence, never falling into line and shouting slogans or marching down the street. The non-Aristotelian physics of classical Haida sculpture, where two creatures can indeed occupy the same space at the same time, is very close to polyphonic musical space. In both arts, there are discords. Things can bump against each other. But the discords pass, and because they pass, they contribute to the shapeliness and wholeness of the whole. It is hard to imagine how, in a world rich with Haida sculpture and polyphonic music, there could be such things as suicide bombers or even their comparatively harmless and equally pitiful academic and journalistic equivalents. But of course there can be, and there are. In any ecology – an ecology of images, an ecology of melodies, an ecology of ideas – just as in the forest itself, things can and sometimes do go wrong. But a real ecology, until it is pushed to the brink of extinction, has the capacity for self-restoration and self-repair.

European polyphony was born at the edge of the forest, just like Haida sculpture. It was born when the fledgling cities of Europe were still within sight of the forest, and when the great groves of stone trees called cathedrals were sprouting on riverbanks and hills across much of the continent. It takes a lot of pride to build Nôtre Dame de Paris, or a Haida village with its memorial poles and frontal poles, or to build a polyphonic mass. But it takes a lot of humility too: a willingness to learn from the forest that you cut and the tuneful silence you invade.

III

Bill Reid was a graceful, thoughtful man. Nevertheless, like all of us who live in the real world – especially those who get things done – he had his share of political and social troubles – another kind of pain, which ought maybe to be called *burning from without* instead of *burning from within*. Much of that pain – and the corresponding joy – came from his position as a member of two cultures. Please remember that those cultures were once openly at war with one another and have lived for over a century under a sullen, *de facto* truce, with one side waiting patiently for a treaty to be signed while the other side, at least through the late 1980s, seemed determined to forget that basic agreements had never been made. This goes some way toward explaining why the two sides are, on some fronts, psychologically still at war. Bill became, little by little, an ex officio member of both, an expert on both, a *creator* of both, and therefore inescapably a conduit between them – which in conditions of monumental mutual ignorance and mistrust cannot be an easy thing to do.

He was not, of course, unique in this regard. Millions of people are raised on the margins between cultures – Muslim and Jewish, Jewish and Christian, Croat and Serb, Bengali and English, Catholic and Protestant, Hutu and Tutsi. Some reach out to both, but many, as we know, choose to deal with cultural boundaries by turning their backs or raising their weapons. Bill was unusual not in the problem that he faced but in the grace and creativity with which he faced it.

The other difference is that most of us have such problems thrust upon us. Bill sought his out. He chose the problem of his own free will.

Many people have interpreted Bill's bicultural position in genetic terms. His first biographer, Maria Tippett, has gone to the other extreme, interpreting his position as, in essence, a charade. Both these perspectives are wrong. Worse than wrong, because both of them are deliberately, willfully shallow.

Bill taught himself the language of Haida visual art. He couldn't have learned it in the old way, by growing up in a Haida village, because by 1920, when he was born, all but three of those villages – one in Alaska, two in Canada – were empty, and the great works of art, along with a lot of the cultural fiber, had been plundered from those which remained. Bill learned the language of that art little by little from books, museum collections, and individual pieces that survived in private hands. He was able to learn it because it is a *human* language and Bill was a human being – one with unusually keen intelligence, curiosity, drive, self-confidence, and an aptitude for fusing spirit and form. He could have been of African, Chinese, or Samoan descent. It happens that he was born here on this coast, raised in British Columbia and Alaska, and it happens that through his mother's Haida relatives and the Provincial Museum collections, he began to see some great as well as mediocre pieces of Haida and Tsimshian and Tlingit art at an early and impressionable age. What he saw took root in his brain. That's how culture works – in broken societies like ours and in healthy ones as well.

There is a lot of cultural rebuilding going on in Haida Gwaii these days: a very exciting thing to see, inspiring to some and apparently terrifying to others. Bill is by no means solely responsible for that rebirth, and it is fashionable now to say that no rebirth occurred, because nothing ever died. That reminds me of the strange language I heard at my grandfather's funeral when I was ten years old. "I look upon this man," said the preacher, "not as dead but as sleeping." Call it a reawakening if you are one of those for whom death is out of fashion. I am happy, myself, to call it a renaissance – and I think it began, unknown to absolutely everyone, in the 1930s in Victoria, British Columbia, in Bill Reid's young and well-made brain.

By his own account, Bill became a Haida artist long before he became a Haida. The consequence was a lifetime of tension between Reid and some of the Haida of Haida Gwaii. There, for half a century, envy and suspicion of Bill Reid ran just as deep as admiration.

An artist Bill resembles in this respect is William Butler Yeats – the principal figure in what is rightly called the Irish Renaissance and the principal bridge between Irish and English literary culture. Reid, though he mastered the visual language of Haida art, never learned to speak or read or write the Haida tongue. Yeats, though he learned to make Irish poetry and drama of the highest order, never learned six words of Gaelic. His close connections in London made him an object of deep suspicion among many Irish nationalists, at the same time that his skill, his success, and his tremendous personal growth as an Irish poet made him a national hero.

Cultures don't mingle by watering each other down. They mingle by thickening the soup, infusing one another with a richer store of references and models, adding facets and perspectives and dimensions to each other. This happens in the music of Béla Bartók as well as in the poetry of William Butler Yeats and in the sculpture of Bill Reid. But let me give you another, more recent, more concrete example.

Just a few weeks ago – in January 2004 – the Perseverance Theater in Juneau, Alaska, mounted a production of *Macbeth*. They did the full play in Elizabethan English, but the entire cast was Tlingit, and the costumes, props, and stage set were all traditional Tlingit: clan houses, crest helmets, Chilkat robes and talking sticks, the works.[5]

You see what this means. It means the world of feudal Scotland has been transposed through the lens of Shakespeare's plot and Shakespeare's English words to the precontact Tlingit world and then unwrapped in the postcontact, multicultural world of Juneau, so that all four worlds can illuminate each other without need for a single word of explanation.

Bill would have loved to see that play. Why? Because it exemplifies the meeting of two cultures at their best instead of their worst, so that their shared humanity shines through.

Because it is full of subtle historical echoes. Because it allows two or three or four conceptions of society to occupy the same stage at the same time, and because both the spark and the balance were struck by native people. Because it neither denigrates nor celebrates; it interrogates; it probes. Because the hostilities are *in the play*, where they belong, and not at the stage door or in the press.

When you accept Shakespeare's script, you accept the fact of human greed as well as normal human hunger. You accept the existence of madness and murder and theft along with sanity and honesty and honor. When you answer the script with Tlingit heraldic architecture and dress, you are implicitly asserting that the range of human character and insight and emotion evoked by Shakespeare is present in Tlingit culture as well, and that art can contain it. In short, you're asserting that humans are humans, and that they don't all have to be homogenized by the shopping mall to prove it.

IV

Reid died nearly six years ago, on March 13, 1998. Ten days after his death, there was a massive public memorial at the Museum of Anthropology at the University of British Columbia: the largest memorial gathering ever inspired by any Canadian visual artist. That tells us something about public perception of Reid's importance in contemporary Northwest Coast society – which is just about as ethnically and culturally diverse as societies can get.

Four months later, Bill's ashes were interred, with massive pageantry, at the empty village of Ttanuu in Haida Gwaii. His memorial is there, where he wanted it to be, among the spirits of the old Haida world and not in the new graveyard. If the renaissance continues, it may catch him up at last. Ttanuu may be repeopled. Such things do happen in Haida myth, and they have happened many times in Haida history.

Bill had his own cherished ideas about the rebirth of the old villages. In 1985, when he and David Suzuki testified at one of the public hearings of the British Columbia Wilderness Advisory Committee, Bill said this:

The Haidas never really left South Moresby or the other areas they once controlled. They only went away for a little while. And now they are coming back....

The Haidas must have their ancient lands back unviolated if they are to reestablish links with their distinguished past and build on it a new future....

Modern methods of logging mean not just cutting trees but murdering the forests – those wonderfully complex organisms which once gone will never return in their ancient form. And in killing the forests, you also kill forever the only authentic link the Haidas still have with their past. You murder once more their symbolic ancestors. That is what I think the land claims are about.

As for what constitutes a Haida – well, Haida only means human being, and as far as I'm concerned, a human being is anyone who respects the needs of his fellow man, and the earth which nurtures and shelters us all. I think we could find room in South Moresby for quite a few Haida no matter what their ethnic background.[6]

Not all parts of that statement went down equally well with all members of the Wilderness Advisory Committee,[7] nor with all members of the Haida nation. Some of his Haida friends and relatives buried their grievances at Ttanuu, where they buried Bill Reid's voice. But his clear, unequivocal pronouncement that *Haida* is not an ethnic category remains just as vivid as it was twenty years ago, and just as politically incorrect.

Is it also true? Yes it is, though it is not, of course, the only truth. Xhaayda – or, in the northern dialect, *xhaada* – is the Haida word for Haida. Like many words in many languages, it is a nest of concentric meanings: a lexical onion whose center disappears when you try to expose it. The Haida mythtellers regularly use this word to speak of anything and everything that lives – animal, plant, or spirit being. They also use it to mean human. And they use it, though not often, to mean Haida-speaking humans, as distinct from those who (in fact or in theory) speak Tlingit or Tsimshian or English. So the word has a generic layer of meaning, a specific layer of meaning, and a narrower meaning circumscribed by race, language, and culture.

Bill alludes to all these layers in the passage I've just quoted. Then he endorses one in particular. It can't be his intention to exclude the other meanings, because his argument depends on them as well. But by taking the word Haida to mean first and foremost "a member of the species Homo sapiens," he is distancing himself from the sectarian fixations that dominate contemporary politics – and that underpin the marketing and academic study of Native American art.

Cultural politics in Haida Gwaii, like cultural politics in the Middle East, is fiercely attached to the principle "us *versus* them." In that kind of atmosphere, Reid's insistence on the seamlessness of humanity will, I hope, appear to some as an inspiration. Others, of course, will see it as a threat.

In November 1999, a Bill Reid symposium was held at UBC. In fact, it met in this very room. There were a number of Haida speakers, a number of academics, and a smattering of friends, but Reid's spirit was notably absent. I had the feeling that if Bill had been alive he would not have been asked to speak, for fear of some of the things he might say. Many of those who did speak made it clear how uncomfortable they were with some of what he had said already, and a few made it clear that they were uncomfortable with his continuing personal fame.

The symposium ended with a statement by Bill's old friend and colleague Guujaaw, President of the Council of the Haida Nation. "I was going to say just one more thing," Guujaaw said, "about the buzz over whether Bill was Haida. Like me, that is what he was – Haida – and there was nothing he could do about it."[8]

If Guujaaw meant that Reid was genetically preprogrammed to act and make art in the Haida way because he was born to a Haida mother, then with all due respect to a very capable Haida leader, Guujaaw was wrong. Bill Reid had a younger brother, Robert, also now deceased, born to the same mother and father. Robert Reid was thought as a child to have greater artistic potential than Bill, and he did, like Bill, become an artist. But Robert chose to become an artist of the commercial, colonial kind, basing his practice in Toronto. That is proof, if any further proof were needed, that Bill Reid's life and art are not explained by genetic predestination.

Perhaps what Guujaaw meant to say is that once the seeds of Haida art took root in Bill Reid's brain – or once Haida culture got its nongenetic start in his genetically human mind – there was no going back, because art has greater power than the humans who create it. I hope that was his meaning, because that's how culture works. Bill had choices and took them both. He had choices because neither of the cultures he was drawn to most strongly ever completely shut him out – though members of both have certainly snubbed him, in life and in death.

v

Bill Reid found home fairly early in his life. That home – the planet, seen from this particular coast – was largely in ruins and needed to be rebuilt. He spent his life doing his bit, like Sandburg's conscript, to rebuild home for himself and all the rest of us – not because he loved us all but because he enjoyed watching people watch his work. And that is reason enough. A lot of others have done their bit as well, and then moved in. Many more have pulled the blinds and changed the channel – certain, evidently, that there is no legacy, that nothing more than chromosomes and money is ever passed from one generation to the next.

Michael Ames, a former director of this university's Museum of Anthropology, has suggested that Bill's charisma was so great that his reputation might not long survive his death. Charisma is a good Greek word, from χάρις, which means grace. But in Haida, charisma is sghaana: the same word that is normally used for a spirit being or its power. In Haida metaphysics, human death is no impediment to sghaana.

Bill Reid was my close friend for a number of years. He was my teacher. He was also, for a time, a kind of stand-in for the father I disowned quite early in my life. Yet what matters to me even more than the man is the art. One reason it matters is that it's beautifully made and therefore a source of joy as well as a record of pain. Another reason it matters is that it's a compass, useful for finding home – something humans often lose, despite the fact that home is everywhere humans touch the planet. The compass of Bill's art was useful to him too. The man was great, but the art is greater; that is why the man was great.

This is all stated very simply in the poem of Rilke's I mentioned before, about the torso of Apollo:

> ... denn da ist keine Stelle,
> die dich nicht sieht. Du mußt dein Leben ändern.

> ... for here there is no place
> that does not see you. You must change your life.

NOTES

1 Reid, *Solitary Raven: Selected Writings*, edited by Robert Bringhurst (Vancouver: Douglas & McIntyre / Seattle: U of Washington Press, 2000): 192–5.

2 John R. Swanton, *Haida Texts: Masset Dialect* (Jesup North Pacific Expedition 10.2, New York: American Museum of Natural History, 1908): 372–3.

3 *Haida Texts: Masset Dialect*, p 373.

4 *Solitary Raven*, p 195.

5 I was able to see the production myself only on videotape. I learned the details from my friend Ishmael Hope, who played the role of Malcolm.

6 *Solitary Raven*, p 217. The original published source is the Advisory Committee's *Proceedings at Public Meeting*, n.p., 1986.

7 People unacquainted with British Columbia politics might assume that the province's Wilderness Advisory Committee would consist of people familiar with and disposed to protect the wilderness. The committee, formed late in 1985, concluded its work in early 1986 and was roundly denounced in the provincial legislature as a smokescreen. It had eight members, all appointed by the Minister of the Environment. One of the eight was a recognizable environmentalist. The remaining seven were representatives of the logging and mining industries.

8 This statement is published now in a book based on the symposium – which is different, of course, in many ways from the actual event. See *Bill Reid and Beyond*, edited by Karen Duffek and Charlotte Townsend-Gault (Vancouver: Douglas & McIntyre / Seattle: U of Washington Press, 2004): 63.

THE SILENCE THAT IS NOT POETRY – AND THE SILENCE THAT IS

"Oh yes, but I don't greatly like poetry myself."
"Why don't you like poetry?"
"You see, poetry resembles metaphysics; one does not mind one's own,
　　but one does not like anyone else's."

　　　　– SAMUEL BUTLER, Notebooks

Yes, light is speech. Free frank
impartial sunlight, moonlight,
starlight, lighthouse light,
　　are language.

　　　　– MARIANNE MOORE, "Light Is Speech"

I

One Sunday morning earlier this year, driving down what
passes for a main road on the island where I live, I came across
the corpse of a blacktail fawn. She had died the night before,
at three or four weeks old, evidently struck by a passing car. It
could have been one of the tourists who infest the coast each
summer; it could have been one of the locals, some of whom

E.J. Pratt Lecture, Memorial University of Newfoundland, St John's
14 October 2005

are less alert to their surroundings on Saturday night than they are during most of the rest of the week; or it could have been anyone fond – as I am myself on certain occasions – of speed for its own sake.

In terms of meat, there is not very much to a young fawn, but the eagles had opened her up, and the ravens had joined them. I reminded myself that being buried bit by bit in the guts of birds is at least as good as going into a hole in the ground, and that fueling an eagle's flight or the voice of a raven is as fine a resurrection as anyone, human or deer, could hope for.

I'm a carnivore too, but I felt no urge to pack the carcass home. The patch of land up on the ridge where I live and work is a place where the deer are welcome. In exchange for the pleasure of their company, I look elsewhere for my meat – and therefore, necessarily, for most of my vegetables as well. Bringing home the roadkilled fawn would have made me feel I had broken my contract. For all I knew, her mother was one of the does I often meet in the dark in the little meadow between the hut I like to write in and the one where I eat and sleep. Still, I wanted somehow, like the eagles and the ravens, to reach out and take my bite. I wanted to assert and to admit that I, like them, was one of her kindred. And I wanted whoever had killed her to do that too. I needed a ritual, evidently – a way of lining up with the other scavengers to receive the roadkill eucharist. And I was much too angry at that moment to dream such a ritual up.

What I thought about all the rest of the day, and the day after that, and the day after that, was the gulf of self-regard that we – not genetically, as a species, but by choice, as a society – have erected between ourselves and everyone else, including the deer. I mean the barriers of law and of social convention which assign to the lives of human beings a theoretically infinite value while they treat the lives of wild creatures as theoretically zilch. I mean our way of assigning value to pets and livestock based on nothing but market price and human sentiment. And I mean the teaching that God said on the sixth day of creation, "Replenish the earth and subdue it: and have dominion over the fish of the sea, and over the fowl of the air, and over every living thing."

Genetics, molecular biology, comparative anatomy, European cave art, Buddhist tradition, shamanic tradition, the theology of St Francis of Assisi and a thousand other mystics (pagan and Jewish, Christian and Muslim), and a hundred different traditions of Native American narrative cosmology all agree that we and the deer have a lot in common. European and colonial civil law, canon law and the sharia (الشريعة al-sharī'a, Islamic law) seem to agree with the Book of Genesis that whatever we have in common with the deer just doesn't matter. In ecclesiastical law, at least this has a rationale: the relationship we are supposed to have with God takes precedence over our relationships with other earthly creatures like ourselves. In statutory law, it is not for any apparent reason except that setting ourselves apart, and taking dominion over all the other creatures, is supposed to make us rich in the short term. That it can only leave us destitute in the long term is something we seem oddly determined to forget.

There would of course have been an exhaustive series of rituals if the corpse had been that of a human. Ambulance crew, the coroner, police, perhaps some laboratory technicians, morticians, mourners, crown counsel, and the courts would have gone through their motions and uttered their spells. All that apparatus to dissipate the shock of one unscheduled human death. As I left the half-eaten fawn, I asked myself, *Why these polar extremes?* Nepotism and self-interest I can understand. Valuing the life of a human being at, let us say, two or three times that of a deer, even ten times that of a deer, I could understand, whether or not I happen to like the chosen ratio. But why do we pretend, in our traditional ritual spaces – in court and in the synagogue, mosque, and church – that the value of the deer's life is zero and that of a human life is infinite? And why, by the way, do some human beings, in and near those same ritual spaces, find it so easy to flip the switch, reclassifying certain of their fellows as infidels or savages and canceling entirely the value accorded to their lives? If life is sacred, as so many people say, can it only have two values, everything or nothing? What kind of sacredness is that?

11

I've told you about the fawn in the hope that this might help to explain what I mean when I say that poetry isn't the business of humans alone.

Poetry is not a cure for death nor a means to eternal life, and all the better for that. Death is the price of life. It is a fair price, evidently, and if so, we should charge it when we must and pay it in our turn without complaint. But a society happy to kill a billion birds or a hundred thousand cattle in the vague hope of saving a single unspecified human life, or to mow down a whole forest to make one day's worth of newsprint, or to sterilize a river in exchange for some ounces of gold, is a society that, I suspect, has lost its sense of what life and death are for: a society that has lost its admiration and its gratitude for life and death alike.

Does poetry have anything to do with this? I think it does. And has it anything to do with the dead fawn – who surely never heard of poetry, and who, even if she had lived to a ripe old age, could not have been coerced into attending a poetry reading or spending an afternoon with a book? Again, it seems to me that the answer is yes.

If poetry is in fact a human invention, or a social construct, or a linguistic epiphenomenon only found in certain ritualized or aberrant and unpractical types of human speech, then poetry can tell us nothing much about the fawn, nothing much about life and death, and probably nothing much about anything else of serious interest. And if poetry were that, I'd be ashamed and disappointed to be known as a poet and ashamed to have spent my adult life exploring the ways in which poetry works.

In the schools, poetry seems to be taught in two ways. In the active sense, under the banner "creative writing," it is taught as a kind of indoor sport, a license to play with language in the same way one plays cards or video games. As writing students grow older, they are also often promised that poetry will help to put them in touch with their inner selves, and that it rivals transactional analysis as a way of working out interpersonal problems. In the passive sense, poetry is taught, by and large, as a somewhat cracked or eccentric or aberrant form of literature, one that tries either much too hard or not nearly hard enough to measure up to its big brother the novel as a window on the human world. Poetry is, like the novel, a way of eavesdropping on other times and places, different regions of society, and the workings of other people's minds. To the extent that it is literature, poetry offers some of the insights of history (with less anxiety attached to sorting out the dates and names), some of the thrills of anthropology (without the discomforts of fieldwork), and some of the titillation of psychology (without the need for clinical expertise). And as literature it provides the opportunity of playing some other games: the game of interpretation and the game of dining out (or in) on literary theory.

One of the ways in which poetry reaches out to other things, and connects us to other things – and so by inference connects us to all the rest of being – is through the good old-fashioned means of art, in the sense of craft. Every trade breeds a sense of moral duty to the material itself: a sense of moral obligation to the inanimate. This may be clearest where the medium is most tangible – among sculptors and boat builders, furniture makers and painters, tailors and aircraft mechanics. It also occurs among poets and novelists, musicians and composers, choreographers and dancers, whose materials are harder to weigh, measure and pin down: image, rhythm, syntax, gesture, tone. Where intangibility is in fashion, the painter and sculptor will say, of course, that they are working in intangible media too: color and line, shadow and light, opacity and transparency, mass and surface, not oil and canvas, metal, wood, or stone.

Where the medium of exchange – money, that is – trumps the medium of artisanship, the arts and crafts are all suborned. The moral rug is pulled out from under them. As the poor sister of the literary family, poetry at least, like Cinderella, has the advantage that no one is going to marry her for her money.

When I practice the trade or craft of poetry, I am manipulating words. That's what you would hear if you listened to me muttering under my breath, and what you would see if you watched me sitting at my desk, scribbling marks on pieces of paper and then crossing most of them out. And if you watched a painter paint, all you might see is a person dabbing pigment onto canvas. That is not exactly the point in either case, but it is the visible surface, and an excellent reference point too, because that surface, like the art that underlies it, is *not us*.

Poet, poem, and *poetry* are Indo-European words, quite different in origin from their counterparts in African, Asian, Native American, Hamito-Semitic, and Finno-Ugric languages. So let us not assume that their Indo-European etymology alone will lead us to some universal truth. What it might lead us to instead is the middle of one of a number of formerly separate, now convergent, piles of old cultural assumptions and associations. But if we are trying to get our bearings, that is one of the places we might look.

The Greek verb ποιέω means to make or to do. The noun of agent descended from this verb, ποιητής [poiētēs], means a maker or a doer. In the Greek of Aristotle and Plato, it is used to mean poet: someone who makes things out of words. In the *Iliad* and the *Odyssey*, the same word is often used, but never to mean poet. It is used instead to speak of other kinds of craftsmen – metalworkers and carpenters especially – and these are usually described as artisans whose work is graced or guided by the gods. That's a way of saying that humans can reach out, by making and doing, to realms beyond the human, and that the things humans make or do can have a presence and a value that might also reach beyond the human realm.

The Arabic word for poetry, شِعْر shi'r, is formed from the verb شَعَرَ sha'ara, which means to know, to realize, to intuit; or to sense, to feel, to perceive. A poet, شاعِر shā'ir, is not a maker but a perceiver: one whose eye or heart or mind is sharp. The Hebrew term for poetry, שירה shīrah, is similar in sound to the Arabic word, but it has a different root: שר shar, which means to sing. The cognate Arabic verb is سار sāra, which means to flow. So a poet in Hebrew is משורר mshôrer, a singer, not a knower. Anglo-Saxon in this respect is closer to Arabic. There a poet is a *scop*, which means a sentry or a seer (in current English, one who *scopes things out*). In Danish, though, a poet is a *digter*, as in German he is a *Dichter*: one who sorts and packs or weaves things into order, or caulks the leaks and cracks.

Once upon a time, I thought it would be useful to collect as many etymologies of this sort as I could, to see what patterns they would form. But language has no secret knowledge of poetry. And the use of words to mean *poet* and *poem* is actually quite recent. These are self-conscious, professional terms. You needn't go back far in any language to reach a point at which there are no words for poetry – not because poetry didn't exist, but because it wasn't a subject that people chose to discuss.

Some etymologies are genuinely helpful. I am glad, for example, to know that *think* and *thank* are variations on a single Indo-European root, and so to be reminded – not by lecturers or preachers but simply by the language I am speaking – that ingratitude and hate and hoarding and begrudging are not thinking. But *poetry*, like *blackness*, is an abstraction, a generalization. The word wasn't formed in the dawn of human time by people pointing directly at the thing, leaving their insight and its symbol like a microlith to be excavated and cherished a thousand generations after their deaths. What it names has always been there, but talking about it, as we are doing here, appears to be a recent aberration.

There are often, perhaps always, names for literary genres: words that are needed to say such useful things as *Tell me a story* or *Sing us a song*. Every indigenous language in Canada has a word that means something like *myth* – a word that is used to refer to stories peopled by spirit beings unconfined by human time. In Haida that word is *qqaygaang*; in Nisgha it is *adaawaq*; in Okanagan it is *captíkʷł*; in Western Inuktitut it is *unipkaaq*. And every indigenous language in Canada has a word that means something like *history* – a word that is used for stories that do take place in human time: tales of personal adventure or of ancestors' deeds, not of the actions of spirit beings or the powers of the land. In Cree that word is *âcimôwin*. In Nootka it is *'oyaqḥmis*. All Native Canadian languages also have a word for *song*. Most, and probably all, in fact, have many words for different kinds of song. None has a word that translates readily as poetry. Yet in every one of those languages, poetry has thrived.

As you may know, unwritten languages also almost never

have grammatical terminology. No words for noun, verb, participle, gerund, preposition, passive voice, or pluperfect subjunctive. But all human languages do have nouns, verbs and complex grammars. Everywhere people are left in relative peace with their environment, they learn to employ those nouns and verbs and grammars in very sophisticated ways. They do this without the need of any overt discussion, any technical instruction, or any linguistic analysis.

Language knows what a verb is, but it doesn't usually say. It may also know what humans are. It does not appear to know what poetry is, nor what language is either. The questions *What is poetry?* and *What is language?*, like the question *What is reality?*, are questions that language never expected to be asked. But that is not the only reason language has no answers. Language does not know what language is, nor what poetry is, because they lie outside its bounds.

III

Twenty years before I was born, José Ortega y Gasset, a far more articulate philosopher than most, set himself the task – unusual for a philosopher – of writing a little book about modern art. Ortega was living in the Spain of Federico García Lorca and Antonio Machado, the Europe of Rilke and Picasso and James Joyce and Gertrude Stein. I encountered his book entirely by accident in 1958 or '59 in the Wasatch Mountains in northern Utah, where no one seemed to have heard of García Lorca or Machado, and few had heard of Joyce, and fewer still had read him. One sentence from Ortega's book lodged in my mind like a grain of sand when I first read it and has been there ever since. The sentence, written in 1925, says *La poesía es hoy el álgebra superior de las metáforas*: "Poetry today is the higher algebra of metaphor."[1]

Ortega's sentence was not meant to embrace all kinds or genres of poems, but it served me well as a simple description of the kind of poetry I grew up choosing to read and attempting to write. I discovered much later that, no matter how wide of the mark it may be as a description of the verse of Johnson and Pope or Byron and Keats, it does pretty well as a description of a great deal of poetry, oral and written, ancient and modern, that Ortega knew nothing about.

The Native American narrative poetry transcribed by mission students and anthropological linguists between the late sixteenth and early twentieth centuries is, on the whole, just as intrinsically metaphorical as the non-narrative poetry of the European avant garde in the 1920s. But because it is mythopoeic rather than lyric, its metaphors belong, metaphorically speaking, to a different species of algebra, or to a wholly different branch of metaphorical mathematics. Perhaps it is more accurate to say this poetry is the advanced integral calculus of metaphor.

In mythtelling, the essential "figure of speech," if you wish to call it that, is personification. Nearly everything – rocks, trees, clouds – is animate enough to speak, to think, to make choices and to pass through transformations. But these figures are not figures of *speech*; they are figures of *thought*. The real masters among the mythtellers are engaged, no doubt about it, in doing serious philosophy, though they never have to resort to abstract terms.

The algebra and calculus of metaphor – a metaphorical form of mathematics, evidently, as well as a quasi-mathematical use of metaphor – is, I should think, essentially silent. Yet when mathematical work starts to go well, we say that it hums. When it really goes well, we say that it sings. That is what happens in the algebra and calculus of metaphor.

That song is the silence of poetry. It is not quite the same as the song that the words in the poem make when you read or recite it. It is a song inside that song: one that your mind hears and to which your mind replies, like half a pair of geese honking in counterpoint, as geese routinely do. It is the resonant silence you hear, and the resonant silence you make in return, when you get the poem and the poem gets you. When you really *see what it means*, what you see is nothing, and the nothing sings a song – one you may want to say you feel instead of hear.

In the oral world, where language is being honed against reality every day, and has no manuscripts or books in which to carry excess baggage, names for abstractions such as *poetry* serve no purpose. Yet poetry is there, in both its human and its elemental form, because oral poets make it happen, and because it is a property of reality itself.

Yves Bonnefoy put it well, just a few months ago, writing from Paris to correct an English critic. In sorting out the poets and non-poets, he said, "it is not the text that counts. However remarkable this text may be, its poetic quality depends on its author having known how to keep alive in it the light of what is beyond language."[2]

The most insightfully sustained writing I have seen on this subject is in Jan Zwicky's recent book *Wisdom and Metaphor*. Poetry is scarcely mentioned there by name, but on every page its nature is illuminated. "Those who think metaphorically," Jan tells us, "are enabled to think truly because the shape of their thinking echoes the shape of the world." And again: "The implied 'is not' in a metaphor points to a gap in language through which we glimpse the world. That which we glimpse is what the 'is' in a metaphor points to."[3]

Metaphor connects things, but it does so in a way that sharpens their own particularity. When you sing a musical interval, you clarify two things by setting them adjacent one another. At the same time, you establish the difference between them as something in itself: their harmony and counterpoint: the agreement and tension between them. Metaphor does the same. This kind of superimposition is the opposite of a chorus line. It asserts the identity "*x* is *y*" in a way that clarifies the vivid singularity of *x* as well as *y*. It clarifies what Ortega could call their *ensimismamiento*, or *in-itself-ness*. The term that Jan would use is "*thisness*." "Thisness," she says, "is the experience of a distinct thing in such a way that the resonant structure of the world sounds through it."[4] And at the geometric center of her book – the 59th of the 118 meditations it contains – is this particularly poignant observation:

A *metaphor can appear to be a gesture of healing — it pulls a stitch through the rift that our capacity for language opens between us and the world. A metaphor is an explicit refusal of the idea that the distinctness of things is their most fundamental ontological characteristic.*

But the distinctness of things is ONE *of their most fundamental ontological characteristics (the other being their interpenetration and connectedness). In this sense, a metaphor heals nothing — there is nothing to be healed.*

IV

I don't dispute that human beings are fascinating creatures. But I have two compelling reasons to behave more like a physicist or a biologist than the Augustan or Romantic poets did: two reasons to spend less time inquiring into the nature of human beings or human society and more time inquiring into the nature of everything else. One reason is that I am a human being myself. This of course is an old problem – familiar to the Augustans, the Romantics and everybody else. It has rarely or never been solved in its entirety, but there are old and well-tried ways to work around it. The other reason is that the world is now – for the first time ever – oversupplied with human beings. It remains to be seen how we are going to deal with that.

"Get to know yourself," the Delphic Oracle said. It's good advice, I'm sure – but advice not to be taken, it seems to me, in too narrow a sense. I have a vested interest in not becoming too interested in a self that can block out my view of the rest of the world. To put it another way, the self I'd like to get to know (and the one I'd rather trust) is not this human being who stands here now, with his ignorance, his fears, and his little, quivering heart; nor any of the social selves he sometimes wears in any of the social worlds in which, to my alarm, he sometimes finds himself immersed; nor the monkeywrenching species to which you and he belong, and which is every day more difficult to escape; but the larger self, consisting of more species, and more incarnations of being, organic and inorganic, than you or I can count.

I do not say this to offend you. No one but another human being is going to read any of my books or learn a poem of mine by heart or do me the great honor of commissioning a lecture and listening to the result. And one of the things I hope those books will tell you is that humans and their visions of what the world is and how it works are much more various than you thought, and that the stories humans tell and the poems they compose are much more various and more interesting than any university on earth is, at the present time, equipped to teach. But what makes them that various and interesting is in large part what they manage to illuminate, or to *connect with*, in the world beyond the human.

Humans, like penguins and seals and lichens and rocks, are interesting because of what they are, but what they really are is in large part a set of interrelations with the world in which they live. The more they recede into a world of their own making, the less truly human they become. Withdrawing into your baggage isn't the same as slimming down to your real self. It isn't *ensimismamiento*; it is not a route to *thisness* but to *thislessness* instead. If the books are only instances or parts of our interrelations among ourselves, instead of instances or parts of our interrelations with the world, they will make us worse rather than better, lesser rather than greater. If that is all they are, I should never have written them to begin with, and if I find that I have written a book like that, I ought to toss it into the fire.

Poetry is a breathing hole in the ice of our identity. It is also – in my dialect at any rate – the name of what passes through that orifice or can be sensed on the other side. "Poetry," like "news," is both the name of the news we get and the name of the route by which we get it.

"Nothing can echo with being," Jan says, "unless it is emptied of itself."[5] *Poetry* is a name I like to use for what she calls "the resonance of being," because that is what the words in the poem are listening for when the poem is being written and on every occasion afterward when the poem is well spoken or well read. If a poem is a text, it is that kind of text: a formulation of words in which the resonance of being can be heard: a text that is lit from within, or perhaps from behind, by the light of what is beyond language. For that to happen, the words must be in some sense emptied of themselves. They must also, in some sense, be emptied of us.

So in writing a poem, as in building a boat or fixing an engine or mapping a river or treating a broken heart, we give ourselves to something else, which is not us. To do so helps to make us whole.

"Matter will be our judge," say Dennis Lee, George Grant, and Simone Weil. Nothing so grand as "the resonance of being" or "the light of the translinguistic"; just good old ordinary *stuff*: hydrogen, nitrogen, carbon, the bread of the universe. That will be our judge.

The deer are animate matter.

So are we of course. But we are we and therefore cannot see us clearly and well through the world's eyes. It is hard enough – some say impossible – to learn to see the deer. There is, however, nothing unusual or uniquely human in all this. The deer, it seems to me, do not see deer as other either. Every species digs a kind of hole for itself, a rut, a trench, by virtue of the fact that it exists. Interspecies communication is quite routine in the natural world, yet it is evidently hard for the adult members of most species to see over that species' lip.

What does it mean to see through the world's eyes? I do not know. I have no hope of ever knowing. I try to do it nevertheless. So I'll tell you my hunch. I suppose that the world's eyes are compound eyes, something like the eyes of insects. I suppose that they are compounded of the eyes of all the species that exist. I also suppose that the world is largely blind, because so many species that used to exist are now extinct, and many others, species that might exist, have not existed yet. So I have a hunch that the world, like a grizzly, has pretty lousy eyesight, but that it still sees many things that all our microscopes and telescopes do not.

There is a beautiful passage about the relations of humans and deer at the beginning of Tim Lilburn's book of meditations *Living in the World As If It Were Home*. This is a sample:

Deer come out of the poplars just as day becomes night; they move in the blue air.... They see me standing by the woodpile. They stare. I stare.

Consciousness walks across the land bridge of the deer's stare into the world of things. This is knowing.... I feel more substantial, less apologetic as a physical thing from having been seen....

When consciousness crosses the divide into the wilderness of what is there, it expects to find a point of noetic privilege: at last a clear view into the heart of things. But what it does find on the other side is further peculiarity, a new version of distance. The deer bend again to eat, then again nod up a stare. The world is a collection of oddnesses, things so gathered into themselves, so ruthlessly at home and separate, they seem to shine with difference....

Looked at by the does in the falling light, I am "seen home," attended closer to the centre of what is.... But at home through the other's look, the things of home seem even more deeply themselves.... The opposite of objective removal from the world is not subjective union but an intensely felt differentiation. The deer show out from around the word "deer" and they have no name.[6]

V

There is nothing new and modern (or postmodern) in the claim that human beings are the fountain of meaning and value, and that the dead fawn is nothing unless it has meaning and value for *us*. Selfishness is not a new disease. In the European literary tradition, it is even ascribed to one of the Presocratics, Protagoras of Abdera.

Plato mentions Protagoras far more often than he mentions Herakleitos, Parmenides or other eminent predecessors. Protagoras haunts two of the dialogues in particular: the *Protagoras* and the *Theaetetus*. Both, however – as usual with Plato – are built like halls of mirrors. τὰ πολλὰ Πρωταγόρας ἔνδον διατρίβει, Sokrates says [311a5]: "Protagoras spends a lot of time indoors"; and Plato always wraps Protagoras up inside a dialogue-within-a-dialogue, so that even in the work that bears his name, he never actually appears.

In the *Theaetetus*, a person named Terpsion reads aloud from a book written by someone named Eukleides. The book,

Eukleides says, is an account, dictated by Sokrates, of a conversation Sokrates once had with a youngster named Theaitetos. This Theaitetos, however, is still too young and easygoing for serious debate; so in talking to Theaitetos, Sokrates has to argue with himself. He does this by inventing a discussion he'd have liked to have with Protagoras. There is a dialogue within a dialogue within a book within a book.

The *Protagoras* itself is a less convoluted structure. There Sokrates simply recounts, to a nameless friend, a conversation he's purportedly just had with Protagoras and his admirers. The recounting is larded, however, with literary allusions, all of which point to the scene in the *Odyssey* where Odysseus recounts to his host Alkinoös discussions he's just had with the spirits of the dead.

The overtly imaginary discussion in the *Theaetetus* returns again and again to a sentence that apparently occurred near the beginning of one of Protagoras' books. No matter how fictional all the conversation may be, this quotation appears to be real; it is mentioned by Aristotle and other sources too. In the quotation, Protagoras says: πάντων χρημάτων μέτρον ἐστὶν ἄνθρωπος· "Man is the measure of all things."

Sokrates argues for sixty pages against this human-centered view. Aristotle's rejoinder, in the *Metaphysics* [1053a31], takes three lines. τὴν ἐπιστήμην δὲ μέτρον τῶν πραγμάτων λέγομεν, he says, καὶ τὴν αἴσθησιν διὰ τὸ αὐτό, ὅτι γνωρίζομέν τι αὐταῖς, ἐπεὶ μετροῦνται μᾶλλον ἢ μετροῦσιν. "We say our understanding is a measure of how things are, and likewise our perception, since that's the way we find our way around, but in fact, instead of measuring, they have their measure taken."

I'm with Aristotle here. I hold that our measurements of things are founded on, and always need to be calibrated against, *their* measurements of *us*. Plato says that Protagoras did a spectacular job of selling the contrary view – but he

315

didn't invent it. There is plenty of evidence, in Homeric epic, Athenian drama, and in countless works of African and Asian, Polynesian and Native American oral literature, that arrogance is a universal and permanent human problem. In that sense, it seems, there is indeed something metaphor might heal, or rather, something it might treat. I don't suppose there are any genuine cures. I don't suppose there are any good scapegoats either. I have suggested, once or twice, that the human hand is central to the problem: that as soon as it was lifted off the ground, reduced to an unemployed foot, the hand had nothing to do but go looking for trouble, and so of course found it. Jan has sometimes sounded equally suspicious of human language – or more precisely, of analytical, nonmetaphorical language: the kind of language that gets involved in manipulation, like the hand, as opposed to the kind of language that connects us to the world, like the foot. Hand and tongue are fertile with human arrogance, to be sure. But neither hands nor human language are required. Everyone who has spent any time with wild animals knows that arrogance is prehuman.

To make matters muddier yet, it seems to me that language is also prehuman. I hold the view, anathema to some of my closest friends, that poetry is a fundamental property inherent in Being itself. Maybe language is that fundamental too. If nucleic acids function as linguistically as geneticists now say, then language – in the elemental, not of course the human sense – is evidently a basic fact and mechanism of life. Perhaps the physicists will tell us, tomorrow or the next day, that quintessentially linguistic transactions are occurring in the nuclei of atoms, just as they are in the nuclei of cells and in the nuclei of sentences. That news would not surprise me.

I do not mean that the world is or might be made of words. I do not mean that the world exists because it is being talked about or described. And I do not mean that reality would be any less real if we and all our books and papers, and all our human languages, were to vanish from the solar system now. I mean that human language is no more unnatural than antlers, hair, or teeth, and that phenomena we encounter in the languages we speak – phenomena with names such as grammar and syntax – may have roots that run much deeper than most of us have looked.

If elemental biological mechanisms really are linguistic, then there are languages in which we are spoken as well as languages we speak. That does not mean that one language, or one kind of language, is interchangeable with another – and it does not mean that language is the most important thing or the only thing that actually exists.

However deep the roots of language are, all they are is roots – and not the only roots at that. Here among us humans, out there among the deer, and down, I think, among the chromosomes and possibly among the mesons, the neutrinos and the quarks, the bird of speech is perched in the tree of ineffability.

Where else would it perch? How else would we see it or hear it? Is there light without darkness? Is there any meaningful sound, or any speech worth hearing, that isn't steeped in silence?

Next question: Does it work both ways? Does the tree of ineffability grow in the soil of language? I do not claim to know. But without language, what could we know of ineffability? Is there darkness without light? Aristotle, like a good Canadian, makes this a question of place. Heterogeneity, as any linguist can tell you, is a precondition of language; if everyone or everything is the same, nothing whatsoever can be said. Heterogeneity is also, according to Aristotle, a precondition of location. There is a passage in the Physics [212a31–b14] that says this: ᾧ μὲν οὖν σώματι ἔστι τι ἐκτὸς σῶμα περιέχον αὐτό, τοῦτό ἐστιν ἐν τόπῳ, ᾧ δὲ μή, οὔ.... τὸ γὰρ που αὐτό τ᾽ ἐστί τι, καὶ ἔτι ἄλλο τι δεῖ εἶναι παρὰ τοῦτο ἐν ᾧ ὃ περιέχει· "If a body is encompassed by another body, external to it, it is in a place, and if not, not…. To have a *where*, a thing must not only exist; it must also be embraced by something other than itself."

Is placelessness prior to place? Is silence prior to music, nonbeing prior to being, ineffability prior to articulation, death prior to life, or vice versa? Easy to say yes; just as easy to say no; not at all so easy to go outside and make sure. But outside, where Protagoras rarely went, is where I think we should be looking.

So if I say that language has been around in some form from the beginning, I don't for a moment mean to suggest that inexpressibility has not been. I don't mean that language trumps the unsayable. It seems to me that language cannot function or exist without the inexpressible to rest on. More than rest on. The ineffable is the blood in language's veins, the air in its lungs. Without the ineffable, no morpheme would have meaning, no phoneme would have shape, no sentence or story would have either shape or meaning. To have anything to say, language must be emptied of itself. It must give itself away, instead of claiming to own the world or itching to control it.

VI

Anthropocentrists routinely suppose that human language is the only language there is, and unhappily, most of the people doing and teaching linguistics, like most of those involved now in literary theory, have been anthropocentrically trained. Carried to extremes, this training leads to the view that *reality is really what we say it is*. In that kind of atmosphere, all talk of the linguistics of reality is deservedly suspect. But if it is meaningful to say (as I do) that *reality speaks*, and if it is plausible furthermore, that reality speaks because the kinds of self-transcending mechanisms *that make language language* are endemic to what-is, then it seems to me that the rug of linguistic privilege is pulled out from under human feet. Then we can start to dance again, like the marginal creatures we are and need to be, on the ground, whose center is everywhere and nowhere.

Poetry isn't language. It is something like a sound, and something like a silence, that reality gives off. I like to think, myself, that this includes pure tones as well as overtones and intervals.

In every tuneful metaphor, an interval is sounded. It is heard in the mind's eye, or the mind's ear, or perhaps in the mind's whole body. Two disjunct constituents of reality are evoked, on top of one another, like two bells rung at once. The interval is the simultaneous consonance and difference between them. When poetry enters language, metaphors tend to occur, not one by one but nested into matrices and strings. That is what is algebraic about them – and that algebra is music.

Poetry isn't language – and so far as I can see, it isn't even linguistic. Language also isn't poetry, though it can certainly be poetic. So can pretty much anything else. In my dialect, however – to confuse the issue further – poetry and music are synonymous in their elemental sense. Poetry and music as we know them in everyday life seem to me to be branches growing out of a common trunk. I call the trunk by the name of either or both of the branches. No doubt this is a sloppy way to talk, but with me it is a long-established habit.

Jan likes to say – as she does in *Wisdom and Metaphor* – that "all genuine understanding is a form of seeing-as: it is fundamentally spatial in organization."[7] I do not see, myself, why understanding cannot just as well be *hearing-as*, or *feeling-as*, in the blind and tactile sense. When we think we understand a thing, we like to say we grasp it. When a fact falls into place, we say it's music to our ears. Those seem to me wise metaphors. Each of these three senses – hearing, touch, and vision – is one of our keys to spatial organization. Evidently for the deer, with their better noses, smell is spatial too. For each key, movement is the test. That is to say, real understanding is dancing.

What's a klutz like me doing talking about dancing? This must be metaphor again. But the dance I have in mind isn't solo performance, where "self-expression" is apt to take over, nor chorus-line dancing, where, as in politics, leading by following is the rule, and the mark of success is to say precisely what one's neighbors say only more so. What makes real understanding real is its connection with reality. Real understanding is dancing with Being – including one's predators, one's prey, and the shared world in which our lives and deaths unfold.

Can such a dance survive translation into the form of a solo performance or pas-de-deux? Can it be re-created on stage? I don't see why not. It can even survive, in some degree, when transposed into language, in the telling of a story or the writing of a text or the singing of a song. I just think it's good to remember that the dance of real understanding doesn't begin or end on the stage, nor on the page, nor in any venue under human control.

In English, Latin, and Greek, the favorite metaphor for understanding is visual. "I see," we say. In Haida, however, when you want to say that you think something, what you normally say is *hl gudang*, "I hear it."

If something is ineffable, that means that it cannot be said. But what cannot be said can sometimes be heard. And in Haida, that is to say that it can be thought. English does not say this, but even in English, that does not make it untrue.

It is not necessary that *the same things* should be ineffable in all languages. It is only necessary that in each language *plenty of things* should be so: unsayable or, at the very least, unsaid.

It seems to me that a kind of speechlessness – the inability to say a quite significant number of things – is actually built into every language. But language is a self-transcending mechanism. It tries, and lets us try, to say what it can't. The survival of poetry depends on the failure of language. The reason language exists, it seems to me, is that poetry – the resonance of being – needs it. If you live in a place that hasn't been pillaged and ruined, the silence of language's failure, and of poetry's success, is present and vivid almost everywhere you listen, almost everywhere you look. Here, however, as always, there is the danger that I have been careless, like a certain unidentified late-night driver, and have said too much.

NOTES

1 Ortega y Gasset, *La Deshumanización del arte / Ideas sobre la novela* (Madrid: Revista de Occidente, 1925): 52.

2 *Times Literary Supplement* (London), 12 August 2005: 13.

3 Jan Zwicky, *Wisdom and Metaphor* (Kentville, Nova Scotia: Gaspereau, 2003): foreword; § 10.

4 *Wisdom and Metaphor* § 55.

5 *Wisdom and Metaphor* § 101.

6 Lilburn, *Living in the World As If It Were Home* (Dunvegan, Ontario: Cormorant, 1999): 3–5. The same passage is quoted at greater length in *Wisdom and Metaphor* § 76.

7 *Wisdom and Metaphor* § 3.

INDEX

ACKNOWLEDGEMENTS

Assembling this book has brought to mind a lot of pleasant memories and a lot of unpaid debts. I would like to express my gratitude to David Abram, Kay Amert, Marilyn Bowering, Mairi Campbell, Bernd Dietz, Gudrun Dreher, Clare Goulet, Sherrill Grace, Heather Hodgson, Ishmael Hope, Amelia Hugill-Fontanel, Susan Ingersoll, Bob Jickling, Sean Kane, Arthur Krentz, Tim Lilburn, Andrew Lyons, Don McKay, Marie Mauzé, Jesús Munárriz, Bill New, David Pankow, Martine Reid, Laurie Ricou, Leslie Saxon, Gary Snyder, Andrew Steeves, Christoph Wolfart, Jan Zwicky – and indeed to many others whose names could fill the page.

Native American Oral Literatures and the Unity of the Humanities was published as a chapbook by the University of British Columbia in 1998. *Prosodies of Meaning* was issued as a small book by Voices of Rupert's Land, University of Manitoba, in 2004; and *Wild Language* by the Institute for Coastal Research, Nanaimo, in 2006.

"Poetry and Thinking" appeared in a different form in the anthology *Thinking and Singing*, edited by Tim Lilburn (Toronto: Cormorant, 2002); and "The Audible Light in the Eyes" in *Coming to Shore*, edited by Marie Mauzé, Sergei Kan, and Michael Harkin (U of Nebraska Press, 2004).

"The Persistence of Poetry and the Destruction of the World" is an English version of something I wrote and delivered in awkward Spanish. The Spanish version first appeared in *Presencia Literaria* (La Paz, Bolivia). "The Polyhistorical Mind" first appeared in the *Journal of Canadian Studies* (Peterborough, Ontario); "The Voice in the Mirror" in *Printing History* (Rochester, New York); "The Tree of Meaning" in the *Canadian Journal of Environmental Education* (Whitehorse); and "Finding Home" in *Canadian Literature* (Vancouver).

❧ This book was designed by Robert Bringhurst and Andrew Steeves. The text face is Rialto Piccolo, designed by Giovanni Di Faccio & Lui Karner. The unserifed face is Quadraat Sans, designed by Fred Smeijers. The Greek is New Hellenic, designed by Victor Scholderer. The Cyrillic is Lazurski, designed by Vadim Lazurski. The Hebrew is Hadassah, designed by Henri Friedlaender. The Arabic is Tasmeem Naskh, created by Thomas Milo and Mirjam Somers. The Chinese type is Monotype Kǎitǐ.

BOOKS BY ROBERT BRINGHURST

· POETRY ·

The Shipwright's Log ⁄ 1972
Cadastre ⁄ 1973
Bergschrund ⁄ 1975
Tzuhalem's Mountain ⁄ 1982
The Beauty of the Weapons: Selected Poems 1972–82 ⁄ 1982
The Blue Roofs of Japan ⁄ 1986
Pieces of Map, Pieces of Music ⁄ 1986
Conversations with a Toad ⁄ 1987
The Calling: Selected Poems 1970–1995 ⁄ 1995
The Book of Silences ⁄ 2001
Ursa Major: A Polyphonic Masque for Speakers and Dancers ⁄ 2003
The Old in Their Knowing ⁄ 2005
New World Suite N° 3 ⁄ 2005

· PROSE ·

Ocean/Paper/Stone ⁄ 1984
The Raven Steals the Light (with Bill Reid) ⁄ 1984; 2nd ed. 1996
The Black Canoe (with Ulli Steltzer) ⁄ 1991; 2nd ed., 1992
The Elements of Typographic Style ⁄ 1992; 2nd ed., 1996; 3rd ed., 2004
A Short History of the Printed Word (with Warren Chappell) ⁄ 1999
A Story as Sharp as a Knife: The Classical Haida Mythtellers and Their World
        (Masterworks of the Classical Haida Mythtellers, vol. 1) ⁄ 1999
Prosodies of Meaning: Literary Form in Native North America ⁄ 2004
Carving the Elements: A Companion to the Fragments of Parmenides
        (with Peter Koch et al.) ⁄ 2004
The Solid Form of Language: An Essay on Writing and Meaning ⁄ 2004
Wild Language ⁄ 2006

· TRANSLATION ·

Ghandl of the Qayahl Llaanas, Nine Journeys to the Mythworld (Masterworks
        of the Classical Haida Mythtellers, vol. 2) ⁄ 2000
Skaay of the Qquuna Qiighawaay, Being in Being
        (Masterworks of the Classical Haida Mythtellers, vol. 3) ⁄ 2001
Parmenides, The Fragments ⁄ 2003
Skaay of the Qquuna Qiighawaay, Siixha: Floating Overhead ⁄ 2007